BIG QUESTIONS IN CREATIVITY 2017

BIG QUESTIONS IN CREATIVITY 2017

Edited by
MARY KAY CULPEPPER
CYNTHIA BURNETT &
PAUL D. REALI

VOLUME 5:
THE BEST OF BIG QUESTIONS 2013-16

ICSC Press
International Center for Studies in Creativity
Buffalo State, The State University of New York
Buffalo, NY, U.S.A.

ICSC PRESS
INTERNATIONAL CENTER *for* STUDIES *in* CREATIVITY

BUFFALO STATE • The State University of New York

ICSC Press
International Center for Studies in Creativity
Buffalo State, The State University of New York
1300 Elmwood Avenue
Buffalo, NY 14222, USA
icscpress.com

© 2013-2017 by ICSC Press

ISBN: 978-0-9849795-8-5 (print edition)

Library of Congress Control Number: 2013907967

Simultaneously published in multiple formats, both print and electronic. For alternative versions and to discover other titles, visit icscpress.com.

Book Design and Graphics: Kevin D. Opp

All trademarks are the property of their respective owners.

While the authors and editors have made every effort to provide accurate Internet addresses at the time of publication, the publisher, editors, or authors do not assume responsibility for changes that occur after publication. Further, the publisher does not control and does not assume any responsibility for author or third-party websites or their content.

Celebrating the 50th birthday of the
International Center for Studies in Creativity
and honoring all the creatives who made it possible.

Contents

Introduction 1

Organizational Creativity

What Might Be the Design of a New Generation of Innovation Models?
Andrés Mejía-Villa 5

Are the Other Benefits of Group Creativity Practices Just as Important as Good Ideas?
David Eyman 31

What are the Natural Relationships Between Creativity and Leadership?
Amy Frazier 45

What If We View Our Education System as an Ecosystem?
Kathryn P. Haydon 65

Personal Creativity

How Does Nature Nurture Creativity?
Jennifer A. Quarrie 83

How to Unlock the Potential of Your Insight?
Mariano Tosso 103

How Can Spiritual Intelligence Help Us Cultivate Creative Potential?
Rebecca DiLiberto 117

Society & Creativity

Does Culture Affect Creativity? An Integrative Literature Review
Mattia Miani 136

Product Measurement: How Do I Know It is Creative?
Eva Teruzzi 151

What is the Correlation Between Mental Health and Creativity?
Julia Figliotti 167

What is Creative Economy?
Irina Mishina 179

What's Next for Creativity?
Mary Kay Culpepper 197

Acknowledgments 213

About the Editors 214

About the International Center for Studies in Creativity 216

About ICSC Press 217

Introduction

Creativity has many effects on those of us who choose to study it. We begin to use the lens of creativity to view both our personal and professional lives—and the result is often asking questions. *Why is that the way it is? What else might we do instead of this? Should that be done another way? How might we change this for the better?* And so on. Inevitably, these questions expand beyond our daily lives and into larger realms—we begin to ask the big questions that define who we are and what we believe.

Each year, students is the Master of Science program at the International Center for Studies in Creativity at SUNY Buffalo State ask and examine a big question in creativity. Since 2013, ICSC Press has had the privilege to publish the best of these papers, showcasing first works from the field of creativity's newest thinkers.

This special volume, created in celebration of the ICSC's 50th birthday, presents the best of the best from those editions, collected into three themes: organizational creativity, personal creativity, and creativity in society.

In this volume, and in the others, you will find yourself both enlightened on these important questions, and, we hope, ready to ask some of your own.

Mary Kay Culpepper
London, England

Cynthia Burnett
Buffalo, NY

Paul D. Reali
Charlotte, NC

ORGANIZATIONAL CREATIVITY

What Might Be the Design of a New Generation of Innovation Models?

Andrés Mejía-Villa
University of La Sabana
Bogotá, Colombia

Originally published in *Big Questions in Creativity 2016*

Abstract

These last three decades have seen a growing body of literature on the topic of creativity and innovation. The two constructs have been positioned as independent, complementary, or interchangeable. But, does the same positioning occur with *organizational* models of creativity and innovation? The answer to this overarching question is formulated throughout this paper. A more precise inquiry focuses on the question: What features should be considered for a new generation of innovation models? With that end in mind, this paper discusses the history and definitions of both constructs; describes the contribution that creativity makes to innovation; explains what comprises creativity and innovation models; identifies their approaches, similarities, and differences; and lists their complementary attributes. Finally, this paper concludes by proposing different features for a new generation of innovation models.

What Might Be the Design of a New Generation of Innovation Models?

"Everything has changed, is changing, and will continue to change" (Mootee, 2013, p. 1). Expressions like this represent the seemingly-ubiquitous term "VUCA"—that is, a world defined by volatility, uncertainty, complexity, and ambiguity (Lawrence, 2013). These conditions have persisted in challenging the growth, productivity, and competitiveness of the business environment. In response to this vexing challenge, companies have discovered that innovation is the major differentiator in the competitive race (Roberts, 2007). It is no surprise, then, that innovative companies have learned to sustain their competitiveness over long periods of time. According to Bowonder, Dambal, Kumar, and Shirodkar (2010), companies such as Bayer, GE, IBM, P&G, Siemens, and Unilever, as well as newer companies such as Apple, Google, Intel, and Microsoft, have also mastered the mantra of sustained growth and intrinsically have rewritten the rules of the game through a series of innovation strategies (Lawton, Finkelstein, & Harvey, 2007).

However, according to the Oslo Manual,* further understanding of the innovation process, and its impact on the economy, is still deficient. For that reason, we need to understand not only if firms are innovative (or not), but we also need to discern how firms innovate and what types of innovations they implement (OECD & Eurostat, 2005). This is important because research suggests that fewer than four percent of the innovation projects undertaken by businesses are proven successful (Kumar, 2012).

Consequently, with the aim to advance the understanding of innovation models and their future developments, this paper seeks to resolve the following research question: *What features should be considered for a new generation of innovation models?* In response, this paper shows a review of the literature to identify the fundamental variables that make up organizational creativity and innovation. Thus, this review considers their separate and sometimes related histories, definitions, approaches, and models to inform features for a new generation of innovation models (see Figure 1). This inquiry not only presents facts about the histories, definitions, approaches, and models of creativity and innovation, but also demonstrates a comparative analysis between the two, which serves as

---

Oslo Manual: Guidelines for Collecting and Interpreting Innovation Data (OECD & Eurostat, 2005) is an international source of guidelines for the collection and use of data on innovation activities in industry.

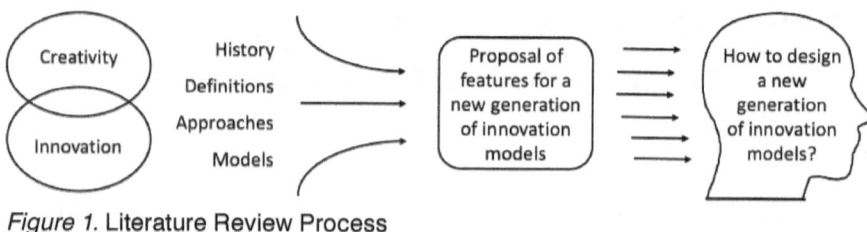

Figure 1. Literature Review Process

a source of knowledge to propose a new generation of innovation models and their characteristics.

Creativity and Innovation: An Ever Closer History

According to Berkhout, Hartmann, Van Der Duin, and Ortt (2006), the economic outlook is changing. They point out that historically, the *classic economy* was based on goods production for local markets through two factors: capital and labor. Subsequently, the increase of production, globalization, competition, the necessity of lower costs, and the demand for specialized products and services served as impetus for a *knowledge economy*, where smarter tools and machines expanded possibilities. Knowledge, therefore, became the third factor of production. For that reason, workforce development evolved as a priority to make companies more efficient. However, Berkhout et al. added, contemporary demands called for another evolution: the *innovation economy*. In this new economy, creativity drove the fourth factor of production. It is important to note that creativity also plays an important role in the knowledge economy, but in the innovation economy, organizational improvement cannot exist without imagination. As Berkhout et al. suggested, one might view the innovation economy as a *creative knowledge economy*.

Xu and Rickards (2007) provided the historical antecedents of the creative knowledge economy by highlighting five stages of evolution: *rational management* (19th-20th century), *incremental innovations* (early 20th century), *humanistic experiments* (mid-20th century), *organizational creativity* (late 20th century), and *creative management* (21st century). The latter of these is considered the study and practice of management, which draws from theories of creative processes and their applications at the individual, group, organizational, and cultural levels. This last stage emerged from the processes embedded in the fourth stage and subsequently offered a focus for revitalizing management theory and practice (Xu & Rickards, 2007). Moreover, one can glimpse the emergence of an integrative process of economics, management, innovation, and creativity.

Creativity and Innovation: Towards a Thematic Conjunction

Predominantly, the literature has defined creativity as the generation of novel and useful ideas, while innovation has been conceived as the production of creative ideas, which is followed by implementation (Amabile, 1996; Shalley & Zhou, 2008; West & Farr, 1990). At the organizational level, creativity is described as "the creation of a valuable, useful new product, service, idea, procedure or process by individuals working together in a complex social system" (Woodman, Sawyer, & Griffin, 1993, p. 293). Meanwhile, the first definition of innovation was coined by Schumpeter (1942) who pointed out that innovation refers to novel outputs; a new good or a new quality of a good; a new method of production; a new market; a new source of supply; or a new organizational structure—all of which can be summarized as "doing things differently." Recently, according to Crossan and Apaydin (2010), innovation was coined as the production or adoption, assimilation, and exploitation of a value-added novelty in economic and social spheres; renewal and enlargement of products, services, and markets; development of new methods of production; and establishment of new management systems. It is both a process and an outcome.* Yet, Anderson, Potočnik, and Zhou (2014) noted the complementary nature of these two constructs. They proffered the following definition:

> Creativity and innovation at work are the process, outcomes, and products of attempts to develop and introduce new and improved ways of doing things. The creativity stage of this process refers to idea generation, and innovation refers to the subsequent stage of implementing ideas toward better procedures, practices, or products. Creativity and innovation can occur at the level of the individual, work team, organization, or at more than one of these levels combined but will invariably result in identifiable benefits at one or more of these levels of analysis. (p. 1298)

The above definition is novel because it incorporates interesting aspects of a systematic view. First, it contains the classic four Ps of creativity (*person, process, product* and *press*) presented by Rhodes (1961) and their innovation counterparts (*people*; repeated creative thinking *processes*; *product* introduction and implementation of strategies; and internal *press* of creation and external

---

*This definition is an abridged version of the current and up-to-date understanding of the concept of innovation as described in the European Commission's (1995) Green Paper on Innovation (pp. 1-2). The original modifier "successful" present in the source was replaced with "value-added" as it would have prevented us from defining innovation ex-ante, before its implementation.

press of the marketplace) proposed by Vehar (2008). Second, this new proposal is in agreement with the *creative change model* described by Puccio, Mance, and Murdock (2010), a systems approach that highlights a set of variables related to organizational creativity (Puccio & Cabra, 2010). Third, this system's view approach is also supported by a multi-dimensional (Crossan & Apaydin, 2010) or multi-level (Drazin, Glynn, & Kazanjian, 1999; Sears & Baba, 2011) view of a creative-innovative process. Finally, the results and benefits of this integrated creative-innovative process are present at all levels (individual, team, organizational, and societal), hence there are partial and final innovation results in each of these levels.

However, Anderson et al.'s (2014) definition does not explicitly consider four relevant topics as seen in the literature review, which is related to a true integration of both concepts: (1) *big purposes,* (2) *open dimension,* (3) *dynamic interaction,* and (4) *leadership and entrepreneurship.* These are important variables to consider in organizational creativity.

Big Purposes

The academic literature positions big purposes in two areas: competitiveness and organizational change. *Competitiveness* is the capacity of people, organizations, and nations to achieve superior outputs and outcomes, and in particular to add value while using the same or lower amounts of inputs (Carayannis & Gonzalez, 2003). From this viewpoint, creativity, innovation, and competitiveness are operationalized at three levels of integration: creativity functions at the individual or micro level, innovation functions at the organizational or meso level, and competitiveness emerges mostly at the national or macro level (Carayannis & Gonzalez, 2003; Tidd, 2001). Similarly, Sears and Baba (2011) pointed out that creativity results from individual innovation, invention from group innovation, adoption from organizational innovation, and organizational and technological change from societal innovation. To be clear, although each level produces its respective outcome, they are integrative and serve the general well-being of the economy. Therefore, it is necessary that this definition have a macro purpose—an all-encompassing view.

The second big purpose is *organizational change.* Creativity and innovation are strategic responses that confront environmental complexity; hence they are considered part of strategic decision making in organizations (Dewett, 2004). Under this perspective, creativity, innovation and organizational change are also integrated. Woodman (2008) presented a *domain model* under which these concepts are integrated in three concentric circles. In the center is organizational creativity, which is surrounded by innovation; and outside this perimeter is organizational change. In this sense, organizational creativity is innovation; all innovation is organizational change; and consequently, all organizational creativity is also change. Similarly, only some organizational changes involve creativity and others innovation. But, innovation always includes creativity. In summary, innovation and organizational creativity support organizational change; and change is vital to support the competitive advantage of organizations (e.g., Damanpour & Schneider, 2006; Damanpour & Wischnevsky, 2006).

Open Dimension

The integrative definition of open dimension provided by Anderson et al. (2014) does not consider the organizations' relationships with other organizations. Their definition of organizational creativity and innovation leaves a space available to recognize the inter- and intra-organizational dimensions of these processes (Camisón & Villar-López, 2014). According to Chesbrough, Vanhaverbeke, and West (2006), *open innovation* is defined as "the use of purposive inflows and outflows of knowledge to accelerate internal innovation, and expand the markets for external use of innovation, respectively" (p. 1). What is more, organizations also need an *open strategy,* which leads them to make strategic sense of innovation communities, ecosystems, networks, and their implications for competitive advantage (Chesbrough & Appleyard, 2007). In sum, a creative-innovative process preconditions an expression of closed and open thinking involving strategy and innovation.

Dynamic Interaction

Although Anderson et al.'s (2014) definition attempts to integrate the creativity and innovation constructs, it does not achieve this objective completely. Cropley and Cropley (2012) explained the classic formula that links both definitions: creativity as the first stage of invention, and after it, innovation as the second stage of exploitation. Thus, invention involves the generation of novel products, processes, systems, and the like, and exploitation involves the implementation of these ideas. According to Rickards (1996), to demarcate creating and implementing is to deny the possibility of organization-wide innovation cultures of "empowered" individuals. For that reason, Rickards asserted that organizations must "stop thinking of the process as divided into the creative bit and the routine bit; start thinking of one unified process in which actions from start to finish are influenced by ideas, and in which ideas are modified by actions and experiences" (p. 22). Rickards also noted that ideas and actions should occur and interact as long as innovation is being pursued. Van de Ven, Polley, Garud, and Venkataraman (2007) proposed viewing innovation as a non-linear dynamic system that consists of a cycle of divergent and convergent activities that may be repeated over time and at different organizational levels. Benner and Tushman (2003) and Burgelman (2002) asserted that creativity and innovation may alternate or occur simultaneously.

Leadership and Entrepreneurship

Anderson et al.'s (2014) integrative definition also does not explicitly include leadership or entrepreneurship. The academic literature has highlighted the relevance of leaders for group and organizational creativity (e.g., Gumusluoglu & Ilsev, 2009; Rickards & Moger, 2006; Sternberg, 2003). According to Puccio, Mance, and Murdock (2011), leadership is the lubricant that allows the other elements to effectively interact or, in some cases, not. Effective leadership begins by establishing a creative atmosphere that supports people as they engage in creative thinking processes. For that reason, Puccio et al. positioned leadership as a fundamental part of their *creative change model*. To be clear, the authors defined *creative leadership* as:

> [T]he ability to deliberately engage one's imagination to define and guide a group toward a novel goal—a direction that is new for the group. As a consequence of bringing about this creative change, creative leaders have a profoundly positive influence on their context and the individuals in that situation. (Puccio et al., 2011, p. 28)

In parallel, Berkhout et al. (2006) explained that entrepreneurship plays a central role: "Without entrepreneurship there is no innovation" (p. 397). Drucker (1998) also highlighted the importance of this topic when he pointed out that "innovation is the specific function of entrepreneurship.... It is the means by which the entrepreneur either creates new wealth-producing resources or endows existing resources with enhanced potential for creating wealth" (p. 3).

Summarizing, the proximity of both constructs requires a cohesive definition that shows creativity and innovation as integrated, interactive, iterative, closed and open processes, guided and motivated by a creative leadership, with different inter- and intra-organizational levels, which work together for the purpose of creating and capturing value.

Functional and Sense Making Paradigms: Two Approaches to Understand Creativity and Innovation

Drazin, Kazanjian, and Glynn (2008) pointed out that social and organizational theories are constructed based upon implicit and explicit assumptions about human behavior. Therefore Wagner and Berger (1985) argued that these assumptions govern what questions we ask, the models we create, and the approach we use to test our models. In that sense, Drazin et al. (2008) presented two schools of thought to explain the organizational processes of creativity and innovation. The first is the *structural-functional paradigm,* which has dominated the sociological and management literature. In this approach, the processes of creativity or innovation are presumed to be in a functional or contributory relationship with a large social system in which it is embedded (Drazin et al., 2008). Thus, this paradigm has a deterministic orientation; behavior is orderly, rational, and constrained by externalities. Outcomes dominate as criteria of action, and change occurs primarily through a division of labor into creative and productive roles that are assumed to integrate harmoniously (Parsons, 1951). In this perspective, creativity and innovation are regarded as important *outcomes* to the social system, and independent variables are considered as factors to be manipulated to improve these outcomes.

In contrast, the second school of thought is *sense making*. This perspective has made significant research progress (Burrell & Morgan, 1979); albeit, the functionalist perspective dominates organizational research (Gioia & Pitre, 1990). Accordingly, Drazin et al. (2008) stressed an understanding of the process through which individuals and organizations develop systems of meaning and how these systems of meaning lead to the emergence of a stream of organizational behavior over time. Thus, the sense making perspective is useful to describe creative and innovative processes. Consequently, under this view creativity and innovation are considered processes rather than outcomes. For that reason, a multilevel organizational analysis under this perspective comprises the same levels as the functionalist approach but focuses on the process of each one rather than their results. Thus, according to Weick (1995), the individual level refers to an *intrasubjective process*—hence the cognitive processes; group level is denominated by an *intersubjective level* because there exist shared frames of references by several people; and the organizational level is the *collective level* that represents the unfolding of change across intersubjective levels.

That said, if these perspectives determine the points of view to understand creativity and innovation, as well as their organizational models, then which are the models under both perspectives?

Innovation and Creativity Models

In this section, different types of innovation and creativity models are presented. In that sense, models such as Stage-Gate (Cooper, 2008), Design-driven Innovation (Verganti, 2009), Design Thinking (Brown, 2008), Theory of Inventive Problem Solving-TRIZ (Mann, 2001), and others, are not considered here because their approaches are related with particular applications, specific aspects, or steps about innovation management rather than general kind of creativity and/or innovation models. Even these could be classified as specific cases or expressions of a general typology of models of creativity and innovation, which are presented below.

Organizational Innovation Models

In the innovation literature, innovation models are subdivided into generations (Berkhout et al., 2006), with the aim of explaining how all models came together to generate commercially viable technologies (Marinova & Phillimore, 2003). Thus, several authors have presented different classifications of these generations. Generally, they present a chronological classification of technological innovation models. In this sense, Rothwell (1994) pointed to the existence of four generations (*Technology Push, Market Pull, Couplin Model,* and *Integrated Innovation*), and proposed a fifth (*Systems Integration and Networking models*), which was formalized and explained by Hobday (2005).

Marinova and Phillimore (2003) described six generations, the largest number found in these studies. Their sequence: *Black Box Model* (Hobday, 2005; Rothwell, 1994); *Linear* models (Technology Push and Market Pull); *Interactive* and *Systems* models (which parallel Systems Integration and Networking models from Hobday, 2005); *Evolutionary Model;* and *Innovative Milieu.* Cropley and Cropley (2012) developed a complete synthesis of these six models based on their foci, strengths, and weakness.

With the same chronological logic, Berkhout et al. (2006) recognized the first three generation models from Rothwell (1994), then proposed a fourth generation: the *Cyclic Innovation Model.* This is characterized by open innovation partnerships, interaction between science and business, hard knowledge of emerging technologies complemented by soft knowledge of emerging markets, new organizational concepts such as skills for managing networks with specialized suppliers and early users, and a central role of entrepreneurship.

From another point of view, Chesbrough (2003) presented two types of models: *Closed* and *Open Innovation* (see also Herzog, 2011). He pointed out that the old model of *Closed Innovation* adhered to the following philosophy: successful innovation requires control. In other words, companies must generate their own ideas which they will then develop, manufacture, market, distribute and service themselves. In contrast, he presented the new model of *Open Innovation,* in which the boundary between a firm and its surrounding environment is more porous, enabling innovation to move easily between the two (Chesbrough, 2003). This might include deploying outside pathways to the market, commercializing internal ideas through channels outside of their current businesses, and using ideas that originate outside the firm's own labs and are brought inside for commercialization.

Organizational Creativity Models

Drazin et al. (2008) pointed out that in the early 1980s and into the 1990s, creativity researchers extended their models beyond the study of individuals (Ford, 1996; Woodman et al., 1993) to include the effects of group or team-level variables (Amabile, 1988). Thus, the *Componential Model of Creativity and Innovation in Organizations* developed by Amabile (1988) is based on individual creativity but also describes the impact of that creativity on organizational innovation. According to Borghini (2005), the implicit idea behind Amabile's model is that creative behavior can be developed only on the individual level and that cognitive and creative skills, and especially motivation, are more important than norms, routines (March, 1991; Nelson & Winter, 1982), and shared behavior.

Another model is *Creative Problem Solving (CPS),* an evolving group of models based on the work Osborn and extended by Parnes and others, comprising at least ten developments and spin-offs (Puccio, Murdock, & Mance, 2005). CPS can be thought of as a cognitive process with applications for individuals and groups. The original CPS model presented by Osborn (1953) included seven steps: (1) orientation, (2) preparation, (3) analysis, (4) hypothesis, (5) incubation, (6) synthesis, and (7) verification. One of the most recent versions was developed by Puccio, Mance, and Murdock (2011), and is called *CPS: The Thinking Skills Model.* It has three major stages (clarification, transformation, and implementation) and seven discrete steps (from Exploring Challenges to Formulating a Plan). The model also includes seven thinking skills (diagnostic, visionary, strategic, ideational, evaluative, contextual, and tactical) and seven affective skills (curiosity, dreaming, sensing gaps, playfulness, avoiding premature closure, sensitivity to environment, and tolerance for risks) associated with the model's seven steps.

In contrast to the above models that are based on individual and group levels, in a very few cases organizational-level variables have been incorporated into models of creativity (Drazin et al., 2008). Factors such as organizational policies, structures, and climate (Burkhardt & Brass, 1990; Tushman & Nelson, 1990), as well as organization-wide training of individuals (Basadur, Graen, & Scandura, 1986; Wheatley, Anthony, & Maddox, 1991) have been linked to creative output. The most comprehensive theoretical model that includes creativity at the organizational level is offered by Woodman et al. (1993), who linked culture, resources, technology, strategy, and rewards to creativity. This process is called the *Interactionist Model of Creativity,* and it considers creativity at the organizational level like a sum of efforts from the group level, and group-level creativity like a sum of individual creativity.

Previous models are based on the functionalist paradigm. In contrast, a sense-making approach (Weick, 1995) is presented by Borghini (2005) who showed a dynamic creative process based on processes of cultural integration, the creation of new knowledge, and the codification of knowledge through integration and sharing. In this process, the solution of problems generates new knowledge, which then develops new competencies, which in turn are shared with different cultural groups within the organization. Consequently, the integration among the different cultures of the dominions in question represent the necessary condition for generating the stock of new knowledge and essential competencies to problem solving (Nonaka, 1991). However, this process represents at the same time the generation of *core rigidities* as a result of codifying knowledge in the organization. These become *organizational rigidities* that mean the inability to abandon rules and consolidated knowledge which have proved to be effective in the past. In a negative way, this affects the creative process. For that reason, the organization requires another kind of process: the destruction of previously-acquired competencies and the manifestation of changes in the cultures of the business sub-systems (Borghini, 2005).

Previously, we studied several different models of creativity and innovation. In the next section, we will develop a comparative analysis of creativity and innovation processes with the aim of finding common and divergent aspects between the two processes.

An Analysis of Organizational Innovation and Creativity Models

Innovation models emerged from the world of economics, which consider innovation as an endogenous change (an internal effort from company to change). Schumpeter (1942), an economist, pointed out that the innovation process was a fundamental driver of economic development, as reflected through his concept of *creative destruction*. To be precise, Schumpeter posited that innovation represents the "process of industrial mutation that incessantly revolutionizes the economic structure from within, incessantly destroying the old one, incessantly creating a new one" (p. 81). Today, after much progress, the economics of innovation seem to concentrate more and more on the effort to elaborate a theory of economic creativity that highlights organizational development and decision (Antonelli, 2014). On the other hand, the study of organizational creative models generally has arisen from psychology because the main studies have been at the individual level. Additionally, other approaches have emerged in social disciplines (Mayer, 1999; Sternberg & Lubart, 1999) such as psychometric, cognitive, social and contextual (including cultural and evolutionary), and experimental. These different foundations of creativity and innovation models explain the gap between both, which is the same that exists between microeconomics and psychology. Therefore, to address the gap, a multilevel relationship could exist in which psychology could serve to underpin the economic dynamic of organizational innovation.

A second point in this comparative analysis is the contrast that exists between the innovation model generations and their additive characters (that is, new models add new concepts to old models, therefore, the old and new knowledge is integrated into one body), and the organizational creativity models which are not integrative (old and new models are not integrated with each other). For example, using Marinova and Phillimore's (2003) generations of innovation models, the Linear Model (as an innovation model) is included in the practices of the next Couplin Model generation; the Integrated Model forms part of the Systems Integration and Networking models; and they too form part of the Innovative Milieu models. Meanwhile, the Cyclic Innovation Model (Berkhout et al., 2006) includes the evolutionary and systemic approach taken from previous models. Therefore, this shows an evolutionary knowledge-building process that makes salient an innovation model phenomenon. In contrast, the different models of creativity are not necessarily interrelated and therefore they are not complementary; rather, they are equivalent. For that reason, an organization could use only the Interactionist Model by Woodman et al. (1993), the Componential Model by Amabile (1988), or the model by Borghini (2005), but an organization could not use an integrated creative model as a result of the union of these models.

A third point is that a model does not exist that fully integrates organizational creativity and innovation models. The Componential Model (Amabile, 1988) links both processes but essentially this is a proposal of individual creativity, which is related to the linear innovation process. Here, creativity is considered the first part of the innovation process but there is not a mix between both models. The Cyclic Innovation Model (Berkhout et al., 2006) includes creativity and it discusses its relevance, but creativity practices are diluted at the midpoint of the innovation process.

Generally, the models of creativity and innovation have been designed from the structural-functional paradigm (according to explanation above). For that reason, they are systems with clearly-identified dependent and independent variables. Models like the linear ones (Technology Pull and Market Pull), Couplin, Integrated, Componential, Interactionist, CPS, Evolutionary, Innovative Milieu, and Cyclic Innovation Model (Amabile, 1988; Marinova & Phillimore, 2003; Puccio et al., 2011; Rothwell, 1994) are based on factors that nurture creativity and innovation in one or various levels. The aim, therefore, is to improve these factors to increase creativity and innovation, which under these conditions are considered outcomes. On the other hand, only the Borghini (2005) creativity model presented a process based on a sense-making approach that features an understanding of the process rather than outcomes (see explanation above).

A final point arises from observations made of the development of both creativity and innovation models that affirm a forward trajectory towards more complex, flexible, and open models, generations more akin to a global business context (see e.g., Gassmann, Enkel, & Chesbrough, 2010; Huizingh, 2011; Niosi, 1999; Tidd, Bessant, & Pavitt, 2005). This occurs because organizations need to respond to the escalating pace and volume of change and the complexity and more intense competition that it brings (Isaksen & Tidd, 2006). The innovation side shows the increase of complexity, flexibility, and openness through the advance between the old Linear Models and the new Systematics, Evolutionary, Cyclic, and Milieu models (Marinova & Phillimore, 2003). On the creativity side, the process has developed, too. It has evolved from Componential (Amabile, 1988) and Interactionist (Woodman et al., 1993) models to CPS: The Thinking Skill Model (Puccio et al., 2011) and Borghini's (2005) creativity model. Both models characterize an exploration of the complexity of cognitive processes, organizational culture and its knowledge management.

Additionally, according to Tidd (2006), the innovation models (and it is possible to include creativity models here, too) are characterized by a partial understanding of the innovation process; as a consequence, the models have been conceived like linear processes and as such miss the potential of incremental innovation, consider innovation as a single isolated change rather than as part of a wider system, and see innovation as product or process without recognizing the interrelationship between the two. In the same way, Tidd et al. (2005) presented the following problems of this partial view of innovation: considering R&D as the main capability; thinking that innovation is only for specialist or key individuals; understanding only the customer needs or only the technology advances; thinking this topic targets only large and single firms; developing only radical innovation; managing innovation only through strategic projects; and considering only a closed or open development of innovation.

Recommendations

Throughout this paper, the contrast between creativity and innovation was shown, related to their histories, definitions, approaches, and models, so that different features can be considered for developing a new generation of innovation models. With this aim in mind, this study uses the *Multi-dimensional Framework of Organizational Innovation* proposed by Crossan and Apaydin (2010) as a basis for its proposal because it offers a clear way to understand different sources and results of innovation. Thus, this framework has ten dimensions to depict innovation as a process and outcome (see Table 1). Additionally, this study has added three dimensions as categories that have arisen from the previous analysis developed in this research; these are: *foundation, sequence* and *purpose*. Table

1 synthesizes the proposal's conclusions along three parts: (1) 13 dimensions as categories of characteristics; (2) current features found as a result of the previous analysis; and, (3) the proposal of features that enhance, complement, and adapt current features to better reflect environmental complexity and dynamism, which will be used in the future for designing a new generation of innovation models. The core of this proposal is the integration and interaction of creativity and innovation processes, as they are complementary and synergetic. This is part of their nature. Therefore, they are not sequential actions (Burgelman, 2002; Rickards, 1996) as the analysis showed above. To distinguish this interaction, this article proposes features for designing a new generation of innovation models as shown on the second column in Table 1 as "Creativity+Innovation (C+I)." Column one lists the current features of creative and innovation models.

As seen in Table 1, the first dimension is *foundation*. Thus, although creativity and innovation have different sources, it is necessary to develop a dialogue in which the economics of innovation considers psychology as its core. In this integration both require a consideration for the functional paradigm and sense making as two perspectives from which is possible to understand C+I (Borghini, 2005; Drazin et al., 2008; Weick, 1995).

The second dimension is *sequence*. Here the linear or cyclic shape of the process is emphasized. The conclusion is that new innovation models could be evolutionary, cyclic, and iterative as responses to a complex and dynamic business environment, which requires constant adaptation (Berkhout et al. 2006; Kumar, 2012; Nelson & Winter, 1982). Likewise, future models should depict an interaction between creativity and innovation along this process (Burgelman, 2002; Rickards, 1996) and through all *levels* of the organization, because C+I is a system in which each one participates and affects the others' levels.

Direction is the dimension that covers the flow of ideas and motivation of this process. Here, participation and commitment come from all people (bottom-up); new processes fuse creative leadership and entrepreneurship, which encourages people, accompanies the C+I process, and obtains effective results (Berkhout et al., 2006; Drucker, 1998; Puccio et al., 2011). With this cyclic, iterative, and interactive process, both customers and technology are *drivers* of a C+I process (Tidd, 2006; Tidd et al., 2005), as the success is achieved when there is fit between value proposition (technology side) and customer segment (Osterwalder, Pigneur, Bernarda, & Smith, 2014). New innovation models, therefore, require the invention and adoption as a *source* to a C+I process. This suggests that there are internal and external sources. Therefore, organizations need to develop a mix between closed and open innovation (Chesbrough & Appleyard, 2007; Chesbrough et al., 2006).

In the same sense, the dimension denominated as *locus* explains the context of the C+I process. The proposal, therefore, suggests developing networks as a response to new conditions under which cooperation, integration, and parallel development are considered effective innovation (Hobday, 2005; Rothwell, 1994;). Likewise, these network are propitious spaces for all kind of organizations (Tidd, 2006; Tidd et al., 2005) which develop a mix of closed and open innovations (Gupta, Smith, & Shalley, 2006).

The *nature* of knowledge for new models suggests that C+I will be a process of learning and unlearning by which people and teams transform and adjust tacit knowledge to explicit knowledge that permits the sharing of mental models to develop the C+I process (Borghini, 2005). The next dimension is the *form* of innovation, which for a next generation would comprise a mix of all types of innovation outcomes as consequence of an integrative, systemic, and complex C+I process that generates outcomes at each level. In the same way, the *purpose* dimension will be defined by the big purpose of C+I process: organizational change at the organizational level (Woodman, 2008), and competitiveness at organizational and macro levels (Carayannis & Gonzalez, 2003).

The *referent* dimension explains that new models will need to consider incremental changes to improve the organization, innovations that reach and discover new markets, and innovations that generate competitiveness within the industry. The *magnitude* dimension proposes a mix of incremental and radical innovations (Tidd, 2006; Tidd et al., 2005). Finally, the *type* dimension represents the difference between creativity and innovation processes based on technical or administrative developments. Today, organizations require many types of C+I based on magnitude, form, level, and purpose dimensions.

In summary, the increase of complexity and dynamism of the business context demands that companies and institutions integrate creativity and innovation through an organizational process characterized by flexibility, continuous learning, open-closed and systemic views, thinking and affective skills, valuation of incremental and radical results, multi-level interaction, and effective leadership and entrepreneurship.

Table 1. *A proposal of features to design a new generation of innovation models*

Dimensions of Innovation	From current features of creativity and innovation (C+I) models...	...to features for designing a new generation of creativity and innovation (C+I) models
Foundation: knowledge foundations	Innovation is based on economics of innovation (Antonelli, 2014; Nelson & Winter, 1982; Schumpeter, 1942).	Dialogue between economics and psychology underpin a new generation of C+I models.
	Creativity is based on psychology and social disciplines (Mayer, 1999; Sternberg & Lubart, 1999).	
	Creativity and innovation approaches are developed from structural-functional paradigm (Drazin et al., 2008).	C+I approach is developed from a structural-functional paradigm and sensemaking perspective (Borghini, 2005; Drazin et al., 2008; Weick, 1995).
Sequence: lineal or cyclic	Linear view of the creativity and innovation processes (Tidd, 2006; Tidd et al., 2005).	Evolutionary, cyclic and iterative view of the C+I process (Berkhout et al., 2006; Kumar, 2012; Nelson & Winter, 1982; Nickles, 2003).
Sequence: stepwise or continuous	Creativity as first stage of ideation, and innovation as second stage of implementation (Amabile, 1988; Bledow, Frese, Anderson, Erez, & Farr, 2009; Cropley & Cropley, 2012; Luecke & Katz, 2003; Roberts, 1988).	Creativity and innovation interact throughout the whole process and through all levels (Burgelman, 2002; Rickards, 1996; Van de Ven et al., 2007).
Level: individual, group, organization or macro	Creativity and innovation is a topic dedicated to specialists and key people (Tidd, 2006; Tidd et al., 2005).	C+I concerns all people from the firm and its partners outside the company.
	Creativity and innovation developed for some levels (Amabile, 1988; Puccio et al., 2005; Woodman et al., 1993).	C+I are developed according to an integrative view. It requires a systemic perspective (Puccio et al., 2007; Sears & Baba, 2011).

(Table continues next page)

Table 1. *A proposal of features to design a new generation of innovation models (continued)*

Dimensions of Innovation (cont.)	From current features of creativity and innovation (C+I) models... (cont.)	...to features for designing a new generation of creativity and innovation (C+I) models (cont.)
Direction: top-down or bottom-up	Creativity and innovation without the core role of leadership and entrepreneurship.	Fusion between creative leadership and entrepreneurship as a core element of the C+I process (Berkhout et al., 2006; Drucker, 1998; Puccio et al., 2011).
Driver: resources or market opportunity	Customers or technology are drivers of creativity and innovation (Tidd, 2006; Tidd et al., 2005).	C+I considered both customers and technology drivers of its process (Tidd, 2006; Tidd et al., 2005); success is reached when there is a fit between value proposition and customer segment (Osterwalder et al., 2014).
Source: invention or adoption	Innovation is a process centered at closed invention.	This is an open and closed (ambidextrous) process that uses invention and adoption as sources of the process (Chesbrough et al., 2006; Chesbrough & Appleyard, 2007).
Locus: firm or network	Creativity and innovation are alone firm issues (Tidd, 2006; Tidd et al., 2005).	C+I is a network issue (Hobday, 2005; Rothwell, 1994).
	These topics are only for big enterprises (Tidd, 2006; Tidd et al., 2005).	This is for all kinds of firms (Tidd, 2006; Tidd et al., 2005).
	Mainly a closed innovation process and sometimes open (Tidd, 2006; Tidd et al., 2005).	A mix of closed and open innovation that develops ambidexterity capabilities (Gupta et al., 2006)
Nature: Tacit or explicit	Creativity and innovation processes uses explicit knowledge.	It is a process of learning and unlearning by which people and teams transform and adjust tacit knowledge; explicit knowledge informs shared mental models to further develop the C+I process (Borghini, 2005).

(Table continues next page)

Table 1. A proposal of features to design a new generation of innovation models (continued)

Dimensions of Innovation (cont.)	From current features of creativity and innovation (C+I) models... (cont.)	...to features for designing a new generation of creativity and innovation (C+I) models (cont.)
Form: product, service, process or business model	This is about product/service or process as outcomes (Tidd, 2006; Tidd et al., 2005).	This is an integrative, systemic and complex process that mixes all ways of innovation outcomes to reach the purposes (Keeley, Walters, Pikkel, & Quinn, 2013).
Purpose: immediate or long term outcomes	Products, services, process, structures, practices, etc, as outcomes.	Competitiveness and organizational change as big purposes of C+I process (Carayannis & Gonzalez, 2003; Woodman, 2008).
Referent: firm, market or industry	The company develops creativity and innovation processes to further its position in the market and to maintain its competitiveness.	The C+I process of a company is a way to change itself. Also, it permits it to reach and discover new markets and to be competitive in its cluster in a specific moment.
Magnitude: incremental or radical	This is a topic of radical innovation (Tidd, 2006; Tidd et al., 2005).	C+I is a process that considers incremental and radical innovations (Tidd, 2006; Tidd et al., 2005).
Type: administrative or technical	Creativity and innovation are developed through strategic projects, mostly at a technological level (Tidd, 2006; Tidd et al., 2005).	C+I is a process developed through projects or incremental effective changes involving many topics. It is developed daily, and along the firm and its industry or cluster.

Note: C+I = The combination, interaction and integration of creativity and innovation processes.
Source: Author's analysis and synthesis, and listed authors as cited.

Acknowledgments

The author appreciates the support received from Associate Professor John Cabra and International Center for Studies in Creativity at SUNY Buffalo State during his visit to the college. Likewise, he appreciates the feedback provided by the Innovation Decisions in the Business Environment Research Group at the School of Economics from University of Navarra (Spain). His visit to Buffalo State and his doctoral studies have been possible by the financial support of the University of La Sabana (Colombia).

References

Amabile, T. M. (1988). A model of creativity and innovation in organizations. In B. M. Staw & L. L. Cummings (Eds.), *Research in organizational behavior* (pp. 123-167). Greenwich, CT: JAI Press.

Amabile, T. M. (1996). *Creativity in context.* Boulder, CO: Westview.

Anderson, N., Potočnik, K., & Zhou, J. (2014). Innovation and creativity in organizations: A state-of-the-science review, prospective commentary, and guiding framework. *Journal of Management, 40*(5), 1297-1333.

Antonelli, C. (2014). *The economics of innovation, new technologies and structural change.* New York, NY: Routledge.

Basadur, M., Graen, G. B., & Scandura, T. A. (1986). Teaching effects on attitudes toward divergent thinking among manufacturing engineers. *Journal of Applied Psychology, 71,* 612-617.

Benner, M. J., & Tushman, M. (2003). Exploitation, exploration, and process management: The productivity dilemma revisited. *Academy of Management Review, 27,* 238-256.

Berkhout, A. J., Hartmann, D., Van Der Duin, P., & Ortt, R. (2006). Innovating the innovation process. *International Journal of Technology Management, 34*(3-4), 390-404.

Bledow, R., Frese, M., Anderson, N., Erez, M., & Farr, J. (2009). A dialectic perspective on innovation: Conflicting demands, multiple pathways, and ambidexterity. *Industrial and Organizational Psychology, 2*(3), 305-337.

Borghini, S., (2005). Organizational creativity: Breaking equilibrium and order to innovate. *Journal of Knowledge Management, 9*(4), 19-33.

Bowonder, B., Dambal, A., Kumar, S., & Shirodkar, A. (2010). Innovation strategies for creating competitive advantage. *Research-Technology Management, 53*(3), 19-32.

Brown, T. (2008). Design thinking. *Harvard Business Review, 86*(6), 84-93.

Burgelman, R. A. (2002). Strategy as vector and the inertia of co-evolutionary lock-in. *Administrative Science Quarterly, 47*, 325-357.

Burkhardt, M. E., & Brass, D. J. (1990). Changing patterns or patterns of change: The effects of change in technology on social network structure and power. *Administrative Science Quarterly, 35*, 1-8.

Burrell, G., & Morgan, G. (1979). *Sociological paradigms and organizational analysis.* London, UK: Heinemann.

Camisón, C., & Villar-López, A. (2014). Organizational innovation as an enabler of technological innovation capabilities and firm performance. *Journal of Business Research, 67*(1), 2891-2902.

Carayannis, E. G., & Gonzalez, E., (2003). Creativity and innovation = competitiveness? When, how and why. In L. V. Shavinina (Ed.), *The international handbook on innovation* (pp. 587-606). Oxford, UK: Elsevier Press.

Chesbrough, H. W. (2003). The era of open innovation. *MIT Sloan Management Review, 44*(3), 35-41.

Chesbrough, H. W., & Appleyard, M. M. (2007). Open innovation and strategy. *California Management Review, 50*(1), 57-76.

Chesbrough, H. W., Vanhaverbeke, W., & West, J. (2006). *Open innovation: Researching a new paradigm.* Oxford, UK: Oxford University Press.

Cooper, R. G. (2008). Perspective: The Stage-Gate idea-to-launch process—Update, what's new and nexgen systems. *Journal of Product Innovation Management, 25*(3), 213-232.

Cropley, D., & Cropley, A. (2012). A psychological taxonomy of organizational innovation: Resolving the paradoxes. *Creativity Research Journal, 24*(1), 29-40.

Crossan, M. M., & Apaydin, M. (2010). A multi-dimensional framework of organizational innovation: A systematic review of the literature. *Journal of Management Studies, 47*, 1154-1192.

Damanpour, F., & Schneider, M. (2006). Phases of the adoption of innovation in organizations: Effects of environment, organization, and top managers. *British Journal of Management, 17*, 215-236.

Damanpour, F., & Wischnevsky, J. D. (2006). Research on organizational innovation: Distinguishing innovation-generating from innovation-adopting organizations. *Journal of Engineering and Technology Management, 23*, 269-291.

Dewett, T. (2004). Creativity and strategic management: Individual and group considerations concerning decision alternatives in the top management teams. *Journal of Managerial Psychology, 19*(2), 156-169.

Drazin, R., Glynn, M.A., & Kazanjian, R. K. (1999), Multilevel theorizing about creativity in organizations: A sense-making perspective. *Academy of Management Review, 24*(2), 286-307.

Drazin, R., Kazanjian, R., & Glynn, M. (2008). Creativity and sensemaking among professionals. In J. Zhou & C. E. Shalley (Eds.), *Handbook of organizational creativity* (pp. 263-282). New York, NY: Lawrence Erlbaum Associates.

Drucker, P. F. (1998). The discipline of innovation. *Harvard Business Review, 76*(6), 149-157.

European Commission (1995, December). *Green paper on innovation*. Retrieved from http://cordis.europa.eu/publication/rcn/361_en.html

Ford, C. M. (1996). A theory of individual creativity in multiple social domains. *Academy of Management Review, 21*, 1112-1134.

Gassmann, O., Enkel, E., & Chesbrough, H. (2010). The future of open innovation. *R&D Management, 40*(3), 213-221.

Gioia, D. A., & Pitre, E. (1990). Multiparadigm perspectives on theory building. *Academy of Management Review, 4*, 584-602.

Gumusluoglu, L., & Ilsev, A. (2009). Transformational leadership, creativity, and organizational innovation. *Journal of Business Research, 62*(4), 461-473.

Gupta, A. K., Smith, K. G., & Shalley, C. E. (2006). The interplay between exploration and exploitation. *Academy of Management Journal, 49*, 693-706.

Herzog, P. (2011). *Open and closed innovation: Different cultures for different strategies* (2nd ed.). Wiesbaden, Germany: Springer Science & Business Media.

Hobday, M. (2005). Firm-level innovation models: Perspectives on research in developed and developing countries. *Technology Analysis & Strategic Management, 17*(2), 121-146.

Huizingh, E. K. (2011). Open innovation: State of the art and future perspectives. *Technovation, 31*(1), 2-9.

Isaksen, S., & Tidd, J. (2006). *Meeting the innovation challenge.* West Sussex, UK: John Wiley & Sons.

Keeley, L., Walters, H., Pikkel, R., & Quinn, B. (2013). *Ten types of innovation: The discipline of building breakthroughs.* Hoboken, NJ: John Wiley & Sons.

Kumar, V. (2012). *101 design methods: A structured approach for driving innovation in your organization.* Hoboken, NJ: John Wiley & Sons.

Lawrence, K. (2013). *Developing leaders in a VUCA environment.* [Unpublished manuscript.]

Lawton, T., Finkelstein, S., & Harvey, C. (2007). Taking by storm: A breakthrough strategy. *Journal of Business Strategy, 28*(2), 22-29.

Luecke, R., & Katz, R. (2003). *Managing creativity and innovation.* Boston, MA: Harvard Business School Press.

Mann, D. (2001). An introduction to TRIZ: The theory of inventive problem solving. *Creativity and Innovation Management, 10*(2), 123-125.

March, J. G. (1991). Exploration and exploitation in organizational learning. *Organization Science, 2*(1), 71-87.

Marinova, D., & Phillimore, J. (2003). Models of innovation. In L. V. Shavinina (Ed.), *The international handbook on innovation* (pp. 44-53). London, UK: Pergamon.

Mayer, R. E. (1999). Fifty years of creativity research. In R. J. Sternberg (Ed.), *Handbook of creativity* (pp. 449-460). Cambridge, UK: Cambridge University Press.

Mootee, I. (2013). *Design thinking for strategic innovation: What they can't teach you at business or design school.* Hoboken, NJ: John Wiley & Sons.

Nelson, R. R., & Winter, S. (1982). *An evolutionary theory of economic change.* Cambridge, MA: Harvard University Press.

Nickles, T. (2003). Evolutionary models of innovation and the meno problem. In L. V. Shavinina (Ed.), *The international handbook on innovation* (pp. 54-78). London, UK: Pergamon.

Niosi, J. (1999). Fourth-generation R&D: From linear models to flexible innovation. *Journal of Business Research, 45*, 111-117.

Nonaka, I. (1991). The knowledge-creating company. *Harvard Business Review, 69*(6), 96-104.

OECD and Eurostat (2005). *Oslo Manual: Guidelines for collecting and interpreting innovation data* (3rd ed.). Paris, France: OECD Publishing.

Osborn, A. F. (1953). *Applied imagination: Principles and procedures of creative thinking.* New York, NY: Charles Scribner's Sons.

Osterwalder, A., Pigneur, Y., Bernarda, G., & Smith, A. (2014). *Value proposition design: How to create products and services customers want.* Hoboken, NJ: John Wiley & Sons.

Parsons, T. (1951). *The social system.* Glencoe, IL: Free Press.

Puccio, G. J., & Cabra, J. F. (2010). Organizational creativity: A systems approach. In J. C. Kaufman & R. J. Sternberg (Eds.), *The Cambridge handbook of creativity* (pp. 145-173). Cambridge, UK: Cambridge University Press.

Puccio, G. J., Mance, M., & Murdock, M. C. (2011). *Creative leadership: Skills that drive change* (2nd ed.). Thousand Oaks, CA: SAGE Publications.

Puccio, G. J., Murdock, M. C., & Mance, M. (2005). Current developments in creative problem solving for organizations: A Focus on thinking skills and styles. *The Korean Journal of Thinking & Problem Solving, 15*(2), 43-76.

Rhodes, M. (1961). An analysis of creativity. *Phi Delta Kappan, 4,* 305-310.

Rickards, T. (1996). The management of innovation: Recasting the role of creativity. *European Journal of Work and Organizational Psychology, 5*(1), 13-27.

Rickards, T., & Moger, S. (2006). Creative leaders: A decade of contributions from Creativity and Innovation Management Journal. *Creativity and Innovation Management, 15*(1), 4-18.

Roberts, E. B. (2007). Managing invention and innovation. *Research Technology Management, 49*(1), 35-54.

Roberts, E. D. (1988). What we have learned managing invention and innovation. *Research Technology Management, 1,* 11-29.

Rothwell, R. (1994). Towards the fifth-generation innovation process. *International Marketing Review, 11*(1), 7-31.

Schumpeter, J. A. (1942). *Capitalism, socialism, and democracy.* New York, NY: Harper & Brothers.

Sears, G. J., & Baba, V. V. (2011). Toward a multistage, multilevel theory of innovation. *Canadian Journal of Administrative Sciences / Revue Canadienne des Sciences de l'Administration, 28*(4), 357-372.

Shalley, C. E., & Zhou, J. (2008). Organizational creativity research: A historical overview. In J. Zhou & C. E. Shalley (Eds.), *Handbook of organizational creativity* (pp. 3-31). Hillsdale, NJ: Lawrence Erlbaum Associates.

Sternberg, R. J. (2003). WICS: A model of leadership in organizations. *Academy of Management Learning & Education, 2*(4), 386-401.

Sternberg, R. J., & Lubart, T. I. (1999). The concept of creativity: Prospects and paradigms. In R. J. Sternberg (Ed.), *Handbook of creativity* (pp. 3-15). Cambridge, UK: Cambridge University Press.

Tidd, J. (2001). Innovation management in context: Environment, organization and performance. *International Journal of Managerial Reviews, 3*(3), 169-183.

Tidd, J. (2006). *A review of innovation models.* Imperial College London. Retrieved from http://ict.udlap.mx/projects/cudi/sipi/files/Innovation%20models%20Imperial%20College%20London.pdf

Tidd, J., Bessant, J., & Pavitt, K. (2005). *Managing innovation: Integrating technological, market and organizational change.* New York, NY: Wiley.

Tushman, M. L., & Nelson, R. R. (1990). Introduction: Technology, organizations, and innovation. *Administrative Science Quarterly, 35,* 1-8

Van de Ven, A., Polley, D., Garud, S., & Venkataraman, S. (2007). *The innovation journey.* New York, NY: Oxford University Press.

Vehar, J. (2008, May). Creativity and innovation: A call for rigor in language. In G. J. Puccio et al. (Eds.), *Proceedings from An International Conference on Creativity and Innovation Management—The Second Community Meeting,* Vol. 2 (pp. 259-277). Buffalo, NY: International Center for Studies in Creativity.

Verganti, R. (2009). *Design-driven innovation: Changing the rules of competition by radically innovating what things mean.* Boston, MA: Harvard Business Press.

Wagner, D. G., & Berger, J. (1985). Do sociological theories grow? *American Journal of Sociology, 70,* 137-158.

Weick, K. E. (1995). *Sensemaking in organizations.* Thousand Oaks, CA: Sage Publications.

West, M. A., & Farr, J. L. (1990). Innovation at work. In M. A. West & J. L. Farr (Eds.), *Innovation and creativity at work: Psychological and organizational strategies* (pp. 3-13). Chichester, UK: Wiley.

Wheatley, W. J., Anthony, W. P., & Maddox, E. N. (1991). Selecting and training strategic planners with imagination and creativity. *Journal of Creative Behavior, 25,* 52-60.

Woodman, R. W. (2008). Creativity and organizational change: Linking ideas and extending theory. In J. Zhou & C. E. Shalley (Eds.). *Handbook of organizational creativity* (pp. 283-300). New York, NY: Lawrence Erlbaum Associates.

Woodman, R. W., Sawyer, J. E., & Griffin, R. W. (1993). Toward a theory of organizational creativity. *The Academy of Management Review, 18*(2), 293-321

Xu, F., & Rickards, T. (2007). Creative management: A predicted development from research into creativity and management. *Creativity and Innovation Management, 16*(3), 216-228.

About the Author

Andrés Mejía Villa is professor of strategic management and innovation at the University of La Sabana, Bogotá, Colombia. Currently, he is pursuing a doctoral degree in Economics and Management at the University of Navarra in Pamplona, Spain. His dissertation is titled, "The role of industry associations as drivers of strategic management of innovation in industry," through which he wants to understand the process of open innovation behind business associations as innovation intermediaries of their affiliated companies. His interest in innovation brought him to Buffalo State as a visiting scholar to deepen his understanding of the relationship between creativity and innovation at the organizational level. Andrés wishes to develop a model that integrates creativity and innovation, which he can then apply to a study of innovation intermediation phenomenon.

Email: andres.mejia@unisabana.edu.co, amejia@alumni.unav.es

Are the Other Benefits of Group Creativity Practices Just as Important as Good Ideas?

David Eyman
International Center for Studies in Creativity
SUNY Buffalo State

Originally published in *Big Questions in Creativity 2015*

Abstract

This paper explores the possibility that additional benefits of group creativity processes—specifically brainstorming—might hold a value that equals or exceeds that of good ideas. This paper describes how to determine what additional outcomes of group creativity might be achieved. More specifically, it reviews six additional outcomes of brainstorming: consensus building, team building, post-session ideas, engagement, motivation, and depth of understanding. Multiple group creativity models such as Creative Problem Solving (Osborn, 1953), design thinking (Curedale, 2013), and community engagement strategy (Block, 2008) are considered in this review. Examples that support research findings are included.

Are the Other Benefits of Group Creativity Practices Just as Important as Good Ideas?

Brainstorming is a frequently misused term that has come to mean anything from a synonym for creativity to group meetings where ideas are supposed to occur but don't (Davis, 2004). Correct use of the word brainstorming would describe a facilitated divergent thinking tool following specific rules to produce new ideas that are further from the expected (Osborn, 1953). Since its birth in the early 1950s, brainstorming has come under scrutiny for efficacy in producing more or better ideas than other forms of ideation. Those who challenge brainstorming have based their opinion and research on proving or disproving efficacy in only one domain: more or better ideas.

So why do we still use brainstorming (by definition) in almost all creative thinking frameworks such as Creative Problem Solving (Osborn, 1953), design thinking (Curedale, 2013), Systematic Inventive Thinking (Boyd & Goldenberg, 2014), and Brainswarming (McCaffrey, 2014)? Some of the newer frameworks (Systematic Inventive Thinking, Brainswarming) even hide the technique under other assertions, yet still use divergence with rules, just as Brainstorming does. The most plausible explanation is that brainstorming works. And it works not only for the production of novel ideas, but for many outcomes such as team building, consensus building, and engagement (which will be discussed in depth in this paper). Additional outcomes have noteworthy value and should be considered when evaluating the effectiveness of brainstorming as a part of any larger problem-solving process. Does an intentional focus on only one output (a novel idea) benefit the group in the same way as group problem solving sessions that yield these other benefits?

What Is at Risk?

Despite debatable evidence on effectiveness (Taylor, Berry, & Block, 1958; Kohn & Smith, 2011), businesses continue to use group creativity processes with successes that transcend the original intent of generating ideas (Faure, 2004; Sutton & Hargadon, 1996). The dispute over the effectiveness of brainstorming revolves around the corporate expectation of producing big ideas desperately needed to compensate for a lack of ongoing innovation. If a big idea does not occur within one short ideation session, the blame is often assigned to the process.

More specifically, brainstorming is often blamed whether or not it is facilitated properly. Critics stereotypically judge the effectiveness of the process based on the success or failure in the production of that big idea and in so doing negate the cumulative value of the group creativity process (Sawyer, 2007; Cain, 2013).

Design thinking, as noted in Sutton and Hargadon's 1996 study of a product design firm, is an exception. In this study, design thinking yielded six important consequences: organizational memory; providing skill variety for designers; supporting an attitude of wisdom; creating a status auction; impressing clients; and providing income for the firm (Sutton & Hargadon, 1996). This study suggests that in the organizational context, idea generation deserves no special status as an effectiveness outcome.

In a lecture regarding creativity in education, Runco (2011), a noted creativity scholar and one of brainstorming's most outspoken critics, professed:

> Brainstorming does not work. Thousands of studies have been done with brainstorming, and it always lowers originality. Always. Across the board. Brainstorming is a pretty good thing…if you want team building and perhaps if you want students to exchange ideas and learn to cooperate, collaborate, and see other perspectives and so on. Those are all good things, and the brainstorming social setting might be good for it. (9:42)

In studying the collaborative effects of brainstorming on decision making, Kramer, Kuo, and Daily (1997) noted, "The use of brainstorming groups in organizations often serves multiple goals besides reaching high-quality decisions, such as team building, consensus building, or increasing participation" (p. 236).

When placing value and priority on critical factors of success such as team building, cooperation, and collaboration, we begin to appraise group creativity practices using a different measure of success than the traditional scales of quantity and quality of ideas. Sponsors of group creativity practice might be more equipped to make such decisions through an understanding of these additional outcomes.

In *Group Genius*, Sawyer (2007) wondered, "If brainstorming isn't the creativity panacea some people have thought it to be, why does its popularity persist?" (p. 66). He attributes this to an illusion of success, yet compelling evidence suggests that brainstorming's additional benefits outweigh any deficiencies in creative efficacy.

Intentions of Group Creativity

Research indicates that we claim that we want revolutionary ideas but often don't adopt them (Mueller, Melwani, & Goncalo, 2011). More frequently, we adopt small evolutionary changes to our present products, services, or ways of being. This research also supports the notion that we enter into brainstorming meetings to garner knowledge, build trust, or organize a strategic plan for achieving success. Participants and sponsors typically suggest that the intention is to generate radical innovation, yet are seldom disappointed if that objective is not met. In fact, Sutton and Hargadon (1996) reported "higher levels of satisfaction with the experience" for group brainstorming despite nominal productivity loss (p. 687). The evidence proposed that we opt for brainstorming not for creativity alone, but that group creativity sessions are superior to other meeting formats in generating other successful outcomes.

Additional Outcomes of Group Creativity

Consensus Building

With consensus, a team builds trust, confidence, accountability, and commitment to the outcome of its project. In the absence of consensus, team members may feel that their individual contributions lack value and may silently sabotage the progress by not performing to the best of their abilities, or they may move forward independently instead of as part of a cohesive team. Building consensus is critical when a project team is working toward a collaborative success, or when operating within a creative leadership model.

Group creativity processes are designed with tools and practices that lend themselves to building consensus by having every member of the team contribute in some way. In some instances, this occurs through initiating ideas and in other cases through building on others' ideas. Whether contributions are directly chosen or merged with the selected ideas, the result is that participants have added to the solution, leading to personal ownership in the outcome.

Finding consensus among group members can be challenging. For instance, people may have different problem-solving preferences (Dyer, Dyer, & Dyer, 2007; Grivas & Puccio, 2012); someone with a discovery-driven style may find it hard to agree or collaborate with someone who has an execution-driven style. And yet, the variety of cultural backgrounds, thinking styles, and even ages contributes to participants' differing opinions, which enhance creative output (Davis, 2004; Grivas & Puccio, 2012; Sawyer, 2007). Group creativity processes are ideally designed for the diversity of participants, and many group creativity tools such as Group Grids and Stakeholder Analysis (Miller, Vehar, Firestien, & Thurber, 2011) are designed to address these differences.

In a systematic group creativity session, using a methodology such as design thinking or Creative Problem Solving, selected ideas are developed by the group. The development process allocates space for further ideational thinking, which often presents further opportunities for each member to contribute. If some participants did not agree beforehand, this is often the place they can contribute the most, thereby coming to consensus with the group as the process unfolds. Compassion towards the initial idea and those who suggested it can be grown in time as the idea comes closer to a solution.

Team Building

Team building helps to foster efficient and open communication, promotes trust among employees, improves attitudes, and builds motivation toward the success of collaborative efforts. Team building is critical when the outcome of a given project is reliant on how well individual team members complement one another in a cooperative effort. Foundations of team building practices such as communication, respect, trust, compassion, support, and understanding are all enhanced by group creativity practices (Dyer, Dyer, & Dyer, 2007).

After a facilitated session, Jennifer Goodin, executive director of the Ronald McDonald House Charities of Cincinnati, noted the enhanced rapport in her group: "I'm so happy we had the entire management team in this brainstorming session. We came away from it like we're all on the same team again and working together better" (personal communication, October 27, 2014). In this session, the team balked at the hardships of implementing some ideas. Although this can be construed as a form of dissent, the team remained positive because of the directive to defer judgment. Given the need for this team's collaborative efforts and the need for iterative innovation as opposed to radically new ideas, allowing such conversations to progress within the brainstorming session helped the group in ways that a traditional team building process might not allow. Team building was the obvious outcome, benefiting the group more than radically innovative ideas.

This example echoes a research study by Henningsen and Henningsen (2013) that concluded, "Our brainstorming groups developed higher levels of cohesiveness in terms of desire to continue working with the group than nominal groups following an idea-generation task" (p. 42). The results of this study did not conclude significant idea generation gains with brainstorming, yet the additional benefits were proven significant.

Expert facilitation requires monitoring many aspects of group dynamics at once, including attending to additional outcomes of sessions. Once informed, the facilitator has the option to add more or less team building as a part of the programming, or to redirect conversations as they may support group interactions. To inspire collaborative teams, the facilitator may encourage interactions by using table teams or small-group brainstorming prior to large-group interactions. Projects may be assigned to give small groups an opportunity to witness a condensed model of their team's interaction. A post-project debrief might include discussion about the team dynamic in addition to reviewing the resulting innovations.

New Thinking and Post-Session Ideas

Creative problem solving can be enhanced by allowing a period of incubation and reflection: reflecting on the problem and gaining insights while not actively engaged in the problem. Csikszentmihalyi (1996) noted that the commercial evidence for incubation is supported in reports where after some time the creator comes to a sudden moment of insight. Participants of group sessions will emerge with ideas hours, days, even months after the session ends. At times, these late-arriving ideas are presented as refined and developed, which may support adoption. Although these ideas appear to spring from unknown sources, the depth of understanding gained in brainstorming sessions can be credited with a significant portion of new thinking.

With a knowledge base of ideas presented in sessions, a participant may also have insights into other problems he or she is presented with, and these ideas may hold value over and above the problem—solutions that were intended in the original course. The value of such ideas is situational, thereby creating a value proposition assessable only by the owner or sponsor of group creativity sessions. Gabe Tzeghai, a global innovation executive with Procter & Gamble, noted:

> The additional benefits [of group creativity] are a great source of future innovation as well. Afterward folks get ideas while driving, in the shower, on vacation, etc. Most of the ideas from the sessions don't go anywhere but the sessions can create trust that creates a broader confidence in other ideas so they may be evaluated and possibly developed into products to market. (personal communication, October 26, 2014)

Procter & Gamble has a rich history in the use of group creativity sessions and continues to employ new processes as they arise. Tzeghai observed the interrelated roles of belief, tenacity, and new product development apparent in such sessions: "Trust is the force multiplier that helps remove naysayers (aka ankle biters) and more importantly creates confidence and pace in the development of good ideas to market" (personal communication, October 26, 2014).

Engagement

Although there is some evidence of social loafing during group brainstorming sessions, there is also evidence of increased levels of project engagement emerging from sessions (Paulus, 2000; Sutton & Hargadon, 1996). Project participation, job commitment, and community engagement are all outcomes that are qualitatively evident from employees of organizations that expect creativity from employees or use group creativity methods (Gilson & Shalley, 2004).

Megan Deal, a director with People's Liberty, a philanthropic organization, has years of experience with group creativity facilitation and participation. On the topic of brainstorming, she observed:

> The results are typically team-building, eagerness, and engagement with the problem/project. I tend to subscribe to the viewpoint that participation fosters empathy and fosters understanding. When individuals are invited to contribute in early stages of brainstorming, their investment towards further stages of the project or subject matter undoubtedly balloons. (personal communication, October 23, 2014)

From this observation, it may be inferred that valuing participant input and the way they feel about participating in group brainstorming fosters future involvement with the project, job, or community. With this knowledge, engagement may become a primary objective of our initiative by shining a light on each participant's contribution. Each member's contribution builds engagement and a commitment to the outcome.

Motivation

During facilitated group creativity sessions, motivation to work on a project tends to grow (Curedale, 2013). In community engagement processes, also a modality of group creativity, this change is described as moving from a viewpoint of personal concern to a group-oriented, compassionate motivation (Block, 2008). Similarly, the design thinking approach emphasizes empathy for end users. More specifically, this approach builds optimism about empathic innovation (Curedale, 2013). Optimistic empathy-building provides motivation to direct one's efforts toward reconciling the needs of others, as well as an intrinsic motivation to succeed at innovating for the benefit of others. One possible explanation is that people are called to be responsible for successful ideation when put in the service of either end users or teammates. This redirects intent from image gain or personal expression toward solving problems on a collective level.

The use of a motivational programming structure ties together many of the additional outcomes of sessions and generates excitement toward systematic success. In *The Skilled Facilitator*, Schwarz (2005) described this possibility of some types of sessions: "In addition to clarifying survey results, these sessions are intended to create momentum and motivation for organizational change" (p. 411). By design, momentum is built into the outcome. Research by Isaksen and Gaulin (2005) affirmed that an adept facilitator is capable of maintaining motivation and group commitment during the session. Experience confirms that this continues into project motivation after the brainstorming ends.

Facilitators allow motivation to happen as a result of participants getting excited about the possibility of their ideas. The tendency is to either promote or control this energy in the room, yet there are opportune times for channeling it in ways that will balance motivation. That power will carry projects ahead at a more efficient pace and with more focus on a successful implementation.

Depth of Understanding

Group creativity promotes depth of understanding of the organization, the problem, and the individual's role in problem solving. We share critical data, build on and remember each other's ideas. We have access to multiple stores of memories and multiple ideas to build on (Brown, Tumeo, Larey, & Paulus, 1998). We ask detailed questions and nurture the collective information share. The conversation is a divergent thinking tool that builds a robust understanding of the data; then we cache pertinent details for use as needed.

At the front end of a recent problem-solving session, a group of trustees for a non-profit organization was introduced to the problem statement. The statement was carefully crafted by consultants and the president of the board. One of the trustees immediately questioned the statement and wondered why they should pursue this topic at all. The facilitators made a conscious choice to allow this comment to progress into a group discussion. The dialog appeared to have more value for the long-term health of the organization than jumping into ideation, so the group moved back into gathering data to see if the vision was worthy of exploration. On an easel pad, they listed objections. A series of questions was formed as a reaction to the complaints, and finally the group-created consensus was that not only was it worth pursuing the challenge, it was critical to do so. In the process of using this impromptu tool and allowing the conversation to unfold, each trustee gained a depth of knowledge that would never have happened outside of that meeting. Typically, this group assembles to address emergencies, report their fundraising successes, or make large decisions. The newly generated knowledge created another list of issues that will eventually need resolution and can be used to expedite all forthcoming problem-solving tasks. In some instances, this group can move to voting on issues without discussion because of knowledge gained in this session. In this particular case, the findings are self-evident, and we maintain that the depth of understanding far outweighs the original intention of the meeting.

This is valuable knowledge, so what might be done with it? For a consultant, selling problem-solving services is a vague pursuit, and the thought that we are now proposing to sell additional services muddles the pitch even further. Rather than suggest these results as by-products, perhaps these outcomes should be considered as part of the overall goals, and incorporated into the design. This might involve a deliberate selection of tools that are more conducive to one of those "additional" outcomes, or designing a new set of tools with particular goals in mind. In the above example, the tool was spontaneously created, yet it could be intentionally built into other sessions.

Conclusion

In many reviews of individual versus group creativity practice, findings might dissuade us from placing so much emphasis on group creativity or brainstorming (Cain, 2013; Dunnette, Campbell, & Jaastad, 1963; Kohn & Smith, 2011; Sawyer, 2007). Even Osborn (1953), who created (and coined the term) brainstorming, touted the merits of individual creativity: "Despite the advances in organized research, the creative power of the *individual* still counts most" (p. 289).

Even so, brainstorming in many modalities persists as the method of choice among organizations (Sawyer, 2007). There are many logical connections to explain this phenomenon, six of which are previously mentioned. We have freedom to assign our priorities to group creativity in an effort to garner the benefits that serve us best. Therefore, it is our charge to place a value on the needs of a project or team and apply the most efficient methodology that we can create. A lack of evidence indicates the need for further research to determine which group creativity tools are most efficient at creating specific, concrete results. This evidence would allow us to target specific outcomes based on our objectives.

In addition to the need for research, there is an opening for the development of tools designed to direct group creativity practice toward augmenting critical domains such as consensus, team building, late arriving ideas, engagement, motivation, and depth of understanding. This group creativity toolkit might find a comfortable home among organizational development practices; a combination of business, leadership, and creativity practices might be in order. Tying organizational development and new brainstorming tools together would support development in all areas of organizational well-being while providing a venue for new thinking.

References

Block, P. (2008). *Community: The structure of belonging.* San Francisco, CA: Berrett-Koehler.

Brown, V., Tumeo, M., Larey, T., & Paulus, P. (1998). Modeling cognitive interactions during group brainstorming. *Small Group Research, 29*(4), 495-526.

Boyd, D., & Goldenberg, J. (2014). *Inside the box: A proven system of creativity for breakthrough results.* New York, NY: Simon & Schuster.

Cain, S. (2013). *Quiet: The power of introverts in a world that can't stop talking.* New York, NY: Broadway Books.

Csikszentmihalyi, M. (1996). *Creativity: Flow and the psychology of discovery and invention.* New York, NY: HarperCollins.

Curedale, R. (2013). *Design thinking: Pocket guide.* Los Angeles, CA: Design Community College.

Davis, G. (2004). *Creativity is forever* (5th ed.). Dubuque, IA: Kendall/Hunt.

Dunnette, M. D., Campbell, J., & Jaastad, K. (1963). The effect of brainstorming effectiveness for 2 industrial samples. *Journal of Applied Psychology, 47*(1). 30-37.

Dyer, W. G., Dyer, W. G., Jr., & Dyer, J. H. (2007). *Team building: Proven strategies for improving team performance* (4th ed.). San Francisco, CA: Jossey-Bass.

Faure, C. (2004). Beyond brainstorming: Effects of different group procedures on selection of ideas and satisfaction with the process. *Journal of Creative Behavior, 38*(1), 13-34.

Gilson, L., & Shalley, C. (2004). A little creativity goes a long way: An examination of teams' engagement in creative processes. *Journal of Management, 30*(4), 453-470.

Grivas, C., & Puccio, G. J. (2012). *The innovative team: Unleashing creative potential for breakthrough results.* San Francisco, CA: Jossey-Bass.

Henningsen, D., & Henningsen, M. (2013). Generating ideas about the uses of brainstorming: Reconsidering the losses and gains of brainstorming groups relative to nominal groups. *Southern Communication Journal, 78*(1), 42-55.

Isaksen, S., & Gaulin, J. (2005). A reexamination of brainstorming research: Implications for research and practice. *Gifted Child Quarterly, 49*(4), 315-329.

Kohn, N., & Smith, S. (2011). Collaborative fixation: Effects of others' ideas on brainstorming. *Applied Cognitive Psychology, 25*(3). 359-371.

Kramer, M., Kuo, C., & Dailey, J. (1997). The impact of brainstorming techniques on subsequent group processes: Beyond generating ideas. *Small Group Research, 28*(2), 218-242.

McCaffrey, T. (2014, March 25). *Why you should stop brainstorming.* Retrieved from https://hbr.org/2014/03/why-you-should-stop-brainstorming

Miller, B., Vehar, J., Firestien, R., Thurber, S., & Nielsen, D. (2011). *Creativity unbound: An introduction to creative process* (5th ed.). Evanston, IL: FourSight.

Mueller, J., Melwani, S., & Goncalo, J. (2011). The bias against creativity: Why people desire but reject creative ideas. *Psychological Science, 23*(1), 13-17.

Osborn, A. (1953). *Applied imagination: Principles and procedures of creative thinking.* New York, NY: Scribner.

Paulus, P. (2000). Groups, teams, and creativity: The creative potential of idea-generating groups. *Applied Psychology, 49*(2), 237-262.

Runco, M. (2011, March 30). *Innovative teaching: Implications of creativity research* [Video file]. Retrieved from https://www.youtube.com/watch?v=3b9p7mBCnT4

Sawyer, R. (2007). *Group genius: The creative power of collaboration.* New York, NY: Basic Books.

Schwarz, R. (2005). *The skilled facilitator fieldbook: Tips, tools, and tested methods for consultants, facilitators, managers, trainers, and coaches.* San Francisco, CA: Jossey-Bass.

Sutton, R., & Hargadon, A. (1996). Brainstorming groups in context: Effectiveness in a product design firm. *Administrative Science Quarterly, 41*(4), 685-718.

Taylor, D. W., Berry, P. C., & Block, C. H. (1958). Does group participation when using brainstorming facilitate or inhibit creative thinking. *Administrative Science Quarterly, 3*(1), 23-47.

About the Author

As both innovation leader and industrial designer, David Eyman brings over twenty years of creative experience. As a catalyst, his expertise lies in developing new products, infrastructures, and innovation teams. His work has led to countless new products, environments, and deeper insights. David holds an Industrial Design degree from the University of Cincinnati, and is pursuing an M.S. in Creativity at the International Center for Studies in Creativity at SUNY Buffalo State.

Website: www.eymancreative.com

What are the Natural Relationships Between Creativity and Leadership?

Amy Frazier
International Center for Studies in Creativity
SUNY Buffalo State

Originally published in *Big Questions in Creativity 2013*

Abstract

A recent global executive survey identified the task of "embodying creative leadership" as the foremost directive for leaders seeking to thrive in an increasingly complex global landscape (IBM, 2010). If this is indeed the case, in order to understand how to harness the combined potential of creativity and leadership in response to complexity, we would be well served by understanding how they interact and what their natural relationships might be. In delving into the question of the connection between creativity and leadership, this paper reviews some of the related cognitive and affective mechanisms involved; provides examples of areas where the two constructs work in tandem; and explores the nature of self-development and internal focus as they pertain to the embodiment of creative leadership.

What are the Natural Relationships Between Creativity and Leadership?

In 2010, in the midst of the global downturn, IBM released its findings from a global survey of CEOs on the most pressing issues facing organizational leaders worldwide. Coming at a time of chaos and contraction, the report, "Capitalizing on Complexity," listed three best practices for succeeding in an increasingly complex environment. The top recommendation: "embody creative leadership" (p. 10).

Two impressions jump out from this compact phrase. The first: the implication that *leadership itself* must be creative—beyond, but certainly including—the need to employ creative thinking; the second: the notable use of the word "embody" to convey a deep-seated sense of both creativity and leadership as arising from within the self, permeating behavior and bearing, and informing engagement with the world.

To discuss creative leadership is, of course, to invite questions on the relationship between the two constructs. How might creativity and leadership be related, and what might be the elements supportive of or relating to their connection? This paper will approach the question from three angles: what are some of the internal cognitive and affective mechanisms which creativity and leadership share in common; in what situations might we naturally find creativity and leadership operating in tandem; and finally, given the deep-seated sense of self mentioned above, how do creativity and leadership align with personal development in the embodying of creative leadership?

Identifiable, but Eluding Definition

We implicitly recognize both creativity and leadership when they occur (Bass, 1990; Sternberg, 2003). As one would expect from their multifaceted natures, however, the study of each has resulted in numerous definitions, diverse theories, and occasionally contradictory historical perspectives (Bass, 1990; Davis, 2004; Sternberg, 2003). Among the current attempts to integrate various theoretical strands of creativity: Sternberg and Lubart (1995), who proposed that creativity manifests in the confluence of intellect, knowledge, thinking styles, personality and environment; Woodman and Schoenfeldt's (1990) interactionist mode, which, similarly, associated the person, situation, behavior and consequences in an effort to weave strands from psychological, cognitive, and social psychological approaches to creativity; and Murdock and Puccio's (2007) ecological approach which assessed creativity within a holistic system of interactions.

The leadership realm also offers unifying perspectives, including those of Avolio (2007), who proposed a deeper integration of leadership theories; Bennis (2007), who stated an urgent need to draw together the strengths of sociological, neurological and cognitive approaches; and Sternberg (2008), whose model of leadership as a synthesis of wisdom, creativity and intelligence drew upon established theories, including trait, behavioral and transformational leadership.

Despite these various attempts to synthesize our understandings of creativity and leadership, universally agreed-upon, comprehensive definitions of either remain elusive. As Bennis (2007) put it, "it is almost a cliché of the leadership literature that a single definition of leadership is lacking" (p. 2). As for defining creativity, "it's like nailing Jell-O to the wall" (M. Murdock, personal communication, June 2009).

Cognition and Affect in Creativity and Leadership

It is in one part the nature of both creativity and leadership which make them challenging to pin down. Attempting to overlay these two multidimensional concepts, then, is certain to provide a boundless stream of possibilities. Since cognition and affect—how we think and how we feel—are so central to our experiences, and since the neurological processes underlying both are themselves deeply intertwined, this seems a good place to begin the exploration of the interrelatedness of creativity and leadership. After all, how may our experiences and capabilities be considered to be in any way "embodied" if taken separately from the vast amounts of information continually flowing into our awareness from the commingling streams of cognition and affect?

Cognition, Creativity and Complexity

Cognition involves the manner in which "ideas (or thoughts or images or mental representations) develop, and how they are stored, accessed, combined, remembered, and...rearranged or distorted by the operations of the human mental apparatus" (Gardner, 1995, pp. 15-16). The study of creativity from a cognitive perspective is concerned with how these cognitive processes "operate on stored knowledge to yield ideas that are novel and appropriate to the task at hand" (Ward & Kolomyts, 2010, p. 93).

Associative mechanisms play an important role in linking images, thoughts, memories and other various bits of stored knowledge (Kaufman, Kornilov, Bristol, Tan, & Grigorenko, 2010). Creative benefits are conferred through the ability to broadly associate, permitting connections across diverse mental categories. "Cognitively complex individuals...use more categories or dimensions to discriminate among stimuli and see more commonalities among these categories or dimensions" (Hooijburg, Hunt, & Dodge, 1997, p. 378). To play among this wide variety of cognitive categories and dimensions opens up the possibility for more and potentially higher-quality novel combinations to emerge (Ranjan & Srinivasan, 2010; Rothenburg, 1973). The more cognitively complex an individual, the greater her chance of producing novel ideas, and of seeding her stores for future creative insights.

Cognition, Leadership and Complexity

Effective leadership in a complex environment requires pattern recognition and the ability to spot opportunities others may miss (Mumford, Connelly, & Gaddis, 2003), as well as being able to transcend cognitive traps which may block these insights (Katz-Buonincontro, 2008). Gardner (1995) heralded the cognitive role of *frames of reference,* especially those encoded in stories, as being key to leadership effectiveness. Duggan (2007) suggested that when faced with novel and complex situations, the leader's encoded knowledge and pattern recognition are made available through creative recombination, in a phenomenon he calls *strategic intuition.* Caughron, Shipman, Beeler, and Mumford (2009) proposed that people who use mental models to "draw attention to change indicators relevant in the situation at hand will be more likely to recognize emergent change events" (p. 15). This ability to identify and draw attention to emerging events was echoed in the IBM (2010) report: "both new threats and emerging opportunities require an ability to see around corners, predict outcomes where possible, act despite some uncertainty and then start over again" (p. 27).

Complexity, as the IBM (2010) report made clear, is not going away any time soon. The most effective method for responding to this complexity, according to Kegan and Lahey (2009), is not to try to tamp down the external complexity of the world, but rather to increase our own *internal* complexity. Not to be confused with becoming a more *complicated* individual, the development of internal *complexity* refers to the elaboration of various ego and personality structures which, taken together, inform how a person makes meaning of the world (Cook-Greuter, 2004). This sort of constructive-developmental approach to leadership is concerned with the way in which a person's stage of development influences how he constructs his world view (McCauley et al., 2006). The development involves not only cognition, but other aspects of the self as well, including awareness of our feelings.

Affect and Emotional Intelligence in Creativity and Leadership

Affect, our emotional or attitudinal valence, serves not only as an inner thermostat of our felt experience, but is also linked to cognition, in a "complex, multifaceted and bidirectional relationship" (Forgas, 2008, p. 99). The self-awareness of affect is one hallmark of emotional intelligence (Mayer, 2006). Developing our emotional intelligence provides us "with the capability to use emotions to contribute to the effective cognitive processing of information" (Zhou & George, 2003, p. 554). Affect helps in "promoting creativity, flexibility, cooperation, integrative thinking, successful negotiation" (Isen, 1987, as cited in Forgas, 2008, p. 99), all of which bear obvious links to the topics at hand.

Affect, Creativity and Complexity

Highlighting the important role of emotional intelligence in creative thinking, Goleman (1998) stated that "coming up with a creative insight is a cognitive act—but realizing its value, nurturing it and following through calls on emotional competencies such as self-confidence, initiative, persistence and the ability to persuade" (p. 100). Indeed, as Zhou and George (2003) succinctly stated: "Creative activities are affect-laden" (p. 545). Puccio, Murdock, and Mance (2007) incorporated the interconnectedness of cognition and affect in their Thinking Skills Model of Creative Problem Solving (CPS), and proposed key affective skills, from "dreaming" to "sensing gaps," to support each of CPS's creative-thinking process steps.

Just as affect can positively support creativity, so too can it impede it. For instance, in the realm of intrinsic motivation, a necessary ingredient for creative behavior: "the undermining of intrinsic interest may result as much from emotion or affect as it does from thoughts or cognitive analysis" (Hennessey, 2010, p. 350), something readily apparent to anyone who has felt deflated or resistant upon being asked to "be creative" amid drudgery.

Inasmuch as developing cognitive complexity supports creativity, so too does a well-differentiated sensitivity to our affective states, by broadening and enhancing the associative process mentioned earlier (Russ & Fiorelli, 2010). In the Thinking Skills Model of CPS, among the three affective meta-skills singled out as necessary for effective creative thinking is "tolerance for complexity" (Puccio et al., 2007, p. 52). In his seminal work on creativity and the state of flow, or optimal engagement, Csikszentmihalyi (1996) interviewed scores of highly creative people in order to distill common traits and behaviors useful in the cultivation of individual creativity. Among his recommendations was to aim for the goal of developing a more complex personality:

> The ability to move from one trait to its opposite is part of the more general condition of psychic complexity.... A creative person is highly individualized. She follows her own star and creates her own career. At the same time she is deeply steeped in the traditions of the culture; she learns and respects the rules of the domain and is responsive to the opinions of the field—as long as those opinions do not conflict with personal experience. Complexity is the result of the fruitful interaction between these two opposing tendencies. (pp. 362-363)

While the complexity Csikszentmihalyi recommends includes (of course) the cognitive complexity found in the rooms of a richly-furnished mind, such qualities as following a star, respecting rules, and demonstrating sensitivity to the environment, all speak to the value of the affective domain. The more elaborated and available our affective qualities and our awareness, the greater our chances for identifying novel associations, our energy for undertaking the creative endeavors that follow, and our ability to both self-manage and learn from our emotional states along the way.

Affect, Leadership and Complexity

In the leadership sphere, awareness of affect, emotional intelligence, and an appreciation for the way in which emotion impacts cognition are likewise important capacities to develop. "Emotions have the potential to affect leader cognition and behavior in a number of ways" (Hoojiburg, Hunt, & Dodge, 1997, p. 383), including when the leader: reverts to familiar emotional scripts; relies upon emotion as a method of interpreting others (especially when the information presented is novel and complex); and is faced with high-emotion situations. Zhou and George (2003) proposed that the missing piece in understanding the basis of leadership behavior is to be found in a deeper appreciation of emotional intelligence. Notably for our discussion, their exploration centered specifically on the ways in which the leader's emotional intelligence may support and enhance employees' creativity:

> Leaders who are high on emotional intelligence will be able to both understand how their followers are feeling and why and take the steps needed to give them the courage, optimism, and enthusiasm to flexibly approach creativity no matter how and when it might manifest itself. (Zhou & George, 2003, p. 563)

We can further clarify this point by applying the value of emotional intelligence to an example drawn from leadership theory; in this case, transformational leadership. It would be hard to imagine how a transformational leader could be successful in the deep work and lofty goals of "elevating the follower's level of maturity and ideals as well as concerns for achievement, self-actualization, and the well-being of others, the organization and society" (Bass, 1999, p.11) without the skillful use of affect and emotional awareness.

On the question of affect in the managing of complexity, we return to Puccio et al., (2007), who stated that the affective skill of "tolerance for complexity" reflects the ability "to stay open and persevere without being overwhelmed by large amounts of information, interrelated and complex issues, and competing perspectives" (p. 53). Further, the ability to tolerate complexity increases as a person evolves through the developmental perspectives and consequent ways of making meaning referred to above (Cook-Greuter, 2004). This has a direct impact on leader effectiveness. Work by Rooke and Torbert (1998) found a relationship between the level of CEO development and positive organizational transformation. In the organizations studied, those which were helmed by CEOs with a lesser ability to manage complexity stalled out or failed in their transformational efforts. Tolerance for complexity is essential to both creative thinking and leadership capacity.

Creativity and Leadership in Tandem

Moving beyond an exploration of the internal mechanisms of cognition and affect, we turn to ways in which creativity and leadership may be seen to be naturally interconnected. Acknowledging again that such complex entities as creativity and leadership will demonstrate themselves in manifold ways, we will focus on three contexts: theoretical perspectives which blend the two; deliberate problem solving methods which implicate creativity and leadership in a process duet; and the particular nested dynamic found in the creative leadership of creative people.

Leadership is Creative; Creativity is Leadership

Sternberg (2003) counted creative intelligence as one aspect of an overall theory of "successful intelligence" which can be lived out in the domain of leadership: "the three key components of leadership are wisdom, intelligence, and creativity, synthesized" (Sternberg, 2008, p. 361). Deepening the connection, Sternberg also related a symbiotic relationship between creativity and leadership: creativity "is by its nature propulsion. It moves a field from some point to another. It also always represents a decision to exercise leadership" (p. 125). Therefore, even a creative act which is merely replicative (reproducing a known work or process with only slight variance) is "at least, a weak attempt to lead" (p. 141).

In their exploration of how creative leaders think, Mumford et al. (2003) showed how leaders employ a particular process in their creative thinking. Inasmuch as this is particular to those in leadership roles, this constitutes a specific skill set: "leader creativity can be viewed as a unique domain-specific form of creative thought" (p. 415). Continuing, they stated: "Leaders are active, key contributors to the production of creative ideas, engaging in creative thought, albeit a rather different form of creative thought than that found to characterize followers" (p. 426). For Puccio et al. (2007), "creative thinking is the fuel that makes leadership work" (p. xii).

To turn from cognition to behavior, Zacko-Smith, Puccio, and Mance (2010), cited research by Gumusluoglu and Ilsev (2009) which demonstrated the predictive association between organizational innovation at the executive level and the leadership behaviors enumerated in Kouzes and Posner's (2002) Leadership Practices Inventory (LPI). In their discussion, Zacko-Smith et al. made the point that many of successful-leader behaviors identified in the LPI, such as searching for opportunities, experimenting and taking risks, treating mistakes as learning opportunities, and envisioning the future (Kouzes & Posner, 2007), share much in common with the behaviors necessary for successful creativity. Puccio et al. (2007) underscored the integration of leadership and creativity by maintaining that "effective leaders embody the spirit of creativity" (p. xii). To embody the spirit of a quality suggests a sense of being positively saturated with it in a way which informs not only behavior, but instills a distinct way of being, self-evident to those who witness it.

In these examples of theoretical perspectives, creativity and leadership in practical context may be seen as relating by degree: wholly coexisting, but varying in the amount of force (or propulsion); as a skill-based subset of creative thinking; and as a way of being, or embodiment.

Creative Process Models and Leadership

Leaders are charged with problem solving in multiple contexts, across various and shifting time frames, impacting diverse stakeholders. Deliberate creative processes such as CPS offer a natural opportunity to link the actions and motives of leadership with the dynamics and skills involved in creative thinking. As research and theories continue to develop this connection, a process-based duet between leadership and creativity is evolving.

Puccio et al. (2007) mapped the process steps of CPS onto a template for leadership in the service of change. Their Thinking Skills Model, not coincidentally, also interweaves cognitive and affective skills, as described above. Basadur (2004) advocated the use of creative problem solving processes as a focus of leadership effort, encouraging leaders to move beyond content influence and into creative process leadership. Notable in Basadur's work is the position that effective leadership emerges through developing competency in creative process. Similarly, Reiter-Palmon and Illies (2004) dug into the question of creative leadership opportunities within the phases of creative problem solving (which they broadly categorized as idea generation and idea evaluation), resulting in both a descriptive analysis of leader behaviors and an advocacy for the use of creative problem solving processes and techniques within the leadership realm. In their clear summation: "leaders must understand the cognitive requirements of creative problem solving" (p. 55).

These examples illuminate the natural fit between the leader's bailiwick of the skillful management of change, and the process dynamics of creative problem solving, and argue for a conscious application of creative thinking in leadership.

Leading Creative People

While some leadership writings seek merely to offer techniques for directing creative employees—such as the slightly tone-deaf advice that the management of "clever people" includes being aware that they "know their worth...have a low boredom threshold...(and) won't thank you" (Goffee & Jones, 2007, p. 6)—Mumford, Scott, Gaddis, and Strange (2002) provided greater insight into the topic: "Leadership of creative efforts seems to call for an integrative style—a style that permits the leader to orchestrate expertise, people, and relationships in such a way as to bring new ideas into being" (p. 738). They identified three areas where leadership both allows for and is implicated in the creative work of employees and teams: idea generation, idea structuring, and idea promotion (pp. 738-739). In each of these areas, the leader's own engaged creativity is essential for success—whether in setting the conditions for productive idea generation, in establishing frameworks to support idea structuring, or in promoting and advocating for the efforts within the organization. Similarly, for Mumford et al. (2003), the leader was "a collaborator who provides a critical perspective" and whose value "derives in part from the unique way in which they generate their contribution" (p. 427). This includes being able to draw upon prior knowledge in the form of experiential cases and being informed by their relationship to the organization's mission.

Creative leadership, as these writings suggest, is creativity manifested by the leader while engaged in leading creative efforts. The findings supersede earlier assumptions that creativity happens at the follower level upon direction of the leader, and bestows upon leadership its own unique creative process. In order to effectively lead creative people and creative efforts, the leadership, too, must be creative.

Inner Source

Sustained creativity and leadership efforts are time intensive and require focused personal energy (Csikszentmihalyi, 1996; Maxwell, 2007). They also represent a decision to manifest change within one's environment (Puccio et al., 2007; Sternberg, Kaufman, & Pretz, 2003; Sternberg & Lubart, 1995). A deep awareness of and sensitivity to the process of change is thus required—as is the will to trust that what appears to be in stasis may in fact be in the midst of transformation; and, conversely, to recognize unproductive or untimely changes as they emerge, and be willing to trim back, pause or redirect. Creativity and leadership also both involve working on an edge between *what is* and *what is emerging* (Scharmer & Kauefer, 2010). Given this unique perspective, the change leader/creator is thus often responding to inputs that others may not yet perceive, and may be met with resistance (Karp, 1996; Sternberg & Lubart, 1995). Courage is called forth in both.

All of these aspects highlight, at a minimum, the benefit of being well-centered in oneself; at the maximum, the necessity of it. Greater understanding of oneself may be deliberately cultivated through conscious self-development. Of self-development and creativity, Maslow (1992) proposed that the frontier-crossing new ideas sought on both an organizational and personal level arise from the deeper self, which is accessed through self-development and integration. Of self-development and leadership, reflective practices such as those described by Torbert (2004) and Kegan and Lahey (2009) are shown to both increase leader effectiveness, and facilitate developmental growth. Joiner and Josephs (2007) offered that "agile leadership and personal development go hand in hand" (p. 226). It's clear through research, scholarship, and what we witness in ourselves and the world around us, that both creativity and leadership have the potential to effect significant personal development.

Creativity and Self-development

The link between creativity and self-development has been elaborated to the point where "the relationship is both a semantic trend and virtually a given" (Davis, 2004, p. 2). Early work done by humanist psychologists such as Maslow (1974) and Rogers (1976) advanced the belief that creativity is not only linked to self-actualization, but in Maslow's (1968) words "seems to be synonymous with health itself" (p. 145). In the words of May (1975), "the creative process must be explored...as the expression of normal people in the act of actualizing themselves" (p. 40). More recently and in the same lineage, Richards (2007) described creativity as "a way of approaching life which can expand our experiences and options, and even deeply affect who we are—and can become" (p. 4).

For Fox (2004), to consider creativity was to consider "the most elemental and innermost and spiritual aspects of our being" (p. 2). In unfolding these aspects of our being, we grow into a deep, personal intimacy with our lives and with the life force itself. Combs and Krippner (2007) expanded the range of such intimate connection with life by linking individual developmental stages with structures of consciousness over time. Asserting that successive stages of consciousness exist both as historical phases (i.e., archaic consciousness, magical consciousness, etc.), and as levels of experience to which we all have access, they stated "each gives birth to unique forms of creative expression…(arising) spontaneously through the structures that unfold across individual development" (p. 131). This is creativity and development writ large across a phylogenic spectrum. Bringing it back to scale, eminent creativity scholar Ruth Richards, speaking on behalf of herself and fellow contributors to an edited publication on everyday creativity, noted:

> For several of us, creativity also represented a path—a personal route to something better and more powerful in our lives…. This path led to some combination of better health and well-being, a stress-free, relaxed and more immediate presence in our world, greater awareness of our interconnection, with enhanced concern and caring for others, and greater awe and awareness of beneficial forces beyond the mundane, with enhanced life meaning, and spirituality. (Richards, 2007, p. 13)

These commentaries, from the mystical to the practical, all circle back to the same understanding: creativity is nothing if not rooted within the self, and the more we engage our creativity, the richer that self becomes.

Leadership and Self-development

While historical approaches to leadership such as the "great man" theory were based on the idea of exceptional attributes constellated in leader personalities (Bass, 1990), there is a current proliferation of theories which conceive of leadership as a developable skill. Among many of these theories are evident themes of self-awareness and self-development, akin to the creative self-actualization theories of Maslow, Rogers, and May. Among these include:

- transformational leadership, mentioned earlier, which is concerned with "achievement, self-actualization, and the well-being of others, the organization and society" (Bass, 1999, p. 11);

- integrative leadership, which, according to Avolio (2007), addresses how leaders and followers "view their actual self and translate that into what could be their possible self or selves" (p. 30);

- intelligent leadership (Sydänmaanlakka, 2008), integrating practical, intellectual, emotional and spiritual components;

- transcendent leadership (Crossan, Vera, & Nanjad, 2008), where leadership of others is interwoven with leadership of the organization and, importantly, leadership of the self, evinced by "a high level of self-awareness and deep judgment" (p. 576);

- spiritual leadership (Fry, 2003) which draws upon a leader's self-knowledge;

- transformative leadership, in which the central focus is on self-creation (Montuori, 2010);

- the Leadership Maturity Framework (Cook-Greuter, 2006), where the leader is increasingly capable of embracing paradox and complexity through self-actualization and evolution of the ego.

These theories not only align leadership with personal development, but position such development as fundamental, calling upon the fabric of one's deep personal orientation to life and the construction of self, meaning and behavior. In the words of Briskin (2012), "Leadership begins with a transformation from within, a shift deep within our own souls." (This is followed by the cautionary remark: "Leadership without the cultivation of the inner world is at the mercy of the forces outside itself.")

While the link between creativity and self-development, as noted above in Davis (2004), is practically a given, one senses in the array of theories listed above a point still striving to be made: that leadership, too, is wed to self-development. In Kegan and Lahey's (2009) words, "too much emphasis has been placed on leadership, and not enough on development" (p. 5). Despite this, as with the case of creativity, there is a sense of rightness to the claim that leadership is rooted in the self, and that awareness and self-development will support and enhance it. To put theory aside and consider our individual experience, both the feelings of accomplishment and the torturous self-questioning we may undergo in the pursuit of both creative efforts and of leadership attest to this connection to our inner world. Both creativity and leadership appear to be rooted in an internal locus, evoking self-development, maturation, mastery, and spiritual growth.

Coinciding, but Not Connected?

Whereas the preceding discussion has explored the shared ground of creativity and leadership, the two constructs part ways in at least one significant aspect: that of how the expression of them necessarily involves other people. While a person may be creative on his own, purely for his own benefit, for the enhancement of quality of life (such as is found in the "happy path" of everyday creativity (Richards, 2007, p. 47)), "the only person who practices leadership alone in a room is the psychotic" (Bennis, 2007, p. 3). Leaders attend to, interact with, support, communicate with, redirect, authorize, guide, mentor, regulate, inspire, empower and evaluate those whom they lead. Put another way, while with leadership you cannot "tickle yourself" (Bavelas, as quoted in Bennis, 2007, p. 3), with creativity you certainly can.

Following on this distinction, might it be that the two constructs merely coincide under certain conditions, without being fundamentally connected? Or, to go further, might there be situations in which creativity and leadership actually stand in each other's way?

Clearly, there are areas within each construct which may operate powerfully without influence of the other. Everyday creativity need not evoke leadership; well-regarded components of leadership such as trustworthiness need not depend upon being creatively deployed, counting more upon consistency of character and stability of execution. Further, acts representative of the dark side of creativity (Sternberg, 2010) not only may be executed without any of the developmental goals of creative self-actualization, but also be absent the transformative goals of many advanced leadership theories as well.

The act of leadership is associated with influence (Bass, 1990). Not (necessarily) so the act of creativity. Despite Sternberg and Lubart's (1995) emphasis on the difference between creative thinking and successful creativity, in that the latter is the actual product of the creative thought and is often brought to bear through skillful influence, it remains that the creative idea may be vital and meaningful on its own, as in the case of everyday creativity (Richards, 2007). Moreover, the creator who inappropriately prioritizes influence may fall prey to some "outside temptations and interruptions," thereby squandering precious energies which are best devoted to the act of creating (Csikszentmihalyi, 1996, p. 551). The leader, on the other hand, who promulgates change and novelty for their own sake risks depriving his or her followers of the establishment of a stable shared ground of meaning, especially if the leadership story keeps changing (Gardner, 1995).

Yes, then: creativity and leadership can operate independently of each other; in some occasions, they need to. The question is not, therefore, whether they always march hand in hand, but whether a compelling case can be made for their natural intersections. We have made the case here that when creativity and leadership conjoin a powerful synergy can arise, imbuing leadership with a sustaining creative awareness, and enlisting our creative energies in the service of change. This synergy both emanates from and enriches our deepest selves, lending a heft and substance to our bearing and actions, emblematic of embodiment.

Conclusion

Abundant creativity and strong leadership are highly desired qualities. They fortify us in the face of change, bring us energy, purpose, drive and satisfaction, and serve as an inspiration to others. Creativity and leadership play important roles in marshaling the vision, imagination and courage necessary to respond to a complex and often troubled world. The IBM (2010) CEO survey authors acknowledged this when they chose the phrase "embody creative leadership" to describe the top recommendation. Yet the recommendation to embody such a thing as "creative leadership" risks becoming a slogan or an aspiration only, fueled by vague but hopeful sentiments about its saving benefits. To counter this, if we suspect that such a thing as "creative leadership" merits the sort of attention given it by the IBM CEO survey and other writings such as those explored here, it falls to us to understand exactly what we mean by the phrase—and how we might expect to see creativity and leadership naturally interrelating, so that we might better seek out those conditions.

By understanding certain similarities in complex cognitive and affective processing, by attuning to the situations which invite a synchrony of creativity and leadership, and by drawing awareness to the internal self-development which supports creativity and leadership, we come to know them on a personal level. From our thinking and our feeling states, our problem solving strategies, our leadership *with* and not just *of* creativity, and an attention to our self-development, the embodiment of creative leadership can then arise, informing our engagement with a complex world.

References

Avolio, B. J. (2007). Promoting more integrative strategies for leadership theory-building. *American Psychologist, 62*(1), 25-33.

Basadur, M. (2004). Leading others to think innovatively together: Creative leadership. *The Leadership Quarterly, 15*(1), 103-121.

Bass, B. M. (1990). *Bass and Stogdill's handbook of leadership: Theory, research and managerial applications.* New York, NY: Free Press.

Bass, B. M. (1999). Two decades of research and development in transformational leadership. *European Journal of Work and Organizational Psychology, 8*(1), 9-32.

Bennis, W. (2007). Challenges of leadership in the modern world. *American Psychologist, 62*(1), 2-5.

Briskin, A. (June, 2012). *Transforming leadership and the heart of collective wisdom.* Presentation at Reimagining, Renewing and Reinventing Leadership conference. Pacifica Graduate Institute, Carpinteria, CA.

Caughron, J. J., Shipman, A. S., Beeler, C. K., & Mumford, M. D. (2009). Social innovation: Thinking about changing the system. *International Journal of Creativity and Problem Solving, 19*(1), 7-32.

Combs, A., & Krippner, S. (2007). Structures of consciousness and creativity: Opening the doors of perception. In R. Richards (Ed.) *Everyday creativity and new views of human nature: Psychological, social, and spiritual perspectives* (pp. 131-149). Washington, D.C.: American Psychological Association.

Cook-Greuter, S. R (2004). Making the case for a developmental perspective. *Industrial and Commercial Training 36*(7), 1-10.

Crossan, M., Vera, D., & Nanjad, L. (2008). Transcendent leadership: Strategic leadership in dynamic environments. *The Leadership Quarterly, 19,* 569-581.

Csikszentmihalyi, M. (1996). *Creativity: Flow and the psychology of discovery and invention.* New York, NY: HarperCollins.

Davis, G. A. (2004). *Creativity is forever.* Dubuque, IA: Kendall/Hunt.

Duggan, W. (2007). *Strategic intuition: The creative spark in human achievement.* New York, NY: Columbia University Press.

Forgas, J. P. (2008). Affect and cognition. *Perspectives on Psychological Science. 3*(2), 94-101.

Fox, M. (2004). *Creativity: Where the divine and human meet.* New York, NY: Tarcher/Penguin.

Fry, L. W. (2003). Toward a theory of spiritual leadership. *The Leadership Quarterly, 14,* 693-727.

Gardner, H. (1995). *Leading minds: An anatomy of leadership.* New York, NY: Basic Books.

Goffee, R., & Jones, G. (2007). Leading clever people. *Harvard Business Review 85*(3), 72-79, 142.

Goleman, D. (1998). *Working with emotional intelligence.* New York, NY: Bantam.

Gumusluoglu, L., & Ilsev, A. (2009). Transformational leadership, creativity and organizational innovation. *Journal of Business Research, 62*, 461-473.

Hennessey, B. A. (2010). The creativity-motivation connection. In J. C. Kaufman & R. J. Sternberg (Eds.), *The Cambridge handbook of creativity* (pp. 342-365). New York, NY: Cambridge University Press.

Hooijburg, R., Hunt, J. G., & Dodge, G. E. (1997). Leadership complexity and development of the leaderplex model. *Journal of Management, 23*(3), 375-408.

IBM (2010). *Capitalizing on complexity: Insights from the global chief executive officer survey.* Portsmouth, UK: IBM Corporation.

Joiner, B., & Josephs, S. (2007). *Leadership agility: Five levels of mastery for anticipating and initiating change.* San Francisco, CA: Wiley.

Katz-Buonincontro, J. (2008). Can the arts assist in developing the creativity of educational leaders? *The International Journal of Creativity and Problem Solving, 18*(2), 67-79.

Karp, H. P. (1996). *The change leader: Using a gestalt approach with work groups.* San Francisco, CA: Pfeiffer.

Kaufman, A. B., Kornilov, S. A., Bristol, A. S., Tan, M., & Grigorenko, E. (2010). The neurobiological foundation of creative cognition. In J. C. Kaufman & R. J. Sternberg (Eds.), *The Cambridge handbook of creativity* (pp. 216-232). New York, NY: Cambridge University Press.

Kegan, R., & Lahey, L. L. (2009). *Immunity to change: How to overcome it and unlock the potential in yourself and your organization.* Boston, MA: Harvard Business Press.

Kouzes, J. M & Posner, B. Z. (2007). *The leadership challenge.* San Francisco, CA: Jossey-Bass.

Koestler, A. (1976). Bisociation in creation. In A. Rothenberg & C. Hausman (Eds.), *The creativity question* (pp. 109-113). Durham, NC: Duke University Press.

May, R. (1975). *The courage to create.* New York, NY: Norton & Co.

Mayer, J. D. (2006). A new field guide to emotional intelligence. In J. Chiarocci, J. P. Forgas, and J. D. Mayer (Eds.), *Emotional Intelligence in Everyday Life* (pp. 3-26). New York, NY: Psychology Press.

Maslow, A. H. (1992). Emotional blocks to creativity. In S. J. Parnes (Ed.), *Sourcebook for creative problem solving: A fifty year digest of proven innovation processes* (pp. 96-105). Hadley, MA: Creative Education Foundation.

Maslow, A. (1968). *Toward a psychology of being* (2nd ed). Princeton, NJ: VanNostrand Reinhold.

Maxwell, J. C. (2007). *The 21 irrefutable laws of leadership.* Nashville, TN: Thomas Nelson.

Mccauley, C., Drath, W., Palus, C., Oconnor, P., & Baker, B. (2006). The use of constructive-developmental theory to advance the understanding of leadership. *The Leadership Quarterly, 17*(6), 634-653.

Montuori, A. (2010). Transformative leadership for the 21st century: Reflections on the design of a graduate school curriculum. *ReVision.* San Francisco, CA: CIIS Press.

Mumford, M. D., Connelly, S., & Gaddis, B. (2003). How creative leaders think: Experimental findings and cases. *The Leadership Quarterly, 14*(4-5) 411-432.

Mumford, M. D., Scott, G. M., Gaddis, B., & Strange, J. M. (2002). Leading creative people: Orchestrating expertise and relationships. *The Leadership Quarterly, 13,* 705-750.

Murdock, M. C., & Puccio, G. J. (2007). Using an ecological approach to creativity assessment: The choice and the challenge. In G. J. Puccio and M. C. Murdock (Eds.), *Creativity assessment: Readings and resources* (pp. 467-477). Hadley, MA: Creative Education Foundation.

Puccio, G. J., Murdock, M. C., & Mance, M. (2007). *Creative leadership: Skills that drive change.* Thousand Oaks, CA: Sage.

Ranjan, A., & Srinivasan, N. (2010). Dissimilarity in Creative Categorization. *Journal of Creative Behavior, 44*(2), 71-83.

Reiter-Palmon, R., & Illies, J. J. (2004). Leadership and creativity: Understanding leadership from a creative problem-solving perspective. *The Leadership Quarterly, 15*(1), 55-77.

Richards, R. (2007). Introduction. In R. Richards (Ed.), *Everyday creativity, and new views of human nature, psychological, social, and spiritual perspectives* (pp. 3-22). Washington, DC: American Psychological Association.

Rogers, C. R. (1976). Toward a theory of creativity. In A. Rothenberg & C. Hausman (Eds.), *The creativity question* (pp. 296-305). Durham, NC: Duke University Press.

Rook, D., & Torbert, W. R. (1998). Organizational transformation as a function of CEOs' developmental stage. *Organization Development Journal, 16*(1), 11-28.

Russ, S. W., & Fiorelli, J. A. (2010). Developmental approaches to creativity. In J. C. Kaufman & R. J. Sternberg (Eds.), *The Cambridge handbook of creativity* (pp. 233-249). New York, NY: Cambridge University Press.

Scharmer, C. O., & Kaeufer, K. (2010). In front of the blank canvas: sensing emerging futures. *Journal of Business Strategy (31)*4, 21-29.

Sternberg, R. J. (2003). *Wisdom, intelligence, and creativity synthesized*. New York, NY: Cambridge University Press.

Sternberg, R. J. (2008). The WICS approach to leadership: Stories of leadership and the structures and processes that support them. *The Leadership Quarterly, 19,* 360–371.

Sternberg, R. J. (2010). The dark side of creativity and how to combat it. In D. Cropley, H. Cropley & J. Kaufman (Eds.), *The dark side of creativity* (pp. 316-328). New York, NY: Cambridge University Press.

Sternberg, R. J., & Lubart, T. I. (1995): *Defying the crowd: Cultivating creativity in a culture of conformity*. New York, NY: Free Press.

Sternberg, R. J., Kaufman, J. C., & Pretz, J. E. (2003). A propulsion model of creative leadership. *Leadership Quarterly, 14*(4-5), 455-473.

Sydänmaanlakka, P. (2008). Intelligent leadership and creativity. *Proceedings of the 2nd Creativity and Innovation Management Conference*. Buffalo, NY: International Center for Studies in Creativity, Buffalo State College.

Torbert, B., et al. (2004). *Action inquiry: The secret of timely and transforming leadership*. San Francisco, CA: Berrett-Koehler.

Ward, T. B., & Kolomyts, Y. (2010). Cognition and creativity. In J. Kaufman & R. Sternberg, (Eds.), *The Cambridge handbook of creativity* (pp. 93-112). New York, NY: Cambridge University Press.

Woodman, R. W., & Schoenfeldt, L. F. (2007) An interactionist model of creative behavior. In G. J. Puccio and M. C. Murdock (Eds.), *Creativity assessment: Readings and resources* (pp. 467-477). Hadley, MA: Creative Education Foundation.

Zacko-Smith, J. D., Puccio, G. J., and Mance, M. (2010). Creative leadership: Welcome to the 21st century. *Academic Exchange Quarterly 14*(4), 133-188.

Zhou, J., & George, J. M. (2003). Awakening employee creativity: The role of leader emotional intelligence. *The Leadership Quarterly, 14*(4-5), 545-568.

About the Author

Amy Frazier is a consultant, teacher, writer, and performer. Through her company Stages of Presence (www.stagesofpresence.com) she offers facilitation and training on creativity and innovation, Creative Problem Solving, leadership development, strategic planning, communications skills, transformation and change. She also contributes subject matter expertise in human resources programming and experience design.

Amy holds a B.A. in Theatre from the University of Denver, and an M.S. in Creativity from the International Center for Studies in Creativity at SUNY Buffalo State. A former professional actress, Amy draws upon theatre skills and practices in an integrated approach to creative learning, training, facilitation, and communications. Focus areas include: creativity and leadership, developmental leadership, creativity and life transitions, storytelling, somatics, archetypal psychology, and creativity as it relates to our conceptions of time. Amy was a founding member of the *Ardeo Theatre Company,* a residential arts community and school housed in a historic chateau in central France, and also served as founding co-artistic director of Seattle's *Theatre Under the Influence*, a company devoted to the production of neglected classics and lesser known works. Amy has presented at conferences in Canada, Europe and the U.S., including a featured presentation of her original one-woman show, *Creativity in Time* based on her master's project: *Memory, Presence, Emergence: Creativity in Time* (http://digitalcommons.buffalostate.edu/creativeprojects/137/) at the Creativity Expert Exchange conference in 2012.

Amy is the current president of the Creative Connections Network, the alumni group of the International Center for Studies in Creativity, and is a contributor at Innovation Bound (www.innovationbound.com).

Linkedin: www.linkedin.com/in/amyfrazier
Twitter: @stagespresence

What If We View Our Education System as an Ecosystem?

Kathryn P. Haydon
International Center for Studies in Creativity
SUNY Buffalo State

Originally published in *Big Questions in Creativity 2015*

Abstract

This paper introduces the Creative Learning Ecosystems model, which was developed using a biomimetic approach to education innovation. The model proposes a foundational structure from which the ideals of creative learning may be realized systemically on a micro or a macro scale. It is designed to illustrate to parents, schools, and organizations that the science of creativity can be used to delineate infrastructures that integrate content and rigorous creativity, and which result in engagement, learner motivation, continuous learning, and positive relationships among constituents. The author articulates the foundational creative learning framework, provides background on the systems model of creativity from which the model is derived, and translates this model into terminology and components related to education. Each component—person, process, press, product, and innovative change—is described as an element of the Creative Learning Ecosystem.

What If We View Our Education System as an Ecosystem?

Though never planted by human hands, the prairie is choked with blossoms, grasses gently pouring over, seeds setting, new shoots growing, runners criss-crossing the earth in a web of decay, growth, and new life. There is no hint of hail damage or drought wilt, no such thing as weeds. Every plant—231 species in this patch alone—has a role and cooperates with linked arms with the plants nearby. I see diversity of form—grasses splaying upward to different heights and widths, a sunflower's bold expanse, a legume's dark leaflets, fernlike in their repetition.

Benyus, 1997, p. 23

The prairie, the natural state of the American plains, teems with life. It is an ecosystem diverse with plants whose individual strengths work in harmony to support the whole. Together, they prevail over harsh elements. Consider this image of a robust, dynamic, self-sustaining prairie: It is a healthy ecosystem of plants, insects, and other species sustaining each other and the land as they bend and wave in the wind.

Biomimicry draws on natural models and systems to help solve complex problems. What if we were to look through the biomimetic lens and study the prairie to inform best practices on nurturing and supporting learning? What if we were to view our education system as an ecosystem?

This paper explores the concept of creative learning as an ecosystem, supporting the call for creativity in the classroom articulated by Beghetto (2010): "[M]ost importantly, there is a need for creativity researchers to assist in the development, testing, and implementation of new pedagogical models that simultaneously support the development of creative potential and academic learning" (p. 459). It also introduces the Creative Learning Ecosystems model. Its theoretical background and related research support its potential to inform the design of sustainable learning infrastructures that integrate creativity and academic content.

Theoretical Foundation

What Is Creative Learning?

While the pedagogy of creative learning is not new, the term *creative learning* has recently gained traction in the United Kingdom, where several organizations contribute to an effort to bring such learning into classrooms throughout the country (Craft, Cremin, Burnard, & Chappell, 2007; Jeffrey & Craft, 2004). Worldwide, the term is still developing into a universally agreed-upon definition.

Broadly defined, creative learning is the integration of creativity, content, self-growth, and collaboration. Jeffrey's (2006) work comes closest to concisely articulating the pedagogy. He amplified his earlier research (Woods & Jeffrey, 2002) that placed creative learning within a humanitarian framework. In this paradigm, personal meaning and relevance to both learners and educators is essential, which follows Amabile's (1983) theory that creative tasks are driven by intrinsic motivation. Amabile's work was influenced by Torrance's (1979b) model, in which creative behavior arises at the intersection of motivation, skill, and abilities. Creative learning is rigorous because it exercises the highest stratum of thinking. Within the last decade, even Bloom's taxonomy (Bloom, Engelhart, Furst, Hill, & Krathwohl, 1956) has been revised to position creativity at the top level of thinking (Krathwohl, 2002). Torrance and Safter (1990) asserted that "the intuitive, creative thinking processes represent mankind's highest thinking ability" (p. 7).

Creative learning, then, can be characterized by four central assertions:

- Learning is meaningful to student interests and needs.
- Students are intrinsically motivated to learn.
- Creativity is integrated with academic content teaching and learning.
- The outcome is a change in thinking: new, meaningful ideas (sometimes expressed in the form of a product), skills, or personal growth.

When one is learning creatively, one is gaining meaningful self-knowledge. As Guilford (1977) stated, "Knowing the nature of your abilities, you will be able to turn them on when you need them and you will learn how to exercise them in order to strengthen them" (p. 12). This knowledge supports the development of solid individuals who are the pillars in a thriving creative learning ecosystem.

While there are scattered examples of schools that seem to function as creative learning ecosystems, these are the exception. Many roadblocks exist that schools perceive as barriers to adopting creative learning methodologies. For example, educators often do not know how to integrate an infrastructure of creative learning into content, assessment mandates, and curriculum standards. In addition, leaders at some schools feel they do incorporate creativity but do not have a way to measure or improve their practices. A rare handful of educators practice creative learning, but find it difficult to share their approaches, which are often developed intuitively. The Creative Learning Ecosystems model proposes a foundational structure from which the ideals of creative learning may be realized systemically on a micro or a macro scale.

Why Creative Learning?

A recent comprehensive literature review (Davies et al., 2013) of several hundred articles and studies concluded that creative learning significantly benefited students. Empirical studies included in the review demonstrated that creative learning led to learners' "improved academic achievement; increased confidence and resilience; enhanced motivation and engagement; development of social, emotional and thinking skills; and improved school attendance" (Davies et al., 2013, p. 88).

Creativity practitioners and researchers, in the past decade or so, have helped raise public awareness about creativity, intrinsic motivation, intelligence, engagement, and the need for a new educational paradigm (e.g., Amabile & Kramer, 2011; Florida, 2002; Robinson, 2009; Wagner, 2012). The essence of their message is that children begin with innate creativity, curiosity, and talents, and that traditional schooling methods tend to inhibit these characteristics and stifle the self in favor of conformity, an assertion that has been supported by decades of creativity research (Beghetto, 2010; Richards, 2010; Torrance, 1959; Wallach & Kogan, 1965). The message is beginning to resonate with more of the general public, due to widespread, accessible media platforms such as YouTube, Facebook, and the Internet in general. Even so, the literature from the field supporting the need for creativity as a central educational goal emerged in the 1950s and continues today in calling for a new educational paradigm that incorporates creative thinking (Beghetto, 2010; Craft et al., 2007; Cramond, Matthews-Morgan, Bandalos, & Zao, 2005; Guilford, 1950; Jeffrey, 2006; Kim, 2006; Krathwohl, 2002; Runco, Millar, Acar, & Cramond, 2010; Torrance, 1979a).

The majority of states in the United States have implemented the Common Core State Standards (CCSS). These standards claim to be "based on rigorous content and application of knowledge through higher-order thinking skills" (Common Core State Standards Initiative, n.d.-a). However, although creativity has been named the highest-level cognitive function (Krathwohl, 2002), a search of the term "creativity" on the CCSS website yields only one result, an off-hand reference buried in the high school math standards (Common Core State Standards Initiative, n.d.-b). Moreover, it has been demonstrated that methodologies such as the standardized assessments that have been developed to accompany the CCSS decrease the chance that creativity will thrive in the classroom (Beghetto, 2010). Studies (Beghetto, 2010; Sawyer, 2004) have shown that fact-based standardized tests beget fact-based, rote learning methodologies, narrower teaching practices and topics, and scripted curricula. Students in low-income areas are most likely to be negatively affected. A creative learning approach offers a strategy that supports higher-order thinking, academic learning, and self-knowledge across a spectrum of learners with widely different needs.

The Systems Model Influence

Over the last 50 years, creativity theories have advanced from a basic understanding to a robust systems model that involves the intersection of Persons, Process, and Press (or environment), to effect a final outcome or Product (Puccio, Mance, & Murdock, 2011; Rhodes, 1961). In the organizational realm, each of these components must be carefully considered to drive new and useful products that, when implemented, create innovative change. The author asserts that to sustain creative learning, one must consider the interactions and connections among the people involved, the conditions of their press/environment (culture and climate as well as physical), and the processes used to facilitate learning. This holistic view is critical to informing the product or outcome: the depth of learning and growth experienced by learners, manifested in its meaningful application to their lives, which leads to change and fuels the iterative cycle of innovation and learning. The Creative Learning Ecosystems model is based on the systems model of creativity.

Creative Learning Ecosystems Model

Diversity allows a prairie to function successfully. The biological diversity of plants, grasses, insects, birds, and animals creates a complex web of interaction that makes the prairie resilient and robust. Species work together to contribute to the health and growth of the whole, and they do this by calling on their individual characteristics and adaptations. The prairie manifests—and often demands—individual growth and freedom of expression. The prairie leverages the adaptations that the species have developed over time, as well as the roles they play in the prairie organization. Only because it works as a system can it gracefully absorb harsh conditions such as flooding and strong winds. If the prairie forsook the primary contribution of each species in favor of fixing weaknesses first, the system would not function. When an outside force (such as humans) uproots individual species, the ecosystem deteriorates.

Similarly, creative learning ecosystems must center on learners by using built-in collaborative structures designed for maximum personal growth along a wide spectrum of intellectual diversity. This can be achieved only within a paradigm that acknowledges that each has a contribution to make and seeks to leverage these assets. Translating the components of the systems model of creativity to educational terminology, following is a description of what each means in an educational setting:

- Persons: instructor attitudes, outlooks, demeanor, approach; student attitudes and outlooks, often derived from instructor modeling; instructor view of students; parent attitudes and outlooks, often taken on cue from instructors

- Process: curriculum; course activities; structure of lesson plans; teaching methodologies

- Press: classroom climate, as determined by teacher norms, attitudes, atmosphere; classroom management practices; physical space

- Product: ideas and knowledge; products created by students that reflect new learning

- Innovation: application of learning to students' everyday lives; joy of learning; sense of progress

Understanding the relationship between education and the components of the systems model of creativity involves how they work together as an interconnected network. Figure 1 depicts the Creative Learning Ecosystems Model. Expanding on the model, Table 1 details each component of the ecosystem, describes its function, and relates it to the systems model of creativity. An elaboration of each component follows, and an exploration of how they all fit within the creative learning ecosystem.

Learners and Leaders, Partners, and Individuals

Like the prairie, the strength of a learning ecosystem begins with finding the positive contributions that each individual has the potential to make. There are three significant categories of individuals involved: educators (teachers and administrators), students, and parents. In a creative learning ecosystem, it is essential to value, acknowledge, and engage their respective strengths to sustain the cycle of continuous learning and growth.

The success of learning in a classroom or a school begins with transformational leadership as modeled by teachers and administrators. A key component of this

Creative Learning Ecosystem

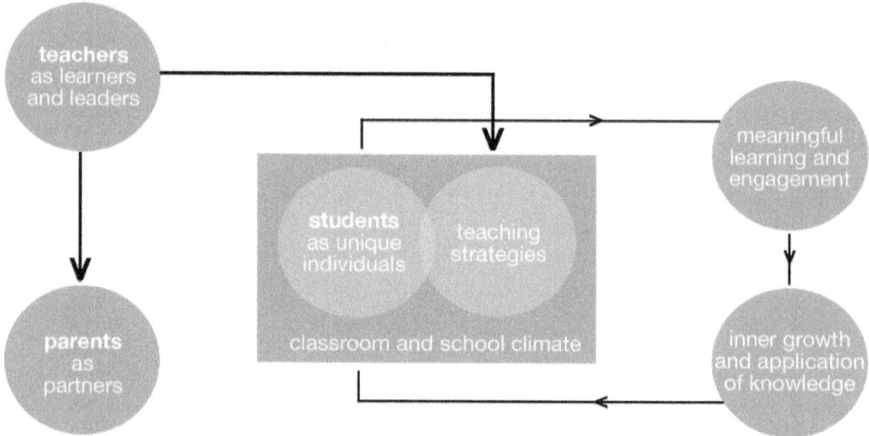

Figure 1. A diagram of the Creative Learning Ecosystems model. Adapted from Puccio, G. J., Mance, M., & Murdock, M. C. (2011). *Creative leadership: Skills that drive change* (2nd ed.). Thousand Oaks, CA: Sage.

type of leadership is valuing the creative characteristics and growth of oneself and others:

> The transformational leader recognizes the inherent value and benefit in promoting individual creativity.... Through their behavior, they create a work climate that supports others' creativity, encouraging followers to pursue their own solutions to problems, to explore complex challenges by reframing problems, and to question decisions and practices. (Puccio et al., 2011, pp. 14-15)

The theory of transformational leadership values creativity as a core leadership quality as well as an outcome. Leaders are most effective when they express characteristics of creativity such as awareness, playfulness, improvisation, joy, curiosity, courage, inspiration, intuition, freedom, humor, and perceptivity (Puccio et al., 2011). Relationships in this paradigm must be built on a platform of mutual respect (Davies et al., 2013).

Educators accept the role that each individual plays in the ecosystem and what they contribute; this includes the need to accept highly creative students who often are misunderstood, penalized for their divergent thinking, or are not well-liked by teachers in traditional classrooms (Kim, 2009; Richards, 2010;

Systems Model of Creativity	Creative Learning Ecosystems Model	
	Label	Description
Persons	Teachers as learners and leaders	Instructor attitudes, outlooks, demeanor, approach
	Parents as partners	Parent attitudes and outlooks, often taken on cue from instructors
	Students as unique individuals	Attitudes and outlooks, often derived from instructor modeling; instructor view of students
Process	Teaching strategies	Curriculum; course activities; structure of lesson plans; teaching methodologies
Press/ Environment	Classroom and school climate and culture	Classroom climate, as determined by teacher norms, attitudes, atmosphere; classroom management practices; physical space
Product	Meaningful learning and engagement	Ideas and knowledge gained that are new and meaningful to students; products created by students that reflect new learning
Innovation	Inner growth and application of knowledge	Application of ideas to students' everyday lives; joy of learning; sense of progress

Table 1. Table depicting each component of the Creative Learning Ecosystems model, its function, and its relationship to the systems model of creativity.

Wallach & Kogan, 1965). These students are akin to species such as trees that grow on the edges of the prairie.

Those who study prairies are often fascinated with the edges, because they are unpredictable and interesting. Prairie expert Mike Fox explained its appeal: "The edges of things are the most visually challenging or interesting, like between concrete and grass. The edge can be a problem or an opportunity because there is no longer a monolithic set of material" (J. M. Fox, personal communication, August 15, 2013). As such, outlier students should be valued for their strengths. For all students, specific feedback can make a significant difference in their lives and growth. Beghetto (2010) observed, "One of the most direct and potentially influential ways that teachers can support the development of students' creative self-efficacy beliefs is to provide informative feedback on their creative potential and ability" (p. 458). When teachers respond positively to the creative activity of their students, creativity is perpetuated (Davies et al., 2013).

Parents are integral to the creative learning ecosystem. Though some researchers cite the lack of consistent empirical results (Fan & Chen, 2001), personal experience strongly affirms that student success is positively influenced by healthy school-home communication. Within the realm of creative learning, parental support is important. Smutny, Haydon, Bolaños, and Danley (2012) asserted that parents "need to know what the classroom teacher is doing in order to play a supportive role in the home" (p. 94). To truly support the creative growth of students, it is critical that educators view parents as partners in the process, and this responsibility falls squarely on the shoulders of educational leadership (including teachers) to set a collaborative tone. Educators need parent insights, and parents need educator insights in order to accurately meet the needs of the students. Often, parents see a very different child at home than is witnessed at school. Dawson (1997) affirmed, "The research does suggest that teachers should listen seriously to parents who claim that their child performs creatively in settings other than school" (p. 151). This information can be leveraged to help engage a child and support his or her learning. When schools and teachers minimize the role of parents, or shut them out for fear of being criticized or controlled, they spawn mistrust and suspicion. The parent is less likely to support the work of the teacher when he or she does not know what is going on in the classroom. The entire ecosystem, including student learning, suffers as a consequence.

Teaching Strategies and Curriculum

Curriculum strategies in a creative learning ecosystem look vastly different from the convergent teaching strategies that seek single right answers and dominate classrooms worldwide (Beghetto, 2010). Creative learning best practices include: authentic projects and problem solving that students perceive as valuable; a balance between structure and freedom of choice; flexibility in time use, including allowing individuals to work at their own pace; clear expectations; opportunities to explore, imagine, discover, invent, and draw original conclusions; novelty; a mix of work and play; field trips outside of the classroom, including the use of outdoor space; and professional visitors and mentors to the classroom (Davies et al., 2013; Torrance & Goff, 1990).

A promising framework to easily integrate creativity and content is the Torrance Incubation Model of Teaching and Learning (Torrance, 1979a), which has seen a recent resurgence in research and application (Cramond, 2013; Keller-Mathers, 2009, in press; Keller-Mathers & Murdock, 2002). Additionally, best practices from the field of gifted education can be applied within the context of creativity and content integration. More than two decades ago, Torrance and Safter (1990) wrote, "Gifted education has nurtured the creativity movement until it is now shared by all areas of education" (p. 3). In the ensuing 25 years, this sharing has become more and more of a reality.

Creative learning necessitates a variety of assessment methods, including creative products. Besemer (1984, 2006) and Besemer and O'Quin (1987) provided foundational work that demonstrated how to assess creative products; such assessments can be built into a rubric that clearly communicates the expectation that students contribute creativity and original thought (Keller-Mathers, 2007, in press). This assessment structure ensures that creativity is not included in name only, but is maintained as a central value held by the teacher leader.

The Classroom and School Environment

Culture, climate, and physical space are three environmental dimensions. Culture and climate are derived from leadership practices and teaching processes. In the educational realm, culture can be roughly defined as school and classroom management practices. Climate can be roughly characterized as the spirit in which teachers respond to students and their ideas, which in turn sets the tone for how students respond to each other. Ekvall (1996) identified measurable dimensions of the creative environment, including freedom, idea time, idea support, challenge, lack of conflict, playfulness/humor, trust/openness, risk-taking, debate, and liveliness. These dimensions clearly overlap with best practices described elsewhere in this paper.

A comprehensive review of the literature related to creative learning environments (Davies et al., 2013) further delineated their essential aspects. The physical environment should be a flexible space that can be changed according to specific needs that arise to best support student creativity. Additional characteristics of an effective creative learning space include openness, small spaces embedded in the overall space, display of student work in progress, use of outdoor space, and access to a wide range of materials and resources, including technology.

Meaningful Learning and Engagement

Some models of creativity and creative learning have defined the "product" aspect to be a tangible piece of work produced by the student (Smith & Smith, 2010). However, this author and others (e.g., Puccio, Mance, & Murdock, 2011) have adopted an expansive view which asserts that the outcome of creative learning may be an actual product, or it may be an idea, which includes new, meaningful learning or insight to oneself in the realm of mini-c creativity (Craft et al., 2007; Kaufman & Beghetto, 2009). Torrance designed his incubation model on just this premise. Each phase of each lesson elicits student curiosity and a desire to dig deeper. He wrote, "For creative thinking to occur and to continue to occur, there must be ample opportunity for one thing to lead to another, and to do something with the information encountered" (Torrance, 1979a, p. 31). There is always a way to give students the opportunity to continue to think about what they have learned and to apply it further. In order for this continued incubation and application to occur, meaning must have been created for the student in the process.

Inner Growth and Application of Knowledge

The prairie is the site of an iterative process that cycles precipitation through the system to create more precipitation, which thereby regulates temperatures and moisture (Savage, 2011). The joy of learning, the satisfaction in attaining greater self-knowledge through learning application, the tangible progress reflected in creative products, and a feeling of collaboration, drive a similar iterative cycle within a creative learning ecosystem. This feeds each dimension of the system so that it can be sustained and reinvigorated over time.

Conclusion

To our knowledge there has not been articulated a systematic model such as the one proposed here, which serves as a framework to develop creative learning infrastructures, and which can be applied on both a micro level (to homes, individual classrooms, and schools) and a macro level (in large districts, and at the level of public policy).

Such a systems approach appears essential to the long-term sustainability of rigorous creativity in education. For example, in an educational system dominated by test taking and homogenization, it is virtually impossible for an individual teacher to sustain a creative learning platform over the long haul. This would be akin to planting a single prairie grass seed in the midst of a manicured garden of annuals. The seed would not have the ecosystem of support needed to grow. It is more plausible for a single school to do so, but still there exist enormous societal pressures to regress toward the mean. Certainly, there are programs and initiatives nationwide that have elements in common with the Creative Learning Ecosystems model; however, as a comprehensive model, it is in its earliest stages. It should be populated with best practices and further researched to create a detailed map that can guide educators to create self-sustaining creative learning ecosystems that can better weather changes in politics, policy, and public opinion.

References

Amabile, T. M. (1983). The social psychology of creativity: A componential conceptualization. *Journal of Personality and Social Psychology, 45*(2), 357-376.

Amabile, T., & Kramer, S. (2011). *The progress principle*. Boston, MA: Harvard Business Review Press.

Beghetto, R. A. (2010). Creativity in the classroom. In J. C. Kaufman & R. J. Sternberg (Eds.), *The Cambridge handbook of creativity* (pp. 447-463). New York, NY: Cambridge University Press.

Benyus, J. (1997). *Biomimicry*. New York, NY: William Morrow.

Besemer, S. (1984). How do you know it's creative? *Gifted Child Today, 32*, 30-35.

Besemer, S. (2006). *Creating products in the age of design*. Stillwater, OK: New Forums.

Besemer, S., & O'Quin, K. (1987). Creative product analysis. In S. G. Isaksen (Ed.), *Frontiers of creativity research: Beyond the basics* (pp. 341-357). Buffalo, NY: Bearly Limited.

Bloom, B. S., Engelhart, M. D., Furst, E. J., Hill, W. H., & Krathwohl, D. R. (Eds.) (1956). *Taxonomy of educational objectives: The classification of educational goals. Handbook 1: Cognitive domain*. New York, NY: David McKay.

Common Core State Standards Initiative (n.d.-a). *About the Common Core State Standards*. Retrieved from http://www.corestandards.org/about-the-standards

Common Core State Standards Initiative (n.d.-b). *High School: Modeling*. Retrieved from http://www.corestandards.org/Math/Content/HSM

Craft, A., Cremin, T., Burnard, P., & Chappell, K. (2007). Teacher stance in creative learning: A study of progression. *Thinking Skills and Creativity, 2*(2), 136-147.

Cramond, B. (2013). The life and contributions of E. Paul Torrance. In E. Romey (Ed.), *Finding John Galt: People, politics, and practice in gifted education* (pp. 25-31). Charlotte, NC: Information Age Publishing.

Cramond, B., Matthews-Morgan, J., Bandalos, D., & Zuo, L. (2005). A report on the 40-year follow-up of the Torrance Tests of Creative Thinking: Alive and well in the new millennium. *Gifted Child Quarterly, 49*(4), 283-291.

Davies, D., Jindal-Snape, D., Collier, C., Digby, R., Hay, P., & Howe, A. (2013). Creative learning environments in education—A systematic literature review. *Thinking Skills and Creativity, 8,* 80-91.

Dawson, V. L. (1997). In search of the wild Bohemian: Challenges in the identification of the creatively gifted. *Roeper Review,* 19, 148-152.

Ekvall, G. (1996). Organizational climate for creativity and innovation. *European Journal of Work and Organizational Psychology,* 5, 105-123.

Fan, X., & Chen, M. (2001). Parental involvement and students' academic achievement: A meta-analysis. *Educational Psychology Review, 13*(1), 1-22.

Florida, R. (2012). *The rise of the creative class, revisited.* New York, NY: Basic Books.

Guilford, J. P. (1950). Creativity. *American Psychologist,* 5, 444-454.

Guilford, J. P. (1977). *Way beyond the IQ: Guide to improving intelligence and creativity.* Buffalo, NY: Creative Education Foundation.

Jeffrey, B. (2006). Creative teaching and learning: Towards a common discourse and practice. *Cambridge Journal of Education, 36*(3), 399-414.

Jeffrey, B., & Craft, A. (2004). Teaching creatively and teaching for creativity: Distinctions and relationships. *Educational Studies, 30*(1), 77-87.

Kaufman, J. C., & Beghetto, R. A. (2009). Beyond big and little: The Four C Model of creativity. *Review of General Psychology, 13*(1), 1-12.

Keller-Mathers, S. (2007, February). *Blending expertise and imagination: The essential creativity ingredient in gifted education.* Paper presented at the Colorado Department of Education State Director's Conference, Denver, CO.

Keller-Mathers, S. (2009). Creative teaching. In B. Kerr (Ed.), *Encyclopedia of giftedness, creativity, and talent* (pp. 197-200). Thousand Oaks, CA: Sage.

Keller-Mathers, S. (In press). *The curious classroom: Weaving creativity into content with TIM.* Buffalo, NY: ICSC Press.

Keller-Mathers, S., & Murdock, M. C. (2002). Teaching the content of creativity using the Torrance Incubation Model: Eyes wide open to the possibilities of learning. *National Association of Gifted Children's Celebrate Creativity, 12*(2), 7-9.

Kim, K. H. (2006). Can we trust creativity tests? A review of the Torrance Tests of Creative Thinking (TTCT). *Creativity Research Journal, 18*(1), 3-14.

Kim, K. H. (2009). The two pioneers of research on creative giftedness: Calvin W. Taylor and E. Paul Torrance. In L. Shavinina (Ed.), *International handbook on giftedness* (pp. 571-583). Dordrecht, Netherlands: Springer.

Krathwohl, D. (2002). A revision of Bloom's Taxonomy: An overview. *Theory into Practice, 41*(4), 212-218.

Puccio, G. J., Mance, M., & Murdock, M. C. (2011). *Creative leadership: Skills that drive change* (2nd ed.). Thousand Oaks, CA: Sage.

Rhodes, M. (1961). An analysis of creativity. *The Phi Delta Kappan, 42*(7), 305-310.

Richards, R. (2010). Everyday creativity: Process and way of life—four key issues. In J. C. Kaufman & R. J. Sternberg (Eds.), *The Cambridge handbook of creativity* (pp. 189-215). New York, NY: Cambridge University Press.

Robinson, K. (2009). *The element: How finding your passion changes everything*. New York, NY: Viking.

Runco, M. A., Millar, G., Acar, S., & Cramond, B. (2010). Torrance Tests of Creative Thinking as predictors of personal and public achievement: A fifty-year follow-up. *Creativity Research Journal, 22*(4), 361-368.

Savage, C. (2011). *Prairie: A natural history* (2nd ed.). Vancouver, BC: Greystone Books.

Sawyer, R. K. (2004). Creative teaching: Collaborative discussion as disciplined improvisation. *Educational Researcher, 33*, 12-20.

Smith, J. K., & Smith, L. F. (2010). Educational creativity. In J. C. Kaufman & R. J. Sternberg (Eds.), *The Cambridge handbook of creativity* (pp. 250-264). New York, NY: Cambridge University Press.

Smutny, J. F., Haydon, K. P., Bolaños, O., & Danley, G. E. (2012). *Discovering and developing talents in Spanish-speaking students*. Thousand Oaks, CA: Corwin.

Torrance, E. P. (1959). Current research on the nature of creative talent. *Journal of Counseling Psychology, 6*(4), 309-316.

Torrance, E. P. (1979a). An instructional model for enhancing incubation. *Journal of Creative Behavior, 13*(1), 23-35.

Torrance, E. P. (1979b). *The search for satori and creativity*. Buffalo, NY: Creative Education Foundation.

Torrance, E. P., & Goff, K. (1990). Fostering academic creativity in gifted students. *ERIC Digest #E484*. Retrieved from http://eric.ed.gov/?id=ED321489

Torrance, E. P., & Safter, H. T. (1990). *The incubation model of teaching*. Buffalo, NY: Bearly Limited.

Wagner, T. (2012). *Creating innovators: The making of young people who will change the world*. New York, NY: Scribner.

Wallach, M. A., & Kogan, N. (1965). A new look at the creativity-intelligence distinction. *Journal of Personality, 33*(3), 348-369.

Woods, P., & Jeffrey, B. (2002). The reconstruction of primary teachers' identities. *British Journal of Sociology in Education, 23*(1), 89-106.

About the Author

Kathryn P. Haydon, founder of Sparkitivity, is an innovative educator and consultant who speaks and writes widely on education and creativity, including co-authoring *Creativity for Everybody* (Sparkitivity, 2015) and *Discovering and Developing Talents in Spanish-Speaking Students* (Corwin, 2012). She holds an M.S. in Creativity from the International Center for Studies in Creativity at SUNY Buffalo State, a B.A. from Northwestern University, and is a published poet.

Website: http://sparkitivity.com
Facebook: https://www.facebook.com/sparkitivity
Creativity Post: http://www.creativitypost.com/authors/list/152/khaydon

PERSONAL CREATIVITY

How Does Nature Nurture Creativity?

Jennifer A. Quarrie
International Center for Studies in Creativity
SUNY Buffalo State

Originally published in *Big Questions in Creativity 2015*

Abstract

The profound relationship between humans and their natural environment has been celebrated since the dawn of humanity, providing inspiration, perspective and sustenance. Neuroscience research indicates that time with nature provokes an alpha wave brain state of alert relaxation that helps humans heal significantly faster compared to exclusively man-made environments. Separate research shows that alpha waves also play a key role in creative thinking, particularly in focusing attention, suppressing sensory input to bolster internal processing, perceiving more clearly, and learning more readily. If natural physical environments that foster self-healing also nurture creativity, we can leverage time with nature as a deliberate tool for fostering creativity. By intentionally integrating nature into our physical environments and thoroughly understanding its influence on our creativity, we may enhance our lives and creatively branch out by merely returning to our roots.

How Does Nature Nurture Creativity?

While nature influences our lives in countless ways, there remains little research on the influence of physical environment on creativity. Conceptually, creativity is the generation of something that is both novel and valuable, evolved from Stein's (1953) original definition. Rhodes' (1961) person-product-process-press construct highlights the influence of environment ("press") on the other aspects of creativity, providing context for people, processes, and products.

The environment includes physical, psychological, and organizational components. Most academic discussion of creative press centers on organizational environments and social dynamics (Amabile, 1983, 1996; Vithayathawornwong, Danko, & Tolbert, 2003). However, the impact of a purer physical and sensory environment on an individual's creative function is not as well understood. Yet emerging discoveries in neuroscience, cognitive science, ecology, biology, and medicine indicate that the physical environments people choose affect conscious and unconscious aspects of health and performance (McCoy & Evans, 2002; Sternberg, 2009).

Research into how physical space fosters creativity has tended to be centered on interior design and architecture (Augustin, 2014; Kristensen, 2004; Leather, Pyrgas, Beale, & Lawrence, 1998; Puccio & Cabra, 2010; Richardson, 2014; Schweitzer, Gilpin, & Frampton, 2004; Ulrich, 2001), with an increasing emphasis on bringing elements of the outdoors indoors. Time spent in nature, one particular subset of the physical environment, facilitates healing and cognitive function (Sternberg, 2009). The implication, which is explored in this paper, is that time spent with nature likely has a direct, positive, multilateral impact on individual and group creativity, and should be utilized as a tool not only to stimulate creativity, but to live more holistic, pleasurable, and productive lives.

Why Are We Drawn to Nature?

Inspiration

Thoreau said, "It is the marriage of the soul with nature that makes the intellect fruitful, and gives birth to imagination" (1927, p. 54). Some of the greatest art, literature, and inventions have derived from witnessing, reflecting, and mimicking nature. Historically, famous creators such as Leonardo da Vinci, Ralph

Waldo Emerson, Benjamin Franklin, and Ansel Adams looked to nature for their deepest revelations. Many eminent creators held daily rituals involving walks in nature, including Russian composer Pyotr Ilyich Tchaikovsky, German pianist and composer Ludwig van Beethoven, American naturalist Charles Darwin, English poet John Milton, English author Charles Dickens, Danish philosopher Søren Kierkegaard, and German philosopher Immanuel Kant (Currey, 2013; Dunne, 2014; Grose, 2013; Nichols, 2014). During a stay along the shores of Lake Como in the Italian town of Bellagio, Franz Liszt wrote, "I feel that all the various features of Nature around me…provoked an emotional reaction in the depth of my soul, which I have tried to transcribe in music" (Csikszentmihalyi, 1996, p. 134). We can all be inspired by nature's profundity, recognize its impact, and use it in our creative work.

Perspective

The link between nature and creativity goes well beyond inspiration. Nature provides a context in its role as a physical environment and context begets meaning. As a result of the awe-inspiring context that nature provides, it is one of our richest sources of meaning. Senge, Scharmer, Jaworski, and Flowers (2004) call this idea "seeing from the whole" (p. 53). At times the scale of nature lends us perspective and reminds us of how small we are within the greater universe. This outlook is key when it comes to creative problem solving, since a higher-level view helps tough problems seem relative and less overwhelming. A global viewpoint also assists emerging patterns and relationships to become more apparent, which can contribute toward finding solutions. It also revives our awareness that we are part of something far greater than our local communities or ourselves. This level of universal connection to others and greater shared goals evokes deep intrinsic motivation to creative problem solving and perpetuates our efforts well beyond what we would otherwise do for ourselves (Pink, 2011). It conveys the message that we are not alone, nor are we the first to attempt solving such problems as many before us have paved the way (Benyus, 2009).

Further, the influence of an environment "is always dependent on the individual's perception," and this "trait × state" combination yields unique and unpredictable outcomes that are valuable for creativity (Runco & Jaeger, 2012, p. 95; Stein, 1953). "Seeing freshly starts with stopping our habitual ways of thinking and perceiving," and nature provides an excellent physical context in which to begin doing so (Senge, Scharmer, Jaworski, & Flowers, 2004, p. 29). Additionally, observing nature helps us to see things in new ways by learning more about them from micro, macro, systems, and other perspectives. Understanding nature at the systems level helps extrapolate the intricacy of the interrelationships to other unassociated systems through interdisciplinary thinking, potentially assisting to generate novel and valuable ideas. Biomimetics, the emerging field that employs this perspective, analyzes nature's elements, designs, systems and processes for the purposes of solving complex problems—which is also a primary objective of creativity (Benyus, 2009).

Biophilia, Ecology, and Restoration

Humans feel intuitively drawn to nature on a deeply emotional level, a condition known as biophilia (Wilson, 1984). Moreover, we are physically equipped to optimally function as part of the ecosystem. Ecology describes how we exist in a state of symbiosis and mutual dependence with our surroundings and other organisms (Ecology, n.d.). There are biological reasons why we feel drawn outside on sunny days, spend hours digging in the yard, and travel long distances to experience a few precious hours by the ocean or mountainside. Our strong attraction to nature has purpose; it draws us to fill some of our most critical physical and psychological deficits, which are a consequence of lives lived increasingly indoors (Kaplan & Kaplan, 1989; Louv, 2012). Our physical links to the ecosystem benefit our bodies and minds in ways that enhance creativity through healing and enhanced cognition (Sternberg, 2009).

On the Same Wavelength: Healing and Creativity

Creative Alpha Waves

To appreciate how our minds and bodies respond to our environment, it is essential to understand what is happening at the cellular level. Neuroscience research uses brain imaging and other technologies to measure brain wave activity. Alpha waves are a type of neural oscillation in the frequency range of 8-12 Hz that predominately originate from the occipital lobe of the brain during wakeful relaxation and are strongest with eyes closed (Olga, 2012).

Since the 1970s, electroencephalography (EEG) research has shown that alpha wave brain activity is correlated with creativity, particularly during those moments in which we focus attention (Carson, 2011), suppress sensory input in order to focus inward (Foxe & Snyder, 2011), and achieve clearer mental perception and learn more easily (Kaul, 2006). In this state, we more readily make associations between previously unassociated concepts and thus generate more novel concepts and solutions.

Neuroscientific studies have shown increased alpha wave activity during specific mental activities associated with creative function. Alpha waves increased their frequency and strength during the formation of novel and valuable ideas such as during creative inspiration (Martindale & Hasenfus, 1978), escalation towards insight (Kounios & Beeman, 2009; Kounios et al., 2006), and creative ideation (Fink & Benedek, 2012). Alpha wave activity also increased when focusing attention on internal thoughts (Carson, 2011) and suppressing external sensory input to allow continued internal focus (Foxe & Snyder, 2011). Further, alpha wave activity increased when confronted with unrecognizable objects, thus showing that alpha waves are a key part of responses to novelty (Vanni, Revonsuo, & Hari, 1997). Research has even become specific enough to show that alpha waves synchronize to periods of top-down processing, where thoughts begin with a general concept and become more specific, in both convergent and divergent thinking (Benedek, Bergner, Könen, Fink, & Neubauer, 2011; Jauk, Benedek, & Neubauer, 2012).

The fact that alpha wave production increases during sensory suppression may also help explain Csikszentmihalyi's (1991) theory of flow, which holds that when an individual is fully immersed, energized, and focused on an activity, the rest of the world falls away, resulting in creativity, deep enjoyment, and an altered perception of time. Both focused and softly-focused attention plays an important role in most types of creative thinking, to include all phases of CPS (Goleman, 2013). Alpha wave activity and focus also increase during meditation (Davidson et al., 2003; Kabat-Zinn, 1994).

Healing Alpha Waves

Our senses provide a constant stream of conscious and unconscious input from the physical environment, and many inputs from nature enable the body's ability to heal (Ackerman, 1991; Sternberg, 2009). A body of medical research indicates that the alpha wave brain state of alert relaxation combats stress and its destructive physiological implications, thus creating an optimal state for healing (Sternberg, 2009). For example, a study on the impact of sunlight showed that, all other variables the same, patients with rooms on the sunnier side of the hospital healed faster and were discharged an average of three days sooner than those with windows on the shadier side (Ulrich, 1984). Several other environmental and sensory inputs that appear to significantly promote healing come from nature and may show a link to the alpha wave state. For instance, the following visual inputs have been shown to promote healing: viewing nature (Cohen & Cohen, 2009; Louv, 2012); observing patterns of fractals, branching, and self-similar repeating patterns found commonly in nature (Sternberg, 2009); and taking in blue and green spectra (the primary spectra for sky, water, and vegetation in nature) for calming (Alter, 2013; Sternberg, 2009).

Immersing in a natural environment in a active or passive way also brings healing benefits, to include such behaviors as exposure to full spectrum sunlight, preferably facing east for higher light intensity (Heschong et al., 1999; Sternberg, 2009; Ulrich, 1984); passive time in garden and forest settings (Corazon, Stigsdotter, Moeller, & Rasmussen, 2012; Li et al., 2006; Ottosson & Grahn, 2005; Simons, Simons, McCallum, & Friedlander, 2006); resting and waking in a way that allows the body clock to align with daily and seasonal circadian rhythms (Cohen & Cohen, 2009; Shiller, 2014); listening to repetitive nature sounds; smelling scents such as lavender, chamomile, geranium, rose, sweet marjoram, and valerian (Sternberg, 2009); or even handling smooth stones or beads (Montagu, 1986). Combining these elements may provide added benefit; for example, waking according to one's own body rhythm and taking in the full spectrum sunlight of the morning while gazing on a lovely natural vista (Cohen & Cohen, 2009). Further, given the stomach's role as our "second brain," the role of nature in our daily nutrition (particularly plants) is another crucial way of bringing nature in as a means to healing (Fuhrman, 2014).

Simultaneous States

Could it be that the very physical environments and sensory input that place the human body into a self-healing state also place it into an ideal state for creative thinking? The nature-inspired alpha wave brain state of alert relaxation that enables the body to direct resources towards healing may simultaneously nurture creativity and problem solving. Healing and creativity share common elements. Both promote internally-driven change in the service of improvement and adaption. They are significantly enhanced by time with nature, are improved via specific processes, require focused energy and investment, center on growth, and involve a connection between body and mind. Healing and creativity are also both paths to self-actualization (Maslow, 1943).

Based on the above, I believe that by moderating our environment, we have the power to influence and improve our own creative function. One might wonder whether habitual creative thinking can invite the alpha wave state and therein induce similar healing effects? Could those who are mentally ill and drawn heavily to creative pursuits in effect be self-medicating by inviting the alpha wave state, lowering cortisol levels and achieving the mental clarity and healing that comes with creative activity? Perhaps widely publicizing creativity's links with nature, healing, and positive psychology may also counter lingering prejudices of an exclusive causal relationship between mental illness and exceptional creativity.

Natural Environments, Creative Tools

How might we leverage the physical environment to nurture our creative functions? Restoring the natural influence in our lives in a deliberate and personalized way not only empowers us as individuals but may also expand our awareness of interconnectedness with our greater society and ecosystem and inspire us to act as creative leaders.

Creative Problem Solving (CPS)

Physical environment plays a key role in every stage of CPS, from exploring the vision to formulating an action plan (Puccio, Mance, Switalski, & Reali, 2012). The Storyboarding tool helps to develop a vision by constructing a detailed physical context that assists in developing the ideal future state, as well as considering environmental influences and helping to identify and remove constraints. Considering the environment while gathering key data and assessing the situation can cast an issue in a new and useful light. Physical environment figures prominently in the Excursions tool, during which one literally uses the physical environment to experience a novel perspective and to prompt fresh reflections on the challenge at hand (Miller, Vehar, Firestien, Thurber, & Neilsen, 2011). The Excursions tool also facilitates relaxation and reduces the amount of immediate sensory stimuli that may distract from deeper thinking. Group work, including CPS, is also impacted by the surrounding physical environment as noted in Schwarz's (2002) Group Effectiveness Model, which lists physical environment as a key element of group context (p. 19).

A natural physical environment that prompts positive emotions can also provide a stimulating yet calming setting for incubation as creators step away from deliberate thinking to allow for periodic defocused and subconscious mental processing. "When persons with prepared minds find themselves in beautiful settings, they are more likely to find new connections among ideas, new perspectives on issues" (Csikszentmihalyi, 1996, p. 136). Anecdotally, when identifying environments in which the best and most creative ideas arise, people most commonly list places like the shower, walks with the dog, or exercising outside. This echoes the daily rituals of the great thinkers, discussed earlier, who took long walks as their primary way of facilitating their personal creativity. The practice of incubation, particularly in a non-judging context such as nature, may also strengthen self-confidence in personal intuition as a complement to cognitive and affective decision-making skills (Francisco & Burnett, 2008).

Variable attention—the ability to readily switch between attention levels where attention is defocused on highly ambiguous tasks and focused on unambiguous tasks—is associated with creative people (Vartanian, 2009). Time in nature may help develop one's variable attention, as the environment demands periodic acute attention to avoid injury yet facilitates a more relaxed state the rest of the time. Poetically, Frost (1921) uses the experience of nature to mirror de Bono's (1970) theory of lateral thinking, the need to jump from our worn paths, when he encourages following the road not taken. More currently, other processes such as design thinking and biomimicry also leverage physical environment. Design thinking includes extensive field observation and empathic immersion in the users' experiences (d.school, 2014). Biomimicry also takes an acute observational approach (Benyus, 2009).

Essential Elements

Interacting with nature directly offers the greatest benefit. Gandhi once said, "To forget how to dig the earth and tend the soil is to forget ourselves" (Gandhi & Attenborough, 1982, p. 5). Yet people have long worked to extract themselves from the dangers, discomforts, and hardships of nature. Indoor environments increase our safety and comfort, while affording the luxury of spending our limited resources on more creative and cognitive pursuits. It is challenging to think divergently when preoccupied with immediate survival; say, when running from a predator, finding food, or constructing shelter. For those without much opportunity to go outside, there are ways to enjoy some benefits of experiencing nature without immersing oneself in it. Studies show that simple interactions such as watering houseplants, interacting with a pet, or even looking at a nature scene, have positive effects on stress attention levels (Kaplan & Kaplan, 1989; Sop Shin, 2007; Ulrich, 2002).

How Nature Can Nurture Creativity

Climate and Cognitive Skills

The majority of currently-popular creative methods are essentially considered to be cognitively-based, despite also having robust affective and intuitive attributes. Physical climate impacts the cognitive skills of creativity on multiple levels, to include learning, memory, awareness, mindfulness, intuition, and intention. By deliberately incorporating physical climate into our creative approach, "we seek the gifts of nature essential for the realization of our full intellectual and spiritual potential" (Louv, 2012, p. 38).

Learning, Memory and Associative Thinking

In education, the "loose parts theory" holds there is a positive relationship between the number of loose parts in an environment and the creativity of play that occurs there (Nicholson, 1971, p. 30). Nature has an almost infinite set of loose parts, particularly in comparison to any man-made environment, and may result in more creative play (Nicholson, 1971, p. 31), and also may "encourage a greater sensitivity to patterns that underlie all experience" (Louv, 2012, p. 34), thus providing the building blocks for future non-obvious associations which drive much of creativity. Some approaches to childhood education, such as Reggio Emilia and nature preschools in Scandinavia, base their learning approach on the concepts that the physical environment is "the third educator after the teacher and parent" according to Susan Lyon, executive director of the Innovative Teacher Project (Garrett, 2013, p. 1; Project Wild Thing, 2014). In them, education is based on interrelationships, and real-life experiences allow deeper questioning and theory development (Garrett, 2013; White, 2007).

The richness of the natural environment also sharpens an observer's powers of perception. Compared to more sterile indoor environments, learners absorb more information somatically, auditorily, visually, as well as intellectually, leading to a much richer understanding (Meier, 2000, pp. 42-50). Being in nature's boundless set of stimuli increases the number of associations an observer is able to make between previously unrelated objects or concepts, thus increasing the potential volume and novelty of ideas (Ulrich, 1993). Additionally, studies indicated that interaction with nature significantly improved memory and attention spans (Berman, Jonides, & Kaplan, 2008; Louv, 2012) and reduced children's Attention-Deficit Disorder symptoms (Taylor, Kuo, & Sullivan, 2001).

Awareness, Mindfulness, and Intuition

The dynamism of nature encourages awareness and mindfulness by rewarding simple observation. By remaining both aware and accepting of our observations, we extend our mental boundaries and open a path to insight. As Rodin said, "To any artist worthy of the name, all in nature is beautiful, because his eyes, fearlessly accepting all external truth, read there, as in an open book, all the inner truth" (Rodin, 1983, p. 20).

Visual thinking tools, which use imagery in various ways, are critical for creative thinking, so much so that the word "imagination" is nearly a synonym for creativity (Davis, 1999, p. 133). However, many of the studies linking imagery with creativity address only mental imagery (thought images, eidetic images, synesthesia, hallucination, dream image, and hypnopompic images) without emphasizing the utility of rich, external imagery (Davis, 1999, p. 133-135). Using nature images as part of the Forced Connections tool provides a powerful prompt for new associations (Miller et al., 2011).

Further, time in nature appears to heighten awareness and awaken more latent senses, thus improving intuition, according to a study of U.S. Marines by the Pentagon-based Joint Improvised Explosive Device Defeat Organization, which supports pre-deployment training (Perry, 2009). More importantly, this awareness extends as much internally toward observing and understanding the self as it does externally to physical surroundings.

Living Deliberately

> I went to the woods because I wished to live deliberately, to front only the essential facts of life. And see if I could not learn what it had to teach and not, when I came to die, discover that I had not lived. (Thoreau, 1854, p. 143)

Deliberately including both nature and creative-thinking habits into daily life increases the likelihood that they will become integral approaches to living fully and holistically. Time in nature may also increase the propensity for deliberate everyday creativity as personal needs arise and individuals work to fulfill them with limited available resources. Habitually spending time in nature may also develop new skill-related knowledge relative to that domain. It is therefore possible that by deliberately spending time with nature, one may increase all three primary psychological components required for creativity: motivation, the ability to make new connections, and skill-related knowledge (Runco & Richards, 1997, p. 234).

Freedom

A common feeling associated with nature is one of freedom. Nature's grand scale can promote a sense of spatial freedom away from the constraint of limited indoor spaces. Further, many are intuitively drawn to explore nature, seeking new locations of solitude or beauty, or particular resources such as certain types of water, plants, or minerals. The freedom of physical movement is an inherent part of natural exploration, not only in regard to moving one's body instead of sitting still, but also the freedom to move throughout the environment in uncharted and non-prescribed ways. Studies have suggested a direct relationship between general physical movement and increased creativity (Berger & Owen, 1988; Green, 1993; Hug, Hartig, Hansmann, Seeland, & Hornung, 2009; Rath, 2013). What's more, "green exercise is like exercised squared"; research has shown that physical movement within a natural environment has far more mental and physical health benefits than indoors on a machine (Selhub & Logan, 2012, p. 116).

Beyond the realm of the physical, nature is free of social judgment, constraint, pressure, and directive; offering a pleasant forum for solitude, concentration, rebellion, or vacation. As a result of spending time without perceived social judgment, one might reduce self-censorship and permit broader and more creative thinking, a key element to successful creative idea generation (Puccio et al., 2012).

Presence

Nature exists in the present; energy is channeled into the current circumstance and the surrounding ecosystem. Those who spend time in the ever-changing environment of nature join their ecosystem by living in the present and paying closer attention to the moment. As a result of spending time with nature, individuals may increase intuitive and mindfulness skills, which are key throughout CPS for identifying needs, understanding priorities, and assessing situations (Francisco & Burnett, 2008; Puccio, Mance, & Murdock, 2011). Presence, living in the moment, is also a key part of positive psychology, notably Csikszentmihalyi's (1997) theory of flow in everyday life, a driver of creativity and problem solving.

Social Impact

While time in nature, particularly for creative pursuits, tends to be associated with solitude, nature also significantly affects social dynamics. Just as we are built to be part of our ecosystems physically, we are also built to be social beings, part of a "mental ecosystem" with others, where we contribute our thoughts to enhance the greater thinking. Jung, for instance, wrote extensively on the collective unconscious and the idea that "part of the psyche was shared by all people, in all cultures, throughout the ages" (Jones, 1999, p. 112).

Practicing non-judgment while in nature also prepares one to maintain that perspective moving forward, continuing to offer compassion and empathy to oneself and others. While empathy is important to problem solving, it is also useful in problem finding: "Empathy with oneself is a means for perceiving inner conflicts and tensions that make good problems" (Runco, 1994, p. 106). Lowering stress hormones changes behaviors and changes one's focus, and as a result individuals in groups may behave more supportively (Sapolsky, 1994). The outdoors has also been identified as an ideal context in which children can maximize socio-cultural learning, create meaning, and learn values, such as: recognition of the equal worth of all humans, equality between the sexes, solidarity, respect for life, tolerance, justice, truth, and honesty (Aasen, Grindheim, & Waters, 2009).

Adaption

Nature offers the ultimate model for embracing change. As H. G. Wells (1945) famously noted, "Adapt or perish, now as ever, is nature's inexorable imperative." Living with this mentality may help the mind become more expectant and accepting of change, and even more responsive to it. Given creativity's role in leading and adapting to change (Puccio et al., 2012), nature not only provides a useful model but also a dynamic partner. As Johann Wolfgang von Goethe noted, "Nature knows no pause in progress and development, and attaches her curse on all inaction" (Holdrege, 2013).

Conclusion

Humans are intuitively drawn towards nature and the need for this interaction has been recognized for centuries across the globe. It is valuable to understand why humans gravitate towards nature for re-centering, creative thinking, problem solving, and healing, as well as why nature works so incredibly well to bring our best thoughts forward. While there is much yet undiscovered, our current knowledge of human-nature dynamics might just be enough to inspire significant changes in the way we choose our physical environments to create lives that deliberately nurture creativity and well-being. As we envision the future and search for the answers to tomorrow's challenges, it is time that the field of creativity focus on what our physical environment might contribute, and highlight the particular benefits that nature brings to nurture creativity.

References

Aasen, W., Grindheim, L. T., & Waters, J. (2009). The outdoor environment as a site for children's participation, meaning-making and democratic learning: Examples from Norwegian kindergartens. *Education 3-13, 37*(1), 5-13.

Ackerman, D. (1991). *A natural history of the senses.* New York, NY: Vintage.

Alter, A. (2013). *Drunk tank pink: And other unexpected forces that shape how we think, feel, and behave.* New York, NY: Penguin Press.

Amabile, T. M. (1983). The social psychology of creativity: A componential conceptualization. *Journal of Personality and Social Psychology, 45*(2), 357-377.

Amabile, T. M. (1996, January). *Creativity and innovation in organizations* [Background note]. Cambridge, MA: Harvard Business School.

Augustin, S. (2014, October 28). *Rules for designing an engaging workplace.* Retrieved from https://hbr.org/2014/10/rules-for-designing-an-engaging-workplace

Benedek, M., Bergner, S., Könen, T., Fink, A., & Neubauer, A. C. (2011). EEG alpha synchronization is related to top-down processing in convergent and divergent thinking. *Neuropsychologia, 49*(12), 3505-3511. doi: 10.1016/j.neuropsychologia.2011.09.004

Benyus, J. (2009, July). *Janine Benyus: Biomimicry in action* [Video file]. Retrieved from http://www.ted.com/talks/janine_benyus_biomimicry_in_action#t-248039

Berger, B. G., & Owen, D. R. (1988). Stress reduction and mood enhancement in four exercise modes: Swimming, body conditioning, hatha yoga, and fencing. *Research Quarterly for Exercise and Sport, 59*(2), 148-159.

Berman, M. G., Jonides, J., & Kaplan, S. (2008). The cognitive benefits of interacting with nature. *Psychological Science, 19*(12), 1207-1212.

Carson, S. (2011). The unleashed mind. *Scientific American Mind, 22*(2), 22-29.

Cohen, M., (Producer and Director) (2009). *The Science of Healing: With Esther Sternberg* [DVD]. United States: Resolution Pictures.

Corazon, S. S., Stigsdotter, U. K., Moeller, M. S., & Rasmussen, S. M. (2012). Nature as therapist: Integrating permaculture with mindfulness-and acceptance-based therapy in the Danish Healing Forest Garden Nacadia. *European Journal of Psychotherapy & Counselling, 14*(4), 335-347.

Csikszentmihalyi, M. (1991). *Flow: The psychology of optimal experience.* New York, NY: HarperPerennial.

Csikszentmihalyi, M. (1996). *Creativity: Flow and the psychology of discovery and invention.* New York, NY: HarperCollins.

Csikszentmihalyi, M. (1997). *Finding flow: The psychology of engagement with everyday life.* New York, NY: Basic Books.

Currey, M. (Ed.). (2013). *Daily rituals: How artists work.* New York, NY: Random House.

d.school. (2014). *Method: What? How? Why?* Retrieved from http://dschool.stanford.edu/wp-content/themes/dschool/method-cards/what-why-how.pdf

Davidson, R. J., Kabat-Zinn, J., Schumacher, J., Rosenkranz, M., Muller, D., Santorelli, S. F., Urbanowski, F., Harrington, A., Bonus, K., & Sheridan, J. F. (2003). Alterations in brain and immune function produced by mindfulness meditation. *Psychosomatic Medicine, 65*(4), 564-570.

Davis, G. A. (1998). *Creativity is forever.* Dubuque, IA: Kendall Hunt.

de Bono, E. (1970). *Lateral thinking: Creativity step by step.* New York, NY: Harper Perennial.

Dunne, C. (2014, July 10). *The daily routines of 26 of history's most creative minds*. Retrieved from http://www.fastcodesign.com/3032874/infographic-of-the-day/the-daily-routines-of-26-of-historys-most-creative-minds

Ecology (n.d.). In *Encyclopædia Britannica*. Retrieved from http://www.britannica.com/EBchecked/topic/178273/ecology

Fink, A., & Benedek, M. (2012). EEG alpha power and creative ideation. *Neuroscience & Biobehavioral Reviews, 44*, 111-123. doi: 10.1016/j.neubiorev.2012.12.002

Foxe, J. J., & Snyder, A. C. (2011). The role of alpha-band brain oscillations as a sensory suppression mechanism during selective attention. *Frontiers in Psychology, 2*, 154. doi: 10.3389/fpsyg.2011.00154

Francisco, J. M., & Burnett, C. A. (2008). Deliberate intuition: Giving intuitive insights their rightful place in the creative problem solving thinking skills model. In G. J. Puccio, C. Burnett, J. F. Cabra, J. M. Fox, S. Keller-Mathers, M. C. Murdock, & J. A. Yudess (Eds.), *Proceedings from An International Conference on Creativity and Innovation Management—The 2nd Community Meeting* (Vol. 2) (pp. 164-175). Buffalo, NY: International Center for Studies in Creativity, Buffalo State.

Frost, R. (1921). *Mountain interval*. New York, NY: Henry Holt.

Fuhrman, J. (2014). *The end of dieting*. New York, NY: HarperCollins.

Gandhi, M. & Attenborough, R. (1982). *The words of Gandhi*. New York, NY: Newmarket Press.

Garrett, R. (2013, July 15). *What is Reggio Emilia?* Retrieved from http://www.education.com/magazine/article/Reggio_Emilia/

Goleman, D. (2013). *Focus: The hidden driver of excellence*. London, UK: Bloomsbury.

Green, J. (1993). *Fostering creativity through movement and body awareness practices: A postpositivist investigation into the relationship between somatics and the creative process* [Doctoral dissertation]. Retrieved from https://etd.ohiolink.edu/rws_etd/document/get/osu1226597858/inline

Grose, J. (2013, May 20). *From Beethoven to Woody Allen—The daily rituals of the world's most creative people and what you can learn from them*. Retrieved from http://www.fastcocreate.com/1682913/from-beethoven-to-woody-allen-the-daily-rituals-of-the-worlds-most-creative-people-and-what-

Heschong, L., Mahone, D., Kuttaiah, K., Stone, N., Chappell, C., & McHugh, J. (1999). *Daylighting in schools: An investigation into the relationship between daylighting and human performance* [Report]. California: Pacific

Gas and Electric Company. Retrieved from http://h-m-g.com/downloads/Daylighting/schoolc.pdf

Holdrege, C. (2014, Spring). *Goethe and the evolution of science.* Retrieved from http://www.natureinstitute.org/pub/ic/ic31/goethe.pdf

Hug, S. M., Hartig, T., Hansmann, R., Seeland, K., & Hornung, R. (2009). Restorative qualities of indoor and outdoor exercise settings as predictors of exercise frequency. *Health & Place, 15*(4), 971-980.

Jauk, E., Benedek, M., & Neubauer, A. C. (2012). Tackling creativity at its roots: Evidence for different patterns of EEG alpha activity related to convergent and divergent modes of task processing. *International Journal of Psychophysiology, 84*(2), 219-225. doi: 10.1016/j.1016/j.ijpsycho.2012.02.012

Jones, K. (1999). Jungian theory. In M. A. Runco & S. R. Pritzker (Eds.), *Encyclopedia of creativity* (Vol. 2). San Diego, CA: Academic Press.

Kabat-Zinn, J. (1994). *Wherever you go, there you are: Mindfulness meditation in everyday life.* New York, NY: Hyperion.

Kaplan, R., & Kaplan, S. (1989). *The experience of nature: A psychological perspective.* New York, NY: Cambridge University Press.

Kaul, P. (2006). Brain wave interactive learning where multimedia and neuroscience converge. In K. Elleithy, T. Sobh, A. Mahmood, M. Iskander, & M. A. Karim (Eds.), *Advances in Computer, Information, and Systems Sciences, and Engineering* (pp. 351-357). Netherlands: Springer.

Kounios, J., & Beeman, M. (2009). The aha! moment: The cognitive neuroscience of insight. *Current Directions in Psychological Science, 18*(4), 210-216. doi: 10.1111/j.1467-8721.2009.01638.x

Kounios, J., Frymiare, J. L., Bowden, E. M., Fleck, J. I., Subramaniam, K., Parrish, T. B., & Jung-Beeman, M. (2006). The prepared mind: Neural activity prior to problem presentation predicts subsequent solution by sudden insight. *Psychological Science, 17*(10), 882-890. doi: 10.1111/j.1467-9280.2006.01798.x

Kristensen, T. (2004). The physical context of creativity. *Creativity and Innovation Management, 13*(2), 89-96. doi: 10.1111/j.0963-1690.2004.00297.x

Leather, P., Pyrgas, M., Beale, D., & Lawrence, C. (1998). Windows in the workplace: Sunlight, view, and occupational stress. *Environment and Behavior, 30*(6), 739-762.

Li, Q., Morimoto, K., Nakadai, A., Inagaki, H., Katsumata, M., Shimizu, T., & Kawada, T. (2006). Forest bathing enhances human natural killer activity and expression of anti-cancer proteins. *International Journal of Immunopathology and Pharmacology, 20*(2 Suppl. 2), 3-8.

Louv, R. (2012). *The nature principle: Human restoration and the end of nature-deficit disorder.* Chapel Hill, NC: Algonquin Books.

Martindale, C., & Hasenfus, N. (1978). EEG differences as a function of creativity, stage of the creative process, and effort to be original. *Biological Psychology, 6*(3), 157-167.

Maslow, A. H. (1943). *A theory of human motivation.* Radford, VA: Wilder.

McCoy, J. M., & Evans, G. W. (2002). The potential role of the physical environment in fostering creativity. *Creativity Research Journal, 14*(3-4), 409-426. doi: 10.1207/S15326934CRJ1434_11

Meier, D. (2000). *The accelerated learning handbook.* New York, NY: McGraw-Hill.

Miller, B., Vehar, J., Firestien, R., Thurber, S., & Neilsen, D. (2011). *Creativity unbound: An introduction to creative process.* Evanston, IL: FourSight.

Montagu, A. (1986). *Touching: The human significance of the skin.* New York, NY: Harper & Row.

Nichols, W. J. (2014). *Blue mind: The surprising science that shows how being in, on or under water can make you happier, healthier, more connected and better at what you do.* New York, NY: Little, Brown.

Nicholson, S. (1971). The theory of loose parts: How not to cheat children. *Landscape Architecture, 62*(1), 30-34.

Olga, B. (2012). Comments for current interpretation EEG alpha activity: A review and analysis. *Journal of Behavioral and Brain Science, 2,* 239-248.

Ottosson, J., & Grahn, P. (2005). A comparison of leisure time spent in a garden with leisure time spent indoors: On measures of restoration in residents in geriatric care. *Landscape Research, 30*(1), 23-55.

Perry, T. (2009, October 28). *Some troops have a sixth sense for bombs.* Retrieved from http://articles.latimes.com/2009/oct/28/world/fg-bombs-vision28

Pink, D. H. (2011). *Drive: The surprising truth about what motivates us.* New York, NY: Riverhead Books.

Project Wild Thing (2014, November). *Project Wild Thing.* Retrieved from http://projectwildthing.com

Puccio, G. J., & Cabra, J. F. (2010). Organizational creativity. In J. C. Kaufman & R. J. Sternberg (Eds.), *The Cambridge handbook of creativity* (pp. 145-173). New York, NY: Cambridge University Press.

Puccio, G. J., Mance, M., & Murdock, M. C. (2011). *Creative leadership: Skills that drive change* (2nd ed.). Thousand Oaks, CA: Sage.

Puccio, G. J., Mance, M., Switalski, L. B., & Reali, P. D. (2012). *Creativity rising: Creative thinking and creative problem solving in the 21st century.* Buffalo, NY: ICSC Press.

Rath, T. (2013). *Eat move sleep: How small choices lead to big changes.* New York, NY: Missionday.

Rhodes, M. (1961). An analysis of creativity. *Phi Delta Kappan, 42,* 305-310.

Richardson, L. (2014, November 2). Fun, creativity at work gets the job done. *The Indianapolis Star.* Retrieved from http://www.indystar.com/story/money/2014/11/02/fun-creativity-work-gets-job-done/18268661/

Rodin, A. (1983). *Rodin on art and artists.* Mineola, NY: Dover Publications.

Runco, M. (1994). *Problem finding, problem solving, and creativity.* Norwood, NJ: Alex Publishing.

Runco, M. A., & Jaeger, G. J. (2012). The standard definition of creativity. *Creativity Research Journal, 24*(1), 92-96.

Runco, M. A., & Richards, R. (Eds.) (1997). *Eminent creativity, everyday creativity, and health.* Santa Barbara, CA: Greenwood Publishing Group.

Sapolsky, R. M. (1998). *Why zebras don't get ulcers: An updated guide to stress, stress-related diseases, and coping.* New York, NY: W. H. Freeman.

Schweitzer, M., Gilpin, L., & Frampton, S. (2004). Healing spaces: Elements of environmental design that make an impact on health. *Journal of Alternative and Complementary Medicine, 10*(Suppl. 1), S71-S83.

Selhub, E. M., & Logan, A. C. (2012). *Your brain on nature.* Mississauga, Canada: John Wiley and Sons Canada.

Senge, P., Scharmer, C. O., Jaworski, J., & Flowers, B. S. (2004). *Presence: Human purpose and the field of the future.* New York, NY: Random House.

Shiller, B. (2014, November 13). *Listening to your body clock can make you more productive and improve your well-being.* Retrieved from http://www.fastcoexist.com/3038029/how-listening-to-our-body-clocks-can-improve-productivity-and-raise-wellbeing

Simons, L. A., Simons, J., McCallum, J., & Friedlander, Y. (2006). Lifestyle factors and risk of dementia: Dubbo study of the elderly. *Medical Journal of Australia, 184*(2), 68.

Sop Shin, W. (2007). The influence of forest view through a window on job satisfaction and job stress. *Scandinavian Journal of Forest Research, 22*(3), 248-253.

Stein, M. I. (1953). Creativity and culture. *Journal of Psychology, 36*, 311–322.

Sternberg, E. M. (2009). *Healing spaces: The science of place and well-being.* Cambridge, MA: Belknap Press of Harvard University Press.

Taylor, A. F., Kuo, F. E., & Sullivan, W. C. (2001). Coping with ADD: The surprising connection to green play settings. *Environment and Behavior, 33*(1), 54-77.

Thoreau, H. D. (1854). *Walden* (Vol. 1). Boston, MA: Houghton Mifflin.

Thoreau, H. D. (1927). *The heart of Thoreau's journals* (O. Shepard, Ed.). Boston, MA: Houghton Mifflin.

Ulrich, R. S. (1984). View through a window may influence recovery from surgery. *Science, 224*, 420-421.

Ulrich, R. S. (1993). Biophilia, biophobia, and natural landscapes. In S. R. Kellert & E. O. Wilson (Eds.), *The biophilia hypothesis* (pp. 73-137). Washington, DC: Island Press.

Ulrich, R. S. (2001). Effects of healthcare environmental design on medical outcomes. In A. Dilani (Ed.), *Design and health: Proceedings of the Second International Conference on Health and Design* (pp. 49-59). Stockholm, Sweden: Svensk Byggtjanst.

Ulrich, R. S. (2002, April). Health benefits of gardens in hospitals. Paper presented at Haarlemmermeer, Netherlands. Retrieved from http://plantsolutions.com/documents/HealthSettingsUlrich.pdf

Vanni, S., Revonsuo, A., & Hari, R. (1997). Modulation of the parieto-occipital alpha rhythm during object detection. *The Journal of Neuroscience, 17*(18), 7141-7147.

Vartanian, O. (2009). Variable attention facilitates creative problem solving. *Psychology of Aesthetics, Creativity, and the Arts, 3*(1), 57.

Vithayathawornwong, S., Danko, S., & Tolbert, P. (2003). The role of the physical environment in supporting organizational creativity. *Journal of Interior Design, 29*(1-2), 1-16.

Wells, H. G. (1945). *Mind at the end of its tether.* London, UK: W. Heinemann.

White, J. (2007). *Being, playing and learning outdoors: Making provision for high quality experiences in the outdoor environment.* London, UK: Routledge.

Wilson, E. O. (1984). *Biophilia.* Cambridge, MA: Harvard University Press.

About the Author

Jennifer Quarrie is a dynamic innovation strategist and creativity expert with a visionary outlook and a knack for metacognition, facilitation, and listening. With a B.A. in Cognitive Science from the University of Virginia and an M.Sc. in Creative Studies from the International Center for Studies in Creativity at SUNY Buffalo State, she incorporates budding areas of mind and creativity research into all of her work. As a leader and speaker she inspires wellness, fosters transformation, and emboldens self-actualization.

Email: NurtureCreativeNature@gmail.com
Twitter: @JQVisionary

How to Unlock the Potential of Your Insight?

Mariano Tosso
International Center for Studies in Creativity
SUNY Buffalo State

Originally published in *Big Questions in Creativity 2014*

Abstract

This paper draws on contemporary research as well as classic studies relating to practices that can help boost insight. Moreover, it examines various aspects of insight-resulting phenomena and potential routes to enhance insight. Rather than providing prescriptive recipes, the author aims instead to build an awareness of the need to nurture insights and the necessity of staying open to possibilities. The author advocates the cultivation of daily habits to begin grasping the full potential of insight.

How to Unlock the Potential of Your Insight?

We don't see things as they are, we see them as we are.

Anais Nin

Exploring how to unlock the full potential of one's insight creates immense opportunities for growth. Put simply, doing so amounts to cultivating one's inner wisdom. This paper summarizes the key concepts in the study of insights. It integrates recent findings with strategies, tips, and sources that may be relevant to discovering a personal path of transformation and change.

Insights and Creativity

What is an insight? The most traditional definition considers insight as involving perceptual and conceptual reorganization, with a sudden transformation (Klein & Jarosz, 2011). The same authors offered a more contemporary characterization, which involved:

> a discontinuous discovery, a non-obvious revision to a person's mental model of a dynamic system, resulting in a new set of beliefs that are more accurate, comprehensive, and useful. Insights do not directly follow from the data available prior to the insight. The person gaining the insight shifts his or her mental model; either new data or a combination of data or a finding of a contradiction leads the person into a conceptual territory that was new in some aspects. (p. 246)

Klein and Jarosz (2011), then, regarded insight as a form of sense-making that involved shifts in understanding and changes in the way a person thinks, acts, sees, desires, and feels.

The 2011 study on which their new definition was based revealed a rich portrait of 120 cases of everyday insights. In one of its most intriguing findings, 44 percent of the respondents reported that insights appeared gradually, while 54 percent said their insights were sudden. Some 30 percent reported their insights as collective, and only 10 percent of respondents said their insights depended on coincidence. A quarter of the reported insights involved some sort of impasse.

More than 80 percent of the respondents were already working deliberately on a problem when insight occurred, and in about two-thirds of the cases, some measure of expertise or experience was required to make the insight possible. Furthermore, the results often showed that a subject's realization of a new connection sometimes overlapped with the discovery of a contradiction or inconsistency (Klein & Jarosz, 2011).

Three main points can be drawn from this study. First, it seems as though one size does not fit all insights; some are gradual rather than sudden. Second, it might be useful to uncover and resolve contradictions to generate insights. Third, deep questioning may trigger insights.

To that end, a process called "assumption busting" (Dunne & Dugan, 2007) may help break patterns and establish new ones. This process consists of a few simple steps. Initially, data representing a challenge or opportunity become key assumptions. Then, the data are deepened by simultaneously surfacing assumptions about them. Finally, all assumptions are systematically reversed and put into "what-if" questioning. As a result, new perspectives may arise, triggering new solutions.

Insights hold the potential for change, which is why they constitute a powerful competitive advantage. Those of a catalytic nature carry within them an unresolved latent tension that, once released, may unlock considerable benefits.

Creativity, the most powerful of human resources, holds the key to that lock. Creativity liberates transformation, choice, and learning, redefining possibilities to change reality across time, while capitalizing on imagination, sensitivity, and motivation. Parnes (2004) pointed out that "the Visioner, in pursuing dreams, discovers and effectively responds to new challenges, goals and opportunities, while simultaneously making new and effective responses to old problems or challenges" (p. 2). In turn, Parnes stated that the deconstruction of repeated thought patterns and the building of new ones using remote associations and analogies can lead to change.

Creativity is also seen as an ability to overcome self-imposed constraints (Ackoff & Vergara, 1981). Khatena and Torrance (1973) described it as "the power of the imagination to break away from perceptual set so as to restructure or structure anew ideas, thoughts, and feelings into novel and associative bonds" (p. 28).

Motivation is one power behind making those bonds. Motivation—thought to be a prerequisite for creativity—has received more attention as the principle of intrinsic motivation in creativity has emerged. People are most creative when they are motivated primarily by the interest, enjoyment, satisfaction, and challenge inherent to the work itself (Hennessey & Amabile, 1998).

Additional factors may influence creativity. Our tendency to see the world in a particular way, and our propensity to select those things that interest us affect how and why we are creative. So does our exposure to different perspectives (Rajah & Jones, 2007).

Incubation: Theories and Suggestions

The role of incubation is discussed by Alex Osborn (1957) in his landmark book *Applied Imagination*:

> The part of the creative process that calls for little or no conscious effort is known as incubation.... Incubation often results in "bright" ideas, and perhaps that's why it is said to invite illumination. And because its flashes are sometimes sudden, it has also been referred to as "the period of luminous surprise." (p. 314)

In the same work, Osborn pointed out that the idea-finding stage of problem solving may also trigger leads that incubation can then transform into valuable ideas.

Topolinski and Reber's (2010) theory about the *aha* moment stated that "positive affect and perceived truth and confidence in one's own judgment are triggered by the sudden appearance of the solution for a problem and the concomitant surprising fluency gain in processing" (p. 402). Testing insight problems with puzzles in laboratory settings suggested that incubation elicits a mindset change which may render insights more likely, regardless of the initial problem fixation (McCarthy, Molony, & Morrison, 2013).

Na Sio and Ormerod (2009) conducted a meta-analytical review of 117 empirical research studies about incubation effects on problem solving and concluded that primarily divergent thinking activities had a positive incubation effect, especially when undertaking low cognitive load tasks. They held that incubation probably facilitates the widening of one's knowledge network search. In contrast, they hypothesized, linguistic and visual tasks provided benefits of a lesser scope.

More recently, Aznar and Ely (2010) identified two creativity engines: a sensitive stance—slow-paced, fuzzy, intuitive—and a dynamic stance, which approximates the creative problem solving model codified by Osborn and Parnes, characterized by divergence and convergence (Parnes, 2004). The sensitive stance has strong emotional implications and consists of three strokes: departure, emergence, and sensitive convergence. The authors recommended particular techniques for the sensitive stance, including storytelling (by individuals or in groups), imaginary travels, and awake dreaming. These techniques engage visual imagery, and bring intuition and emotions to the fore. The authors considered other techniques useful for both sensitive and dynamic stances—making metaphors, viewing matters from a different perspective, and constructing collages.

Further insight-building techniques proposed by Parnes (2004) included drawing, symbolizing, deconstructing dreams, and using pictures as triggers. Some of these employ sensory stimuli, while others heighten personal awareness and creative movement, non-verbal imagination, relaxation, and fantasy.

The Incubation Model of Teaching and Learning (Torrance & Safter, 1990) can be useful especially with regards to the gradual process of fostering insights. Multiple aspects of the model make it relevant beyond teaching, especially since its heightening anticipation stage may enhance awareness, nurture curiosity, and facilitate dealing with uncertainties. The result is an additional openness and willingness to deepen expectations, to explore changes, and to extend learning (Walsh, 2007).

The Role of Rest

Rest is a key component of incubation. Osborn (1957) suggested that "sleeping well, above all else, helps court illumination, for it tends to step up our power of association as well as to recharge our mental energy" (p. 319). His point of view is underscored in a study (Cai, Harrison, Kanady, & Mednick, 2009) that showed quiet rest involving REM sleep enhances creative problem solving by integrating unassociated information. Dreams are often reported to be an aid to incubation. One study reported that almost a tenth of dreams contribute to solving waking life problems (Schredl & Erlacher, 2007), while another suggested that lucid dreams may also assist creativity and problem solving (Stumbrys & Daniels, 2010).

Osborn (1957) acknowledged other potentially helpful incubation strategies: yoga, shifting activities, allowing longer time, taking a walk, and keeping a notebook. Helpful as those strategies are, Osborn emphasized that years of dedication and deliberative thinking might be necessary to reach those points of illumination, proposing the idea that domain expertise can be a crucial contributing factor.

News from Neuroscience

Neuroimaging studies proposed that what happens in the brain in the presence of an *aha* experience arises from a culminating process of brain states and processes operating at different timescales (Kounios & Beeman, 2009). While such studies conducted with functional magnetic resonance imaging (fMRI) and electroencephalogram recordings (EEG) bring new understanding, they do have some limitations. To measure brain activity, test subjects must remain still, which makes the research most suitable for impasse and puzzle problems.

That said, neuroscientific studies tantalizingly offer clues about where in the brain insights occur. In a study focused on verbal problems solved with insights, researchers found heightened activity in the right hemisphere anterior superior temporal gyrus—the region recognized as being responsible for distant or novel semantic or associative relations. They also suggested that the brain processes involving insight follow discrete steps: "Although all problem solving relies on a largely shared cortical network, the sudden flash of insight occurs when solvers engage distinct neural and cognitive processes that allow them to see connections that previously eluded them" (Jung-Beeman et al., 2004, p. 500).

In another *aha*-puzzle neuroimaging study, task-related processing depended on the characteristics of the prior resting state, leading researchers to suggest that contextual manipulations positively influence cognitive strategies (Kounios et al., 2008). In fact, those who were about to produce an insight turned their attention inward while those who later followed an analytical solving path focused their attention outward, activating the high cortex visual areas (Kounios et al., 2008). In another study, people with a positive mood were shown to solve more problems and to have more insights (Subramaniam, Kounios, & Parrish, 2008), while other research found that in solving anagrams, eye movement reveals knowledge of a solution several seconds prior to perceived insight (Ellis, Glaholt, & Reingold, 2011).

Imagery, Priming, and Mindset

Methods that enhance awareness and perceptions of the sensitive, astute, and powerful subconscious—including imagery, priming, and mindset—can help identify and solve problems, leading to breakthrough innovations, inventions, and understanding.

Wenger and Poe (1996) proposed an "image streaming" system of thought and perception, involving a combinatory play composed by sense impressions, visual images and memories, muscular sensations, emotion, and intuition. Only in the final stages is productive thought translated into words and equations. The authors submitted that the unconscious expresses itself in sidebands of thought and perception; in their understanding, the mind continually sorts through its entire database for the best insights, which are subsequently expressed through imagery. Wenger (1998) advised describing one's perceptions aloud to a listener if feasible, and claims that doing so heightens "conscious perception of our inner subtleties in a way no other procedure can" (p. 21).

A different approach consisted of using external visual stimuli to tap the unconscious, as an external stimulus may also "prime" unconscious resolution. With respect to priming effects, even subliminal presentation of a stimulus seems to positively influence performance in a creativity task (Forster, 2009).

A recent study indicated that priming participants with novelty has beneficial effects when the unrelated creativity task conducted later was a divergent activity. However, results showed that familiarity or neutrality prior to an unrelated convergence activity casts an inhibitory effect of novelty on creativity (Gillebaart, Forster, Rotteveel, & Jehle, 2013).

In light of these findings, it would be ideal to use a broad variety of visual stimuli with the purpose of creative stimulation and priming, and this selection should be based on the participant's profiles, the nature of the challenge, the environment available, and other factors such as length of the task. A body of knowledge of cognitive research and creativity suggests that inducing people to access more abstract levels of representation, carrying out conceptual expansion tasks, and constraining the most readily accessible solutions can lead to increased originality in creative outputs, as can working with metaphors especially when dealing with discrepant and opposing conceptual combinations (Ward & Kolomyts, 2010).

Another approach is to selectively manipulate mindset to generate targeted improvement. A series of "seeing is believing" studies (Langer, Djikic, Pirson, Madenci, & Donohue, 2010) confirmed that even visual acuity can be improved by altering mindset. Kiefer and Constable (2013) suggested careful listening as a way to cultivate a state of mind in which insights happen more frequently. Their "fresh thought hunt" exercise requires working with a partner, and involves one participant voicing the fresh thought while the other one listens for insights, followed by reflective pausing.

Deliberate stimuli should be more broadly reframed, though, so that priming and altering mindset are potential shortcuts to insight. Such stimuli might include symbolic images or artifacts, environment cues, instructions, guided grounding, and listening journeys to help connect to unconscious wisdom. In particular, I believe surrealistic imagery may provide a level of ambiguity that helps surface unconscious impressions.

Enhanced Awareness, Mindfulness, and Context

Self-awareness—such as the experience of walking mindfully through a labyrinth, with deliberately pre-set intentions—is another path to unlocking insights. A novel self-guidance system with a labyrinth path called LABgraphic (Boelhower, Miguez, & Pearce, 2013) blends change management and emotional intelligence, providing a transformative technology to access the awareness, vision, and realization of one's inner wisdom.

Mindfulness may grant access to inner wisdom. Ostafin and Kassman (2012) hypothesized that certain types of mindfulness meditation may facilitate insight problem solving, and that insight is partially mediated by a state of mindfulness. The authors found a statistically significant positive correlation between mindful awareness and insight problem solving. Even after controlling for positive affect, the relationship between mindfulness and predicted insight problem solving was also significant. This study suggested that mindfulness training may improve insight problem solving, and it claimed to be the first research to scientifically bring evidence of a direct link between mindfulness meditation and creativity. The authors believed the effect occurred because mindfulness meditation promotes a low-level awareness, which involves habitual verbal-conceptual processing of ongoing experiences. Indeed, being in the moment reduces the chances of being constrained by past experiences, and may lead to approaching insight problems with a fresh or beginners type of mindset.

In the search for consumer insights, understanding the broader context and competitive environment is important. Consumers often have trouble articulating repressed needs, though these can reveal underlying motivations behind usage (Lee & Park, 2013). Contextual cues can help infer potential needs beyond the usual consumer-expressed needs captured by traditional market research. A family of techniques based on observation, like ethnography or the building of empathy maps, is especially suitable to discover non-obvious consumer needs (Osterwalder & Pigneur, 2010). An empathic connection is essential to truly understand customers, and has facilitated design challenges in the frame of the consumer-centric Design Thinking approach (Mootee, 2013).

Conclusion

In my exploration of insight, I was surprised by the amount and quality of research and practical knowledge surrounding insights. I realize not just one route leads to the achievement of insight. Instead, constellations of access points, opportunity paths, tools and practices light the way.

This abundance reflects different ways in which the multiple facets of insights and dimensions of creativity can be encouraged and influenced. Facilitators, mentors, coaches, leaders, and anyone seeking self-discovery would benefit from exploring diverse angles, to try what works best for specific purposes, adapting or developing new alternatives, and sharing their learning.

The number of tools to foster insights contrasts with their limited popularity in practice, at least in organizations. I believe true adoption remains elusive, and speculate this is due to lack of awareness, lack of confidence in the tools' effectiveness, misjudgment regarding predictability and control of potential insight, and an inability to support the learning of new habits and routines.

Among these factors, I wish to focus on one critical final question: how might we make accessing insight a regular part of life? I suggest that future research and practices focus on overcoming the barriers that inhibit the acceptance of effective daily insight-cultivating systems and the successful widespread adoption of their practices.

I remain open-minded and curious about insight, and wish for others to join me in a deliberate choice to persevere through enhanced awareness to integrate insight-cultivating habits every day. Championing the architecture of insight's awakening and consistently catalyzing changes in assumptions and beliefs on a daily basis may open limitless possibilities for the emergence of sustainable breakthroughs and radical leaps charged with purposefulness, heightened awareness, wisdom, excitement, growth, renewal, choice, and value creation. For that, I say this is a rewarding time to welcome our insights.

References

Ackoff, R., & Vergara, E. (1981). Creativity in problem solving and planning: A review. *European Journal of Operational Research, 7,* 1-13.

Aznar, G., & Ely, S. (2010). *The sensitive stance in the production of creative ideas.* Paris, France: Editions Crea Universite.

Boelhower, G., Miguez, J., & Pearce, T. (2013). *Mountain 10: Climbing the labyrinth within.* North Charleston, SC: Mountain 10 Resources.

Cai, D. C., Harrison, E. M., Kanady, J. C., & Mednick, S. C. (2009). REM, not incubation, improves creativity by priming associative networks. *PNAS, Proceedings of the National Academy of Sciences of the United States of*

America, 106(25). Retrieved from http://www.pnas.org/cgi/doi/10.1073/pnas.0900271106

Dunne, T., & Dugan, M. (2007). *Assumption busting: Breaking patterns to find new ideas.* Retrieved from http://www.instantbrainstorm.com/bust_assumptions.html

Ellis, J. J., Glaholt, M. G., & Reingold, E. M. (2011). Eye movements reveal solution knowledge prior to insight. *Consciousness and Cognition, 20*(3), 768-776.

Forster, J. (2009). The unconscious city: How expectancies about creative milieus influence creative performance. In P. Meusburger, J. Funke, & E. Wunder (Eds.), *Milieus of creativity: Knowledge and space* (Vol. 2, pp. 219-233). Retrieved from http://link.springer.com/chapter/10.1007%2F978-1-4020-9877-2_12#page-1

Gillebaart, M., Forster, J., Rotteveel, M., & Jehle, A. C. M. (2013). Unraveling effects of novelty on creativity. *Creativity Research Journal, 25*(3), 280-285. Retrieved from http://www.taylorandfrancis.com/

Hennessey, B. A., & Amabile, T. M. (1998). Reality, intrinsic motivation, and creativity. *American Psychologist, 63*(6), 674-675.

Jung-Beeman, M., Bowden, E. M., Haberman, J., Frymiare, J. L., Arambel-Liu, S., Greenblatt, R., Reber, P. J., & Kounios, J. (2004). Neural activity when people solve verbal problems with insight. *Plos Biology, 2*(4), 0500-0510. doi:10.1371/journal.pbio.0020097

Khatena, J., & Torrance, E. P. (1973). *Thinking Creatively with Sounds and Words: Norms-technical manual* (Revised ed.). Lexington, MS: Personal Press.

Kiefer, C., & Constable, M. (2013). *The art of insight.* San Francisco, CA: Berret-Koeler Publishing.

Klein, G., & Jarosz, A. (2011). A naturalistic study of insight. *Journal of Cognitive Engineering and Decision Making, 5*(4), 335-351. doi:10.1177/1555343411427013

Kounios, J., & Beeman, M. (2009). The aha! moment: The cognitive neuroscience of insight. *Current Directions in Psychological Science, 18*(4), 210-216. doi:10.1111/j.1467-8721.2009.01638.x

Kounios, J., Fleck, J. I., Green, D. L., Payne, L., Stevenson, J. L., Bowden, E. M., & Jung-Beeman, M. (2008). The origins of insight in resting-state brain activity. *Neuropsychologia, 46,* 281-291. doi:10.1016/j.neuropsychologia.2007.07.013

Langer, E., Djikic, M., Pirson, M., Madenci, A., & Donohue, R. (2010). Believing is seeing: Using mindlessness (mindfully) to improve visual acuity. *Psychological Science, 21*(5), 661-666. doi:10.1177/0956797610366543

Lee, K. J., & Park, Y. (2013). User-centric service map for identifying new service opportunities from potential needs: A case of App Store applications. *Creativity and Innovation Management, 22*(3), 241-264.

McCarthy, S., Molony, J., & Morrison, R. G. (2013). Insight follows incubation in the compound remote task. In *Proceedings of the 35th Annual Conference of the Science Society* (pp. 1-6). Retrieved from http://www.researchgate.net/publication/236631535_Insight_Follows_Incubation_In_The_Compound_Remote_Associates_Task/file/3deec518902f65c3f4.pdf

Mootee, I. (2013). *Design thinking for strategic innovation: What they can't teach you at business or design school.* Hoboken, NJ: Wiley.

Na Sio, T., & Ormerod, T. (2009). Does incubation enhance problem solving? A meta-analytic review. *Psychological Bulletin, 135*(1), 94-120. doi:10.1037/a0014212

Osborn, A. (1957). *Applied imagination.* New York, NY: Scribner.

Ostafin, B. D., & Kassman, K. T. (2012). Stepping out of history: Mindfulness improves insight problem solving. *Consciousness and Cognition, 21,* 1031-1036.

Osterwalder, A., & Pigneur, Y. (2010). *Business model generation: A handbook for visionaries, game changers, and challengers.* Hoboken, NJ: Wiley.

Parnes, S. (2004). *Visionizing.* Buffalo, NY: Creative Education Foundation Press.

Rajah, K., & Jones, L. (2007). Creativity, enterprise and socio-economic change. In K. Jones (Ed.), *Complex creativity* (pp. 21-27). London, UK: University of Greeenwich Press.

Schredl, M., & Erlacher, D. (2007). Self-reported effects of dreams on waking-life creativity: An empirical study. *The Journal of Psychology, 14*(1), 35-46.

Stumbrys, T., & Daniels, M. (2010). An exploratory study of creative problem solving in lucid dreams: Preliminary findings and methodological considerations. *International Journal of Dream Research, 3*(2), 121-129.

Subramaniam, K., Kounios, J., & Parrish, T. B. (2008). A brain mechanism for facilitation of insight by positive affect. *Journal of Cognitive Neuroscience, 21*(3), 415-432. doi:10.1162/jocn.2009.21057

Topolinski, S., & Reber, R. (2010). Gaining insight into the "Aha" experience. *Current Directions in Psychological Science, 19*(6), 402-405.

Torrance, E. P., & Safter, T. H. (1990). *The incubation model of teaching: Getting beyond the aha!* Buffalo, NY: Bearly Limited.

Walsh, S. (2007). Curiosity unlocks innovation. In K. Rajah (Ed.), *Complex creativity* (pp. 173-190). London, UK: University of Greenwich Press.

Ward, T. W., & Kolomyts, Y. (2010). Cognition and creativity. In J. C. Kaufman & R. J. Sternberg (Eds.), *The Cambridge handbook of creativity* (pp. 93-112). New York, NY: Cambridge University Press.

Wenger, W. (1998). *Discovering the obvious.* Gaithersburg, MD: Project Renaissance.

Wenger, W., & Poe, R. (1996). *The Einstein factor: A proven new method for increasing your intelligence.* Roseville, CA: Prima Publishing.

About the Author

With an extensive background in research and development in the categories of food and pet care, Mariano Tosso has more than 15 years of experience leading consumer-driven innovation teams. As a master's degree candidate at the International Center for Studies in Creativity, he has refined his passions for designing and orchestrating creativity training programs and crafting creative learning experiences for organizations. Email: marianotosso@gmail.com, LinkedIn: https://www.linkedin.com/in/marianotosso.

How Can Spiritual Intelligence Help Us Cultivate Creative Potential?

Rebecca DiLiberto
International Center for Studies in Creativity
SUNY Buffalo State

Originally published in *Big Questions in Creativity 2016*

Abstract

The nature and nurture of human potential, intellectual abilities, and creative achievements have long been topics of interest in the science of human behavior. In particular, there is an emerging effort to understand the relationship between spiritual intelligence and creativity. Research suggests that developing our spiritual intelligence is quite relevant to the cultivation of our creative potentials. There appears to be a current desire by many people for a higher intellectual level of spirituality, and an eagerness to learn how to develop creative potentials, enhance one's senses of purpose, and deepen one's connections to the world. The purpose of this paper is to provide a comprehensive and contemporary overview of spiritual intelligence, and the relationship of spiritual intelligence to creativity and one's sense of purpose and meaning.

How Can Spiritual Intelligence Help Us Cultivate Creative Potential?

There is an imbalance in the forms of intelligences recognized by our culture. General intelligence (often measured as an intelligence quotient, or IQ) is perceived as the predominant form of intelligence, outweighing less tangible abilities and intelligences such as visual-spatial intelligence (Gardner, 1983), emotional intelligence (EQ; Goleman, 1995), spiritual intelligence (SQ; Zohar, 2000), creative thinking ability, and others. This imbalance is compounded with Western cultural values such as immediate gratification and the "quest to be the best." The result is a narrowed perspective on the importance of these other intelligences and abilities—and, in the case of SQ, a discounting of its value. Meanwhile, there is a culturally-driven yearning to find a purposeful life. People in all walks of life appear not only to desire and appreciate a higher intellectual level of spirituality, but are eager to learn how to cultivate their creative potentials, enhance their senses of purpose, and deepen their connections to the world.

Contemporary literature and scholarly opinion suggest that SQ is a vital and valid form of intelligence, which can influence creative achievement and enhance a sense of life purpose. But have we fallen for the misconception of defining creativity, spirituality, and intelligence as mutually exclusive? How might SQ influence creativity? With these questions in mind, the primary overarching question to address is: Are we developing our SQ to cultivate our creative potentials and senses of life's meaning? The intent of this paper is to explore the concept of SQ and discuss how it is related to creativity and enhancing one's sense of purpose and meaning in the world.

Spiritual Intelligence

The concept of SQ is rooted in the idea of spirituality. Spirituality is distinct from religion in that it encompasses universal domains of humanity and is not confined to religious practices or beliefs (Elkins, Hedstrom, Hughes, Leaf, & Saunders, 1988; Wigglesworth, 2012). The wide range of understanding surrounding spirituality has influenced its definition. Spirituality has been associated with terms ranging from *supernatural* to *the essence of being* (King, 2005; Sriraman, 2009). In line with the humanistic understanding of spirituality, and most congruent with the concept of SQ, Wigglesworth (2012) defined spirituality as "the innate human need to be connected to something larger than ourselves, something we consider to be divine or of exceptional nobility" (p. 8).

Contemporary SQ Ideologies

The various views and interpretations of spirituality contribute to the diversity of SQ ideologies. Many studies, theories, and definitions of SQ have been developed and applied to the fields of academics, business, and leadership. However, primary characteristics of SQ have emerged from the literature to form the contemporary ideology (Table 1).

Perhaps due to the many primary characteristics of SQ, it remains controversial if SQ is truly an independent and measurable intelligence. It is nevertheless instructive to consider what some scholars have said about SQ: it is intimately related with creativity; creativity is an important and fundamental aspect in the nurturing of SQ; and the components of SQ strongly complement our quests for deep self-awareness, appreciation for inner knowing, higher states of consciousness, universal interconnectedness, and insight into existential questions for attaining meaningful goals and a sense of purpose (Emmons, 2000a, 2000b; Green & Noble, 2010; Noble, 2009; Sinetar, 1992, 2000; Vaughan, 2002; Wigglesworth, 2012; Zohar & Marshall, 2000, 2004). The contemporary ideology of SQ is primarily influenced by humanistic and transpersonal psychology, paying strong tribute to the spiritual natures of transcendent experience and "plateau experience" (Maslow, 1971, p. 281). Such experiences are thought to be of great importance in encouraging greater well-being, self-actualization, and creative and spiritual growth. Accordingly, engaging in problem solving, observing continuous spiritual and creative thinking practices, and practicing leadership should simultaneously nurture both SQ and creativity. Therefore, it is reasonable to think that developing SQ is highly relevant to developing one's creative potential.

Sisk and Torrance (2001) developed a comprehensive and holistic understanding of SQ that is representative of contemporary ideology and of the relationship between SQ and creativity. They associated the essence of SQ to a deep self-awareness and an inner experience of the continuously-evolving self. They explained, "A person leading a spiritual life wants to feel connected, to feel a sense of community, to be free of restrictions, to experience inner freedom and a life of meaning" (p. 8). Through the expression of SQ, they continued, one becomes more aware of the inner processes of the self to develop and nurture higher values, motivations, intentions, and aspirations. More conclusively, Sisk and Torrance highlighted four areas that resonate with the authentic meaning and concept of SQ: *inner knowing, deep intuition, oneness with nature and the universe,* and *problem solving.* The following sections will explore how these focal areas are related and can influence one's creativity.

Inner Knowing

"Inner knowing is to know the essence of consciousness and to realize that this inner essence is the essence of all creation" (Sisk & Torrance, 2001, p. 11).

Without our conscious awareness, our imaginations, creativity, intelligences, and senses of self are void. Our abilities to reflect on the past, to be mindful of the present, and to imagine the future are dependent on our different levels of consciousness. "To achieve a life filled with meaning, you must figure out how to be more conscious; only then do you become the author of your own destiny" (Chopra & Tanzi, 2012, p. 57). Inner knowing can strengthen our ability to unlock different levels of consciousness, to listen to our intuition, to problem-solve life's big questions, and to direct our creative potentials toward a meaningful life.

Inner knowing is often associated with intuition, gut feeling, inner voice, or sense of self (Burnett, 2010), but it is not to be confused with deep intuition. Vaughan (1979) explained how intuitive experiences could funnel into physical, emotional, mental, and spiritual levels of awareness. *Physical intuition* refers to body responses, sensations, and conscious awareness of one's physical being and surrounding environment. *Emotional intuition* is concerned with empathy, feelings, and a heightened ability to recognize synchronicity experiences. *Mental intuition* is associated with creativity, problem solving, imagery, and the process where unconscious patterns become conscious. Each of these are associated with inner knowing. However, the fourth form of awareness—*spiritual intuition*—is more closely associated with deep intuition. Vaughan wrote, "Pure, spiritual intuition is distinguished from other forms by its independence from sensations, feelings, and thoughts" (p. 77).

Having faith in one's intuitions is an important quality of SQ, creative thinking, and problem solving. Interestingly, Kaufman (2013) found that faith in intuition, superstitious thinking, and impractical expectations "are not always irrational.... They are often conducive to reaching one's goals.... Faith in intuition is associated with a reduced latent inhibition, which in turn, is associated with higher levels of creative achievement" (p. 304). Burnett (2010, 2014) advocated intuition and mindfulness as being prevalent throughout the Creative Problem Solving (CPS) process, with particular attention drawn to the affective skills. Mindfulness in CPS allows for a greater awareness of intuition, and helps to balance the ebb and flow of the affective and cognitive skills. Hence, the intuition in inner knowing, embedded in SQ, does not replace one's creative thinking skills, but works as an internal resource influencing change along one's spiritual creative journey.

Table 1. SQ Ideologies Primary Characteristics

SQ Primary Characteristics	SQ Ideologies					
	Emmons, 2000a, 2000b	Green & Noble, 2010; Noble, 2009	Sinetar, 1992, 2000	Vaughan, 2002	Wigglesworth, 2012	Zohar & Marshall, 2000, 2004
Abilities to Nurture & Develop	X	X	X	X	X	X
Creativity is Fundamental			X	X		X
Creativity Relevance/Associations	X	X	X	X	X	X
Existential Questions/Thinking	X	X	X	X	X	X
Higher Conscious Expansion	X	X	X	X	X	X
Humanistic/Transpersonal Psychology Influence	X	X	X	X	X	X
Codependent Intelligence					X	
Measurable					X	X

Characteristic							
Personal Meaning/Purpose	X	X	X	X		X	X
Problem Solving	X	X	X	X		X	X
Psychological Health Well-being	X	X	X			X	
Self-Awareness/Inner Knowing	X	X	X	X		X	X
Spiritual Change Agent/Leadership			X			X	X
Spiritual Practitioner	X	X	X	X		X	X
Spiritual/Transcendent/Plateau Experiences	X	X	X	X		X	X
Transcendental Awareness/Capacity	X	X	X	X		X	X
Universal Awareness/Interconnectedness	X	X	X	X		X	X

Note: Cells with an X denote when authors included the corresponding primary characteristic in their SQ ideology.

Deep Intuition

SQ assists in overlooking the egotistical self to employ deep intuition in developing solutions for the greater good (Sisk & Torrance, 2001).

Deep intuition in many aspects fits Vaughan's (1979) definition of spiritual intuition, Harman's (1988) M-3 Transcendental Monism (from his three metaphysical perspectives), and Jung's (1959/1980) concept of the collective unconscious. Each author discussed how our rational minds could hinder our ability to access higher states of consciousness that transcend true awakening. It is at this level that consciousness transcends the sense of self, ego, or the concept of "I."

Deep intuition strongly contributes to self-actualization. To foster deep intuition, one must seek experiences of spiritual growth to remove the clutter and suppressed creative energy from all levels of consciousness. Csikszentmihalyi (1990) included forms of this throughout his lists of attributes prevalent during optimal or flow experiences; for instance, concentration on the task at hand; the removal of anxiety from the mind, and the loss of self-consciousness; and the loss of inhibitions and consciousness of the self. Flow or peak experiences can result in rewarding and lasting impressions, due to their spiritual natures (Csikszentmihalyi & Rathunde, 1990). Noble (2000) has even argued that spiritual experiences not only facilitate self-actualizations but are precursors to spiritual intelligence. Deep intuition assists in the process of self-actualization through the production of spiritual and transcendent experiences, and integrates one's unrestricted creativity with the collective being.

Through deep intuition, one has the capability to reach beyond self-actualization and strengthen one's potential for self-transcendence. Rogers (1979) believed that every individual has actualizing tendencies, and that the knowledge and experiences of our authentic consciences impact our personas. He stated, "we are tuning in to a potent creative tendency which has formed our universe.... And perhaps we are touching the cutting edge of our ability to transcend ourselves, to create new and more spiritual directions in human evolution" (p. 8).

Maslow's efforts to promote creativity are evident in his concept of self-actualization. His insights into spirituality are further heightened in his Theory Z, with the spiritual nature of the "plateau experience" and transcending self-actualizers (Maslow, 1971, p. 281). Maslow further proposed that self-actualized transcenders exceed the expectation of self-actualized non-transcenders. Feuerstein (1997) wrote that self-actualized transcenders "are motivated by the desire to realize their true identity, which is the identity of all beings and things—the transcendental Self" (p. 139).

With the support of deep intuition in SQ, one can transcend the ego, past unconscious notions and the illusion of reality, to direct his or her potential and cultivate solutions in benefit of the greater good.

Oneness with Nature and the Universe

SQ harmonizes with nature and the world around us to find a purpose in life that is intrinsically motivating (Sisk & Torrance, 2001).

Everything is a process, from nature and the universe to spirituality and creativity. The quest for spiritual and creative growth becomes vital when life's processes and motivations start to become unbalanced. Oneness with nature and the universe "urges us to search for wholeness, a sense of community and relationship, to create an identity, and to search for meaning; and out of this search for meaning will come a sense of empowerment" (Sisk & Torrance, 2001, p. 12).

To live a creative life of meaning, an individual must venture into the realms of his inner world in conjunction with the outer world (Robinson & Aronica, 2013). According to Amabile (1997), "maintaining your own creativity in your work depends on maintaining your intrinsic motivation" (p. 55). In many creative endeavors, inspiration is a key component in maintaining intrinsic motivation (Kaufman, 2013) and orchestrating SQ (Sinetar, 2000; Vaughan, 2002). Creative inspiration transpires in the outer world of the self and often provokes an intuitive sense of opening, an awakening of new perceptions, and a connection to one's inner world (Kaufman, 2013; Rogers, 1961). Vaughan (2002) explained that SQ "facilitates the integration of subjective insights and illuminations with ways of being and acting in the world" (p. 7). In the end, our individual pursuits of meaning and purpose are lost without the connection to each other and the world. Csikszentmihalyi (1990) explained:

> Just as we have learned to separate ourselves from each other and from the environment, we now need to learn how to reunite ourselves with the other entities around us without losing our hard-won individuality. The most promising faith for the future might be based on the realization that the entire universe is a system related by common laws and that it makes no sense to impose our dreams and desires on nature without taking them into account. Recognizing the limitations of human will, accepting a cooperative rather than a ruling role in the universe, we should feel the relief of the exile who is finally returning home. The problem of meaning will then be resolved as the individual's purpose merges with the universal flow. (p. 240)

We are a trivial part of an infinite world and universal process that is far greater than ourselves. Looking at our place in the universe guides the attitudes of openness to novelty and tolerance for ambiguity and complexity, to put our problems into perspective. In turn, this generates novel ideas and cultivates meaningful solutions for the purpose of a collective ambition (Quarrie, 2015). The oneness with nature and the universe component of SQ complements and guides our internal creative processes and our senses of purpose and meaning to the external world.

Problem Solving

SQ guides one's life's purpose and meaning throughout the entire problem solving process (Sisk & Torrance, 2001).

Problem solving and change is an inevitable occurrence in human life, and could even be thought of as the entire process of being alive, with our selves as the evolving innovative solutions. SQ "is not amoral, it engages us in questions of good and evil and affords us opportunities to dream, to reconfigure, to look beyond the boundaries of a situation to what it could be" (Sisk & Torrance, 2001, p. 12). Not only do we ask questions of meaning and purpose in hopes to put our lives in perspective, but these perceptions, behaviors, and motivations have powerful influences in the world around us. SQ provides insight into harmonizing one's sense of purpose and peace across multiple life contexts in the pursuit of generating creative change for the world.

Creativity is change, thus it can easily be argued that the great spiritual warriors were not just change agents but *creative* change agents. Mahatma Gandhi, Nelson Mandela, Martin Luther King Jr., and Mother Teresa were solving problems with meaning and value to the world, not just to themselves. They embodied the spirit of creativity within their own SQ. As Sisk and Torrance (2001) wrote, SQ "has the capacity to integrate these intelligences and enable them to achieve the highest realization of human nature" (p. 7). At this point creativity becomes a way of living and being, "the force that drives all life" (Chopra & Chopra, 2011, p. 119). SQ arguably is the necessary and overarching intelligence of CPS.

In addition to creative spiritual warriors internalizing the principles of creativity, three qualities remain primary: love, wisdom, and compassion. According to Wigglesworth's (2012) research on SQ, love is comprised of wisdom and compassion. Love nurtures creativity within ourselves and others. Wisdom and compassion allow love and creativity to flourish and extend human meaning and purpose towards a greater good. In relation to creativity, love is commonly associated with the internal desire or passion that propels an individual's creative ability (Amabile, 1997; Sternberg, 1988; Torrance, 1995). And wisdom in creativity can be linked with the importance of a positive attitude, knowledge, and evaluation supported by a vision and deliberate practice (Parnes, Noller, & Biondi, 1977; Puccio, Mance, Barbero Switalski, & Reali, 2012). On the other hand, there seems to be little emphasis on the direct connection between creativity and compassion. To be compassionate is "to suffer with another; sympathy for the suffering of others, often including a desire to help" (Dossey, 2007, p. 1). The strongest component of compassion is the desire to help; this motivation alone proactively promotes imagination, creative thinking, problem solving, and leadership. Correspondingly, Kaufman (2013) researched creative achievement and openness to experience, finding correlations with compassion. With these ideas in mind, compassion—and even the combination of love, wisdom, and compassion—may warrant further research to heighten the instrumental correlation between SQ, creativity, CPS, and creative leadership.

Nurturing the Creative, Spiritual Life

All humans are innately spiritual and creative, and have the ability to deliberately strengthen those natural tendencies or let them weaken. As one focuses on nurturing one's own creative potential, it is important to remember that accessing one's inner awareness, personal obstacles, and individual processes are driving forces in the progression and direction of growth. Taking the time to practice inner knowing, deep intuition, oneness with nature and the universe, and problem solving to harmonize the creative being is a spiritual journey of continuous transformation. In an effort to guide one's spiritual, creative journey, Sisk and Torrance's (2001) suggest seven ways to nurture and develop SQ:

1. Think about your goals, desires and wants, to bring your life into perspective and balance, and identify your values.

2. Access your inner processes and use visualization to see your goals, desires and wants fulfilled, and experience the emotion connected with this fulfillment.

3. Integrate your personal and universal vision and recognize your connectedness to others, to nature, to the world, and to the universe.

4. Take responsibility for your goals, desires, and wants.

5. Develop a sense of community by letting more people into your life.

6. Focus on love and compassion.

7. When chance knocks at your door, let it in and take advantage of coincidences. (p. 180)

It is through the development and understanding of these SQ ambitions that we can reawaken our inner compasses to direct our creative potentials and guide our paths to self-actualization, self-transcendence, and the greater good. Ultimately, this will allow us to lead more creative and spiritual lives of meaning and purpose. As one's sense of purpose and life direction evolves, so will one's spiritual, creative journey.

Conclusion

The nature and nurture of human potential, intellectual abilities, and creative achievements has long been a topic of interest in the science of human behavior. Many human behaviors and motivations are spiritual in nature, such as love, wisdom, compassion, inspiration, openness to experiences, self-actualization, and the cultivation of one's creative potentials. SQ is an oft-neglected but important type of intelligence that is related to both creativity and one's sense of purpose in life. Considerable scholarly works have helped shape and develop contemporary SQ ideology, as well as identify the components of SQ within all of us that are important in assisting self-actualization, creative potential, and the greater good. To nurture our SQ we must expose ourselves to experiences that best complement our unique creative natures. And to nurture our creative natures, we must expose ourselves to experiences that enhance our SQ.

References

Amabile, T. M. (1997). Motivating creativity in organizations: On doing what you love and loving what you do. *California Management Review, 40*(1), 39-58.

Burnett, C. (2010). *Holistic approaches to creative problem solving.* [Unpublished doctoral thesis.] Toronto, Canada: University of Toronto.

Burnett, C. (2014). The missing link: Teaching the creative problem solving process. In J. Piirto (Ed.), *Organic creativity in the classroom: Teaching to intuition in academics and the arts* (pp. 285-297). Waco, TX: Prufrock Press.

Chopra, D., & Chopra, G. (2011). *The seven spiritual laws of superheroes: Harnessing our power to change the world.* New York, NY: HarperCollins.

Chopra, D., & Tanzi, R. E. (2012). *Super brain: Unleashing the explosive power of your mind to maximize health, happiness, and spiritual well-being.* New York, NY: Crown Publishing Group.

Csikszentmihalyi, M. (1990). *Flow: The psychology of optimal experience.* New York, NY: HarperPerennial.

Csikszentmihalyi, M., & Rathunde, K. (1990). The psychology of wisdom: An evolutionary interpretation. In R. J. Sternberg (Ed.), *Wisdom: Its nature, origins, and development* (pp. 26-51). New York, NY: Cambridge University Press.

Dossey, D. (2007). Compassion. *EXPLORE: The Journal of Science and Healing, 3*(1), 1-5.

Elkins, D. N., Hedstrom, L. J., Hughes, L. L., Leaf, J. A., & Saunders, C. (1988). Toward a humanistic-phenomenological spirituality: Definition, description, and measurement. *Journal of Humanistic Psychology, 28*(4), 5-18.

Emmons, R. A. (2000a). Is spirituality an intelligence? Motivation, cognition, and the psychology of ultimate concern. *The International Journal for the Psychology of Religion, 10*(1), 3-26.

Emmons, R. A. (2000b). Spirituality and intelligence: Problems and prospects. *The International Journal for the Psychology of Religion, 10*(1), 57-64.

Feuerstein, G. (1997). *Lucid waking: Mindfulness and the spiritual potential of humanity.* Rochester, VT: Inner Traditions International.

Gardner, H. (1983). *Frames of mind: The theory of multiple intelligences.* New York, NY: Basic Books.

Goleman, D. (1995). Emotional intelligence: Why it can matter more than IQ. New York, NY: Bantam Books.

Green, W. N., & Noble, K. D. (2010). Fostering spiritual intelligence: Undergraduates' growth in a course about consciousness. *Advanced Development Journal, 12*(1), 26-49.

Harman, W. (1988). *Global mind change: The promise of the last years of the 20th century.* Indianapolis, IN: Knowledge Systems Inc.

Jung, C. G. (1980). *The archetypes and the collective unconscious* (2nd ed., R. F. C. Hull Trans.). Princeton, NJ: Princeton University Press. (Original work published 1959)

Kaufman, S. B. (2013). *Ungifted: Intelligence redefined.* Philadelphia, PA: Perseus Books Group.

King, P. (2005). Spirituality. In C. Fisher & R. Lerner (Eds.), *Encyclopedia of applied developmental science* (Vol. 2, pp. 1047-1047). Thousand Oaks, CA: Sage Publications.

Maslow, A. H. (1971). *The farther reaches of human nature.* New York, NY: Viking Press.

Noble, K. D. (2000). Spiritual intelligence: A new frame of mind. *Advanced Development, 9,* 1-29.

Noble, K. D. (2009). Spiritual intelligence. In B. Kerr (Ed.), *Encyclopedia of giftedness, creativity, and talent* (pp. 821-823). Thousand Oaks, CA: Sage Publications.

Parnes, S. J., Noller, R. B., & Biondi, A. M. (1977). *Guide to creative action.* New York, NY: Charles Scribner's Sons.

Puccio, G. J., Mance, M., Barbero Switalski, L., & Reali, P. D. (2012). *Creativity rising: Creative thinking and creative problem solving in the 21st century.* Buffalo, NY: ICSC Press.

Quarrie, J. A. (2015). How does nature nurture creativity? In M. K. Culpepper & C. Burnett (Eds.), *Big questions in creativity 2015* (pp. 93-112). Buffalo, NY: ICSC Press.

Robinson, K., & Aronica, L. (2013). *Finding your element: How to discover your talents and passions and transform your life.* New York, NY: Penguin.

Rogers, C. (1961). *On becoming a person: A therapist's view of psychotherapy.* Boston, MA: Houghton Mifflin.

Rogers, C. R. (1979). The foundations of the person-centered approach. *Education, 100*(2), 98-107.

Sinetar, M. (1992). *A way without words: A guide for spiritually emerging adults.* Mahwah, NJ: Paulist Press.

Sinetar, M. (2000). *Spiritual intelligence: What we can learn from the early awakening child.* Maryknoll, NY: Orbis Books.

Sisk, D., & Torrance, E. P. (2001). *Spiritual intelligence: Developing higher consciousness.* Buffalo, NY: Creative Education Foundation Press.

Sriraman, B. (2009). Spirituality. In B. Kerr (Ed.), *Encyclopedia of giftedness, creativity, and talent* (pp. 823-824). Thousand Oaks, CA: Sage Publications.

Sternberg, R. J. (1988). Three-facet model of creativity. In R. J. Sternberg (Ed.), *The nature of creativity: Contemporary psychological perspectives.* (pp. 125-147). New York, NY: Cambridge University Press.

Torrance, E. P. (1995). *Why fly?* Norwood, NJ: Ablex Publishing Corporation.

Vaughan, F. (1979). *Awakening intuition.* New York, NY: Anchor Press.

Vaughan, F. (2002). What is spiritual intelligence? *Journal of Humanistic Psychology, 42*(2), 16-33.

Wigglesworth, C. (2012). *SQ21: The twenty-one skills of spiritual intelligence.* New York, NY: Select Books.

Zohar, D., & Marshall, I. (2000). *SQ: Connecting with our spiritual intelligence.* New York, NY: Bloomsbury Publishing.

Zohar, D., & Marshall, I. (2004). *Spiritual capital: Wealth we can live by.* San Francisco, CA: Berrett-Koehler Publishers.

About the Author

Rebecca DiLiberto earned an M.S. in Creativity from the International Center for Studies in Creativity at SUNY Buffalo State, and a B.A. in Art/Design, with a Minor in Computer Applications from SUNY Cortland. Rebecca ascribes to the philosophy "you do not have to be unique to be creative; rather we are all uniquely creative." This philosophy guides her in cultivating the principles of creativity and proactively inspiring different ways of thinking to promote meaningful change in herself and others. Rebecca's ultimate vision is to foster personal growth and creativity in others, to lead them toward a more purposeful life and greater well-being.

Email: AllUniquelyCreative@gmail.com

SOCIETY & CREATIVITY

Does Culture Affect Creativity? An Integrative Literature Review

Mattia Miani
International Center for Studies in Creativity
SUNY Buffalo State

Originally published in *Big Questions in Creativity 2016*

Abstract

This paper presents an integrative literature review of the study of cross-cultural issues in creativity. It analyzes five areas: conceptions of creativity across cultures, effect of culture on creativity production, effect of multicultural experience on individual levels of creativity, validity of creativity methods across cultures, and the relationship between studies in creativity and studies in differences in thinking patterns across cultures. For each of these areas, the paper offers a view of the questions that remain unanswered in the literature and makes recommendation for further research. "Does culture affect creativity?" is the overarching question this paper attempts to answer. The conclusion is that the construct of culture is very important in illuminating creativity in a global perspective, but, at the same time, it may conceal other forces that shape the different forms that creativity takes around the world.

Does Culture Affect Creativity? An Integrative Literature Review

Phenomena such as the globalization of business, the international mobility of the highly-skilled workforce, and the multiplication of social and economic exchanges made possible by the new media, make the introduction of a cross-cultural perspective in the study of creativity particularly important (Westwood & Low, 2003; Zhao, 2012).

This paper presents an integrative literature review of studies on cross-cultural issues in creativity to answer the broader question of whether culture affects creativity. According to Torraco (2005), "the integrative literature review is a form of research that reviews, critiques, and synthesizes representative literature on a topic in an integrated way such that new frameworks and perspectives on the topic are generated" (p. 356).

This paper first presents how the review was conducted, and what was and was not included. Second, it presents how the topic was structured in previous reviews published in journals and handbooks. Third, it presents a sample of the literature available today in a number of key areas, in part already addressed in previous reviews and in part neglected. This will ultimately lead to answering the question about the relationship between culture and creativity.

How This Review Was Conducted

This review considers *creativity* to be a general mental and social process (Sawyer, 2006; Torrance, 1979). As a consequence, scholarly works on the creative industries and domain specific creative manifestations (e.g., fine arts) were excluded.

The term *cross-cultural* in this paper takes on two meanings: it refers to comparative studies of creativity in different cultures, and also refers to studies that focus on creativity in cultures different from North America and Western Europe. The assumption being made is that the academic literature on creativity, at least in English-speaking publications, has a perspective dominated by studies conducted in English speaking countries and universities based in Western Europe.

With these limits in mind, the work began by searching the indices of major creativity journals: *Journal of Creative Behavior, Creativity Research Journal, Thinking Skills and Creativity, Creativity and Innovation Management,* and *International Journal of Creativity and Problem Solving.*

Many more articles were found scattered among a variety of journals ranging from management to philosophy, found using targeted keyword searches on the online databases of SUNY Buffalo State and RMIT University. The keywords "multicultural," "culture," and "cross-cultural" were used in conjunction with "creativity" and "creative." Further documents, in particular a few books and proceedings, were identified using a "snowball" approach, by identifying new sources mentioned in the bibliographies of works under examination. Also added were references to books on creativity methods developed by authors outside North America and Western Europe.

The result was an extensive collection of around 70 references. Most came from literature published over the past 20 years, clearly showing a growing interest in the subject. This review does not present findings from all literature identified, but does focus on what the author considered to be the most representative pieces of research.

Previous Literature Reviews on Cross-Cultural Issues and Creativity

A number of reviews of this topic were published between 1990 and 2010. Niu and Sternberg (2002) developed a review comparing both implicit and explicit theories of creativity across cultures. Their conclusion is that people in different countries have similar, but not identical views of what creativity is (essentially agreeing with the results of Rudowicz & Hui, 1997). In particular, people living in the Far East tend to associate creativity more with moral and social values while people living in the West tend to associate the concept of creativity more with individual accomplishments. When it comes to testing explicit theories of creativity, the authors showed skepticism in employing divergent thinking tests across cultures (including the Torrance Tests of Creative Thinking; Torrance, 1966), since they are based on a specific view of creativity, and suggested that more meaningful results might be achieved using product-oriented tasks and consensual measurement. From this point of view, the plethora of studies that seem to favor the Westerner in divergent thinking tests may not be more significant than standardized IQ tests administered to people not familiar with the Western educational system and testing.

Westwood and Low (2003) analyzed different conceptions of creativity across cultures; social structural factors that may relate to creativity and innovation (e.g., the educational or religious systems); creativity as an aspect of cognition and personality; and the relationship between creativity and cultural values. Overall, the authors downplayed the role of cultural differences, contending that the literature on cultural values leads to oversimplified, one-dimensional comparisons (e.g., individualistic vs. collectivist societies), and emphasized the social and institutional factors (e.g., the educational system) that can affect how creativity is valued and practiced in a society.

Lubart (1990, 2010) has paid much attention to the phenomenon and has written a number of extensive reviews. In an early work, Lubart (1990) focused on the effect of cultural environments on creativity, addressing four topics from a cross-cultural perspective: definitions of creativity, the creative process, the direction in which creativity is channeled, and the degree to which creativity is nurtured. Later, Lubart (2010) structured the relationship between culture—mostly national culture—and creativity in three main areas of inquiry: conceptions of culture across cultures, relationship between culture and amount of creativity expressed, and the effects of multicultural experiences (e.g., living abroad) on creativity.

Conceptions of Creativity

Niu and Sternberg (2002) asked, "Is there a truly global concept of creativity?" (p. 270). The answer that emerges from the literature is both a qualified "yes" and a qualified "no." The dimension of novelty seems to be associated with the concept of creativity almost universally (Lubart, 2010). The disagreements begin emerging when further qualifications of the concept (e.g., usefulness of the new idea) come into play.

Lubart (1990) claimed that Western definitions are prominently product-oriented, while in Eastern definitions it is impossible to separate the product and the individual. For example, in Hinduism creativity is seen more as a psychic state than as a process or product. Lubart further explained that sometimes creativity can be accepted in a well-defined niche (e.g., dance for the Samoan people studied by Margaret Mead), but the same culture can actually squelch creative practices in other areas (e.g., education for the Samoans).

One interesting commonality across cultures is what can be called the "doublespeak" about creativity. Many countries and societies praise creativity, yet suppress and discourage creative contributions (Staw, 1996; Thompson, 2014). This tendency has been documented, for example, in the school setting. Dawson, D'Andrea, Affinito, and Westby (1999), citing previous research conducted mainly in North America, summarized that

> teachers tend to dislike children who display the characteristics of the creative personality.... On the other hand, this research might be

seen as quite surprising, given that teachers generally acknowledge the importance of creativity as an educational goal. (p. 58)

Similarly, Chan and Chan (1999) reported that characteristics normally associated with creative individuals (e.g., nonconformity and expressiveness) are disliked by Chinese teachers in their pupils. Nearly identical conclusions were drawn studying Korean students and teachers (Lim & Plucker, 2001).

Even the way in which the concept of creativity itself is framed in a study is subject to the cultural bias of the researcher. For this reason, it is refreshing that there is increasing interest in studying creativity among Asian scholars (as shown by Lau, Hiu, & Ng, 2004; Ng, 2001, 2004; Singh 2004; Sinha 2008).

It may remain difficult to disentangle the conflicting views on creativity in a specific context because of the hybrid nature of globalized culture and multiple influences that exercise their power on individuals working in transnational and multicultural environments. However, at least to some extent, cultural orientations seem to affect the perception and definition of creativity.

Creativity and National Cultures

It has become almost a commonplace to state that individuals in the West (English speaking countries and Western Europe) are more creative than individuals in the East (China and Confucian heritage societies). A Singaporean scholar educated in Australia, Ng (2001), showed that Asian societies squelch individual creativity more than Western societies. Ng (2001) described two ideal types of individuals struggling between creativity and conformity:

> By yielding their personal autonomy to the social group in this way, they gain its approval, as well as preserve its internal unity and harmony. However, conducting themselves in this restrained and somewhat self-deprecating manner will limit their capacity for creative / critical thinking.
>
> This is in marked contrast to the non-conforming and group-independent individuals, who show a psychological need for autonomy, independence and separation from the social group.... By behaving this carefree and self-gratifying manner, they risk the censure of the group, as well as threaten its internal unity and harmony. However, maintaining their personal autonomy from the group enables these individuals to engage in creative / critical thinking. (p. 56)

Needless to say, according to Ng, Asians tend to fall into the first ideal type, Westerners into the second. Ng is hardly the first scholar to note these differences. Weber (1915/1951) was perhaps the first to identify this difference between East and West when he analyzed the religions of China. He claimed that the social conservatism of the Chinese stemmed from their valuing status over performance and achievement. Many scholars link the lack of individual creativity in Confucian heritage societies to the Confucian values of conformity and obedience (Kim, 2007; Lubart & Sternberg, 1998; Weiner, 2000).

However, establishing such one-dimensional causal connections between two very complex constructs such as creativity and culture may be misleading. In some cases, these differences may not be due to cultural factors per se, but may be related to other social and economic factors. Mar'I and Karayanni (1983), reviewing two decades of research, noted that while Westerners seem to score better than individuals from the Middle East in divergent thinking tests, actually the same differences may be found among individuals of Arabic culture when comparing subjects who are more or less modernized. This suggests that modernization factors (e.g., freedom of expression, access to a variety of media, higher disposable income, time for leisure) can be the real differentiating factor behind divergent thinking scores.

History tends to confirm this view; depending on the chosen chronological point, the same country or region can show a great deal of creativity, or not. One example is Japan, which used to be seen as a country of imitators, but in the 1980s became highly regarded for its creative outputs in industry, design, and popular culture (Tatsuno, 1989).

One final example will prove the difficulty in making causal statements when it comes to connecting culture and creativity. Lubart (2010) suggested that "collectivist values may foster, via processes involving compromise, incremental innovations (as opposed to radical innovations), with people working together toward creativity in a collective interest" (p. 274). A surface reading of this statement could lead one to claim that collectivist societies prefer incremental creativity and individualistic societies favor radical innovation. Is it true? Let's take Japan, a society that unquestionably falls at the high end of the collectivist scale, and test the hypothesis on a random domain: fountain pens (Gerosa, 2012; Lambrou & Sunami, 2012). Japanese craftsmen are known for applying the millenary arts of urushi (a type of lacquer) and maki-e (a type of painting on lacquer) to fountain pens. They have been perfecting this specific application since the 1930s when Namiki pens were chosen by Dunhill, of London, for export into the Western markets. But if you look closer, you can easily find a number of breakthrough innovations coming from Japan: in 1963 engineers at Pilot invented a fountain pen with a retractable nib that remains in production today, and is regarded as a design icon (sometimes referred to as "capless" or "vanishing point"). Another pen company, Platinum, has recently introduced the "slip and seal" mechanism to cap its fountain pens in a hermetic way, thus preventing the ink from drying for an unprecedented length of time. Sailor has pioneered the use of unusual materials to build groundbreaking fountain pens, including amber, ceramics, and susutake (a type of bamboo), and has introduced a series of never-seen-before nibs. In summary, when it comes to fountain pens, Japanese industries and craftsmen can be either incremental or radical innovators; one does not exclude the other. This simple sketch cannot be used to formulate a general rule, but is enough to disprove the initial generalization, and shows how difficult it is to establish causal connections between culture and creativity in its various dimensions (including its extension in innovation processes).

Cross-cultural Experience and Creativity

The literature on the effect of multicultural exposure on individual levels of creativity would support a separate review; this paper will rely on a few exemplary studies.

Maddux and Galinsky (2009) found that Western students who spent time overseas were more likely to come up with innovative insights upon their return. Fee and Gray (2012) tested the hypothesis of a link between creativity and expatriate experience in a longitudinal study. They measured changes in the creative-thinking abilities of a sample of expatriates over the first 12 months of their placement. When compared with a control group of non-expatriates, the expatriates showed significant increases in overall creative-thinking abilities and cognitive flexibility, although not originality, elaboration, or ideational fluency (Fee & Gray, 2012).

These studies are quite typical as they measure the impact of time spent abroad. However, the time spent abroad itself may not be the direct variable influencing gains in creativity. In a contiguous field, cross-cultural competence, it has been demonstrated that only "reflective" cultural experiences abroad will have lasting effects on one's cross-cultural competence; this means that students abroad or expats hanging out with other individuals from their home country will not be particularly affected (Hammer, 2012, p. 126). The same could apply to gains in creativity.

Chua (2011) contributed an interesting perspective: what counts is not living abroad, but developing multicultural professional networks. However, his findings are limited to tasks that require cross-cultural knowledge.

Certainly more research is needed in this area, taking into account that multicultural exposure may now take many forms, such as working in a multicultural team or organization, virtually connecting with people living abroad for leisure or business, and adopting fashions and ideas originated in another cultural context.

Creativity Methods in Cross-Cultural Perspective

One area of inquiry that has received limited attention so far is the effectiveness of creativity methods across cultures. Lubart (1990), one of the few authors to mention the problem, quoted only three studies; and of these, only one suggested alternatives to the classic four-stage process (Wallas, 1926).

Some research on the cross-cultural effectiveness of the Osborn-Parnes Creative Problem Solving (CPS) process exists. (For a history of CPS, see Puccio, Murdock, & Mance, 2005). In a very early study, Lindgren and Lindgren (1965) used individual-group-individual brainstorming, and assessed its effects on ideation and originality in a group of art students from the Middle East in Beirut. By comparing the outcomes with a previous study conducted with students in San Francisco, they concluded that "the method may be considered to have been even more successful with the Middle East subjects, inasmuch as gains in number of responses were achieved by both sexes in the experimental group" (Lindgren & Lindgren, 1965, p. 26). They also warned that results may not be replicable in languages different than English since other languages may lack the same level of directedness.

Puccio & González (2004), discussing creativity issues in the East, claimed that "practices that have been developed for nurturing creative thinking in the West, and primarily in the United States, [can] be directly applied to audiences in the East" (p. 407). This idea is shared by many CPS facilitators who have worked with organizations in Asia (B. Miller, personal communication, October 3, 2013).

Some research seems to support this position. Basadur, Wakabayashi, and Takai (1992) measured divergent thinking attitudes in a group of Japanese managers before and after training in CPS. The experimental group of 60 people showed significant gains on these measures versus two control groups. Compared to North American managers from similar studies, the Japanese managers appeared to make at least equal gains after training. Later on, Basadur, Pringle, and Kirkland (2002) used the same research design with a group of South American managers, with the group again showing significant gains in divergent thinking measures. This led the authors to conclude that "the concepts and methods of similar training provided in previous Japanese and North American research are applicable to Spanish-speaking South American managers" (Basadur et al., 2002, p. 395), and hinted at broader applicability if replicated in other countries.

Other research questions that have been neglected so far have to do with the cultural origin of these methods. Are creativity methods a domain of North American and European thinkers? It is fairly easy to answer no. However, in many cases, for many decades, researchers in the West did not have access to foreign creative-thinking methodologies due to political and linguistic barriers. For example, it is not an accident that TRIZ methodology (Altshuller, 1999) became popular outside its home country, Azerbaijan, and the states of the former Soviet Union, only after the fall of the iron curtain. Another example is the K-J Method, which originated in Japan in the 1960s (Kawakita, 1991) and was first mentioned in the West by Torrance (1979), but remained inaccessible until recent times when articles and training courses in English appeared outside Japan (Kunifuji, 2013; Nomura, 2013; Scupin, 1997).

The questions that remain to be answered are whether these methods differ in any significant way and whether the differences may be explained by cultural factors. At first glance, similarities seem to outmatch differences, such that a synthesis is possible (Sawyer, 2013). For example, in many of these methods it is possible to find rounds of divergent and convergent thinking, clustering, and transformative processes (Nomura, 2013).

The social and cultural context seems to clearly influence at least some of these methods. For example, Radjou, Prabhu and Ahuja (2012) popularized the term "Jugaad" to indicate frugal innovation. Jugaad is a Hindu term that indicates an ingenious fix derived from a very limited pool of resources. While the concept is clearly situated in the reality of a developing country, the concepts of Jugaad have been embraced by major corporations worldwide on a mission to solve engineering problems in more cost-effective ways.

Creativity and Thinking

One area of inquiry that is relatively untouched is the relationship between creativity and culturally-influenced modes of thinking.

Research supports the view that cognitive differences are the deepest and most challenging sources of misunderstanding and conflict in cross-cultural groups (Shweder, 1991). Nisbett (2003) came to conceptualize a "geography of thought" in which remarkable differences between Westerners (North Americans, in his studies) and Asians (Chinese, Japanese, and Koreans) could be found in an impressive number of experiments on attention, perception, and cognition. Kase,

Slocum, and Zhang (2011) applied this line of inquiry to the field of managerial cognition and found major differences in the thinking models applied by Western and Eastern managers. In brief, what they found was that Asian managers were more inductive in their thinking, while American and European managers were more likely to adopt a deductive thinking pattern (Kase et al., 2011).

Arguably, this research can be useful for creativity scholars. Rather than using complex and indistinct constructs such as *Confucianism* or *Western culture*, this literature provides evidence of differences in basic mental operations that can more easily be related to creative thinking patterns.

Conclusions

Cross-cultural issues in the study of creativity have become increasingly part of the research agenda of scholars in the field. As this paper has shown, the past 20 years have witnessed an increasing number of studies and an increasing cultural diversity in the authorship of these studies. So, is there a causal link between culture and creativity? Research has established a few interim conclusions that seem to support, at least to some extent, certain effects of culture upon creativity: conceptions of culture may subtly vary across cultures; different institutional settings may, to a certain extent, foster or squelch creativity; and exposure to cross-cultural experiences may increase the level of individual creativity, at least under certain circumstances.

These conclusions, however, can be seen only as interim achievements, since research is still dominated by a number of simplified assumptions about the relationship between culture and creativity. Much of the time culture is examined only at the national level, where it is a much more complex construct. Many areas of inquiry remain open for researchers. More research on the cross-cultural validity of creativity methods would be useful, given that many of these methods will likely be used in today's increasingly-common multicultural groups and international businesses. Further, studies on cross-cultural variations in basic psychological processes can offer creativity scholars very useful benchmarks for advancing a research agenda on the cross-cultural nature of creative thinking.

While studying the connection between creativity and culture seems to mean dealing with sometimes-muddy concepts, it is still a rewarding exercise since it can help us to improve mutual understanding between diverse groups and achieve breakthrough results when working across cultures or in multicultural teams. While it may not be possible to answer the initial question in a definitive way at this time, focused studies will help us better understand where and how culture and creativity are interrelated and affect each other.

References

Altshuller, G. (1999). *The innovation algorithm: TRIZ, systematic innovation, and technical creativity.* Worcester, MA: Technical Innovation Center.

Basadur, M., Pringle, P., & Kirkland, D. (2002). Crossing cultures: Training effects on the divergent thinking attitudes of Spanish-speaking South American managers. *Creativity Research Journal, 14*(3-4), 395-408.

Basadur, M., Wakabayashi, M., & Takai, J. (1992). Training effects on the divergent thinking attitudes of Japanese managers. *International Journal of Intercultural Relations, 16*(3), 329-345.

Chan, D., & Chan, L. K. (1999). Implicit theories of creativity: Teachers' perception of student characteristics in Hong Kong. *Creativity Research Journal, 12*(3), 185-195.

Chua, R. Y. J. (2011). *Innovating at the world's crossroads: How multicultural networks promote creativity* (Working Paper No. 11-085). Retrieved from Harvard Business School: http://www.hbs.edu/faculty/Publication%20Files/11-085.pdf

Dawson, V. L., D'Andrea, T., Affinito, R., & Westby, E. L. (1999). Predicting creative behavior: A reexamination of the divergence between traditional and teacher-defined concepts of creativity. *Creativity Research Journal, 12*(1), 57-66.

Fee, A., & Gray, J. S. (2012). The expatriate-creativity hypothesis: A longitudinal field test. *Human Relations, 65*(12), 1515-1538.

Gerosa, A. (2012). *Maki-e: A story waiting to be written.* Milan, Italy: Ops.

Hammer, M. (2012). The Intercultural Development Inventory: A new frontier in assessment and development of intercultural competence. In M. Vande Berg, R. M. Paige, & K. H. Lou (Eds.), *Student Learning Abroad* (pp. 115-136). Sterling, VA: Stylus Publishing.

Kase, K., Slocum, A., & Zhang, Y. (2011). *Asian versus Western management thinking: Its culture-bound nature.* New York, NY: Palgrave Macmillan.

Kawakita, J. (1991) *The original KJ method* (rev. ed.). Meguro, Tokyo: Kawakita Research Institute.

Kim, K. H. (2007). Exploring the interactions between Asian culture (Confucianism) and creativity. *Journal of Creative Behavior, 41*(1), 28-53.

Kunifuji, S. (2013). A Japanese problem solving approach: the KJ Ho Method. In A. M. J. Skulimowski & J. Kacprzyk (Eds.), *Proceedings of the 8th International Conference on Knowledge, Information and Creativity*

Support Systems (pp. 333-338). Kraków, Poland: Progress & Business Publishers.

Lambrou, A., & Sunami, M. (2012). *Fountain pens of Japan*. El Paso, TX: Andreas Lambrou Publishers Limited.

Lau, S., Hiu, A., & Ng, G. (Eds.) (2004). *Creativity. When East meets West*. Singapore: World Scientific Publishing.

Lim, W., & Plucker, J. A. (2001). Creativity through a lens of social responsibility: Implicit theories of creativity with Korean samples. *Journal of Creative Behavior, 35*(2), 115-130.

Lindgren, H. C., & Lindgren, F. (1965). Creativity, brainstorming, and orneriness: A cross-cultural study. *The Journal of Social Psychology, 67*, 23-30.

Lubart, T. I. (1990). Creativity and cross-cultural variation. *International Journal of Psychology, 25*, 39-59.

Lubart, T. I. (2010). Cross-cultural perspectives on creativity. In J. C. Kaufman & R. J. Sternberg (Eds.), *The Cambridge handbook of creativity* (pp. 265-278). New York, NY: Cambridge University Press.

Lubart, T. I., & Sternberg, R. J. (1998). Creativity across time and place: Life span and cross-cultural perspectives. *High Ability Studies, 9*(1), 59-74.

Maddux, W. W., & Galinsky, A. D. (2009). Cultural borders and mental barriers: The relationship between living abroad and creativity. *Journal of Personality and Social Psychology, 96*(5), 1047-1061.

Mar'I, S. K., & Karayanni, M. (1983). Creativity in Arab culture: Two decades of research. *Journal of Creative Behavior, 16*(4), 227-238.

Ng, A. K. (2001). *Why Asians are less creative than Westerners*. Singapore: Prentice Hall.

Ng, A. K. (2004). *Liberating the creative spirit in Asian students*. Singapore: Prentice Hall.

Nisbett, R. E. (2003). *The geography of thought*. New York, NY: Free Press.

Niu, W. H., & Sternberg, R. J. (2002). Contemporary studies on the concept of creativity: The East and the West. *The Journal of Creative Behavior, 36*(4), 269-288.

Nomura, T. (2013). Introduction to KJ-Ho: A Japanese problem solving approach. *Creativity & Human Development*. Retrieved from www.creativityjournal.net/index.php/contents/articles/item/201-kj-ho_japanese_problem_solving

Puccio, G. J., & González, D. W. (2004). Nurturing creative thinking. Western approaches and Eastern issues. In S. Lau, A. Hiu, & G. Ng (Eds.), *Creativity: When East meets West* (pp. 393-426). Singapore: World Scientific Publishing.

Puccio, G. J., Murdock, M. C., & Mance, M. (2005). Current developments in creative problem solving for organizations: A focus on thinking skills and styles. *Korean Journal of Thinking and Problem Solving, 15*(2), 43-76.

Radjou, N., Prabhu, J., & Ahuja, S. (2012). *Jugaad innovation: A frugal and flexible approach to innovation for the 21st century.* New Delhi, India: Random House India.

Rudowicz, E., & Hui, A. (1997). The creative personality: Hong Kong perspective. *Journal of Social Behavior & Personality, 12*(1), 139-157.

Sawyer, K. (2013). *Zig zag: The surprising path to greater creativity.* San Francisco, CA: Jossey-Bass.

Sawyer, R. K. (2006). *Explaining creativity: The science of human innovation.* New York, NY: Oxford University Press.

Scupin, R. (1997). The KJ method: A technique for analyzing data derived from Japanese ethnology. *Human Organization, 56*(2), 233-237.

Shweder, R. (1991). *Thinking through cultures.* Cambridge, MA: Harvard University Press.

Singh, K. (2004). *Thinking hats and coloured turbans: Creativity across cultures.* Singapore: Prentice Hall.

Sinha, K. (2008). *China's creative imperative: How creativity is transforming society and business in China.* Hoboken, NJ: Wiley.

Staw, B. M. (1996). Why no one really wants creativity. In C. M. Ford & D. A. Gioia (Eds.), *Creative action in organizations: Ivory tower visions and real world voices.* Thousand Oaks, CA: Sage Publications.

Tatsuno, S. M. (1989). *Created in Japan. From imitators to world-class innovators.* New York, NY: Ballinger.

Thompson, D. (2014, October 10). *Why experts reject creativity.* Retrieved from http://www.theatlantic.com/business/archive/2014/10/why-new-ideas-fail/381275

Torraco, R. J. (2005). Writing integrative literature reviews: Guidelines and examples. *Human Resource Development Review, 4*(3), 356-367.

Torrance, E. P. (1966). *Torrance Tests of Creative Thinking: Norms-technical manual research edition—Verbal Tests, Forms A and B—Figural Tests, Forms A and B.* Princeton, NJ: Personnel Press.

Torrance, E. P. (1979). *The search for satori and creativity*. Buffalo, NY: Creative Education Foundation.

Wallas, G. (1926). *The art of thought*. New York, NY: Harcourt, Brace & Company.

Weber, M. (1951). *The religion of China* (H. H. Gerth, Ed. and Trans.). Glencoe, IL: Free Press. (Original work published in German in 1915).

Weiner, R. P. (2000). *Creativity and beyond: Cultures, values and change*. Albany, NY: State University of New York Press.

Westwood, R., & Low, D. R. (2003). The multicultural muse: Culture, creativity and innovation. *International Journal of Cross Cultural Management, 3*(2), 235-259.

Zhao, Y. (2012). *World class learners: Educating creative and entrepreneurial students*. Thousand Oaks, CA: Corwin.

About the Author

Mattia Miani is based in Vietnam where he designs, develops, and delivers learning programs for industry and government with a focus on creativity and leadership. He holds a degree in Communication Sciences and an EMBA from the University of Bologna (Italy) and a Master of Science in Creativity from SUNY Buffalo State.

Mattia is a certified trainer, instructional designer, and lecturer, having achieved an Australian Graduate Certificate in Tertiary Teaching and Learning, an American Graduate Certificate in Instructional Design, an Australian Diploma of Training Design and Development, and an Australian Certificate IV in Training and Assessment. He has logged more than 4,000 hours of teaching at all levels: executive, postgraduate, undergraduate, and vocational.

For his work in Vietnam in 2014 he received the Firestien Family Creative Achievement Award from the International Center for Studies of Creativity.

Email: mattiainasia@gmail.com

Product Measurement: How Do I Know It is Creative?

Eva Teruzzi
International Center for Studies in Creativity
SUNY Buffalo State

Originally published in *Big Questions in Creativity 2014*

Abstract

The product is the most important of the four Ps, as it is the proof of the existence of creativity. While a number of definitions and theories exist, there is a need for a well-structured frame for interpreting the field, and for answering the question of how to define and measure the creative product. The purpose of this paper is to provide a clear-cut frame for creative product measurement. Obtained by opposing the work of two influential creativity scholars, Besemer (1998, 2000, 2006) and Amabile (1982, 1983, 1996), this frame organizes the rest of the work in the field around them. The author highlights how researchers from other disciplines—specifically, industrial design scholars Horn and Salvendy (2006, 2009)—positively contribute to the field by synthesizing and adding to Besemer's and Amabile's positions. The paper closes by examining some of the key questions that still lay ahead for creative product research.

Product Measurement: How Do I Know It is Creative?

When an idea becomes embodied into tangible form, it is called a product. Each product of a man's mind or hands presents a record of his thinking at some point in time.... And by probing backward from the moment of inspiration, it may be possible to trace the thoughts and the events leading up to the idea. Products are artifacts of thoughts.

Mel Rhodes

Rhodes' 53-year-old way of looking at creativity through the lenses of person, process, product, and press (1961) defined the four specific streams of research still used today. Other scholars (e.g., Amabile, 1979; MacKinnon, 1978; Taylor & Sandler, 1972; Treffinger & Poggio, 1972; Ward & Cox, 1974), underlined the importance of the product stream. However, Plucker and Makel (2011) stated, "assessment of creative products receives much less attention [than the other Ps] in the literature" (p. 58).

Yet, creative products afford a direct route to understanding creativity. They can illuminate, for example, a creator's way of thinking; the transformation of creative ideas; the workings of creative process; and aspects of the creative environment. This paper is an attempt to argue for the importance of assessing creative product, and to point out ways to make that assessment more universal. A new approach for measuring creative product, springing from creativity and industrial design literature, is suggested with the goal of opening fresh perspectives for research.

Advocating for Product

The limited body of knowledge about creative product could be due to the fact that almost exclusive attention has been devoted to highly creative individuals and their products (Barron, 1955; MacKinnon, 1978; Simonton, 1999). In addition, the idea that creative products can be effectively evaluated only by domain experts is widespread in the field (Amabile, 1982, 1983, 1996; Csikszentmihalyi, 1991).

As a creativity student, I can hardly subscribe to such an elitist perspective. How could it be possible that we all are creative (Treffinger, Isaksen, & Firestein, 1983), but only a few of us can effectively judge creative outputs? How effective are consumers in that role? How open are expert judges, the gatekeepers (Cross & Parker, 2004) of a domain, in assessing new and disruptive creative products that might jeopardize their positions?

Notwithstanding the limited development of the creative product stream, my view is that person, process, and press are but the enablers—or inhibitors—of the creative product. As Simonton (2004) noted, when Einstein won the Nobel Prize in 1921, it was his "...ideas that were being honored, not his cognitive process or character quirks" (p. 15).

As does MacKinnon (1978), I see the creative product as "the bedrock of all studies of creativity" (p. 120), and concrete evidence that creativity exists. The importance of creative product was also acknowledged by Runco (1989): "The analysis of the creative products may address the inconsistent psychometric quality of other forms of creativity measurement" (p. 59).

As the goal of psychometrics is to predict the ability to produce creative outputs, the assessment of creative products is fundamental to validate the measures obtained from the other Ps. That is, measuring the creative product is fundamental to establishing a valid criterion by which to assess creativity itself.

The field of creativity would greatly benefit from the development of more research on the creative product, as well as from more creative ways of presenting the existing body of knowledge. I believe existing literature on the creative product—which is scattered across myriad domains—could be more effectively presented if it concentrated on polarities. For example, two experts with opposing points of view should be able to articulate the polarities around which the field is arrayed. This polarity approach would necessitate clarifying the differences between the authors' positions while defining the boundaries of the field. Subsequently, connections among others in the field could be traced by locating them on an ideal scale developed between the two polarities. Moreover, the field would benefit also from exposure to and the consolidation of work produced outside the creative studies domain.

What Is the Creative Product Made of?

Among creativity experts, novelty plays a key role in defining what is creative. Kneller (1965) asserted that creativity in a product exists if the product is new to the individual who created it. Boden (2003) widened that perspective by making a distinction between two types of novel ideas: H-creative (historical) ideas new to mankind, and P-creative (psychological) ideas new to the person in whose mind they arose. By contrast, Csikszentmihalyi (1991) posited that novelty is domain specific, and does not exist as an objective entity. By extension, a creative product can exist only in the relationship between the field, the domain, and the individual creator. Within such a perspective, a product can be called creative only when domain experts judge it as such.

Of course, someone must recognize the novelty of the product for it to be creative. But novelty and the existence of an assessor alone are not sufficient for creativity, which is why other scholars have identified additional attributes of a creative product. "The traditional psychological definition of creativity includes two parts: originality and functionality" (Kersting, 2003, p. 40). Those characteristics are the same ones used to describe the creative product. The attribute of originality tends to be constant, while functionality is more varied. To some scholars (Amabile, 1983; Nickerson, Perkins, & Smith, 1985; Sternberg & Lubart, 2002), it meant appropriateness. To others (Plucker, Beghetto, & Dow, 2004), it signified utility "as defined within a social context" (p. 90), or value (Boden, 2003; Wiggins, 2006), or quality (Oman & Tumer, 2009).

Other experts described creative product with more than two attributes. Cropley and Cropley (2000), and Cropley, Kaufman, and Cropley (2011) called out novelty, relevance, effectiveness in problem solving, elegance, and opening perspectives. Cropley and Cropley (2008) elaborated on the aesthetics of assessing a creative product. They stressed that the creative product solicits "admiration in the beholder" (p. 156), which is key to its efficacy and is distinct from elegance. Maher (2010), who wrote about design computing, named novelty, value, and surprise as criteria, while Briskman (1980), a political philosopher of scientific and artistic creativity, named novelty, value, and acceptability (that is, solving problems consistent with some standards). According to Briskman, a really creative product must also be outstanding, as it transcends the very tradition from which it emerges.

Helpful as these definitions are, they fall short of forming a common definition. While few scholars have developed a comprehensive approach to defining and measuring the creative product, Susan Besemer (1981) and Teresa Amabile (1982) are among the first and are still the most relevant to the field. To thoroughly examine their work, it is important to understand the relationship between their theoretical stances, models, and tools.

Objectivity Versus Subjectivity

Usually creativity tools have a model they refer to either implicitly or explicitly. A model is usually connected to a philosophical stance, while a tool is the operationalization of a model for some assessment purposes. To clarify and simplify this examination of creative product research, two polarized philosophical stances will be used: objective and subjective. This is not to say that scholars classify themselves in this way. However, by analyzing their writings one can deduce it.

Objective Stance: Besemer and the CPAM

In my opinion, Besemer adopted an objective stance. (Note that I refer only to Besemer for simplicity; however, she has published with a variety of coauthors, including O'Quin, who is currently an Associate Dean at SUNY Buffalo State). Besemer believed that creativity is a normally distributed trait (Parnes, Noller, & Biondi, 1977), which can be identified and described by analyzing the creative product. As the result of the creative person's natural abilities, "the product can be indicative of the level of creativity in the maker" (Besemer & O' Quin, 1986, p. 115). Actually, Besemer held (as did Rhodes) that investigations should proceed only from product to person (Besemer & Treffinger, 1981). She stressed that the creative product's attributes can be identified and made explicit: "If there really is a group of characteristics which contribute to the creativeness of a product, then it must be possible to identify those qualities" (Besemer & Treffinger, 1981, p. 160). Besemer assumed that creative products of any kind (e.g., artifacts, ideas, etc.) could be characterized by universal, explicit attributes. They can thus be analyzed and measured as independent, objective entities.

The newest version of the Creative Product Analysis Matrix (CPAM; Besemer, 2006; Besemer & Thompson, 2013), wove the dimensions of novelty, resolution, and style with nine attributes: surprising, original, logical, and useful (with novelty); valuable and understandable (with resolution); and organic, well-crafted, and elegant (with style). The CPAM model addressed what a creative product was made of. Besemer assumed her objective model holds across domains, cultures, and judges.

CPAM (Besemer, 2006; Besemer & Thompson, 2013) was influenced by earlier creativity literature (especially Jackson & Messick, 1965; and Taylor, 1975), as well as patent office reports, and fields as diverse as advertising, dance, and science. Searching for evidence to support a cross-domain approach, she wondered why people might call "one product and not another, creative" (Besemer, 2006, p. 41). She built her model by identifying commonalities among the wide variety of criteria she found.

The model's first dimension is novelty, which can be original and/or surprising. Originality does not need to be extreme or radical, as creative products usually come from existing ones; in real life, the progression from line extensions to revolutionary products, such as 3M sticky notes (Besemer, 2006), is usually gradual. The facet of surprise can be interpreted as information that is unexpected or unanticipated. According to Besemer (2006), surprise was not necessarily positive. In some fields, like fashion or fine arts, a high degree of surprise is mandatory. In others, surprise can yield negative reactions in clients. In the world of industrial design, the acronym "MAYA" (Besemer, 2006, p. 104) was a reminder that one rule of success can be "More Advanced, Yet Acceptable" to a customer, as suggested by the work of the 20th century industrial designer Raymond Loewy (Loewy, 1979).

Resolution is the model's second dimension. People want products that can help them solve problems, or as the Harvard economics professor Theodore Levitt used to tell his students, "People don't want to buy a quarter-inch drill. They want a quarter-inch hole!" (Christensen, Cook, & Hall, 2006, p. 1). Resolution is composed of four attributes mostly focused upon problem resolution. A solution must be logical, useful, valuable, and understandable.

The CPAM's third dimension is style, and is Besemer's most creative contribution to the definition of creative product. Style has to do with how a product is presented. According to Besemer (2006), style became integrated into mass-produced consumer goods after World War II; afterward, all other things being equal, consumers started to select new products based on style.

The attributes of style are both important and complex, and beg explication. Organic, the first one, addressed the sense of wholeness of a creative product, "the integration of all the parts of the product's design" (Besemer, 2006, p. 88). Well-crafted is the second attribute of style. Well-craftedness is present if a customer perceives quality in the product, if he perceives that time and effort has been devoted to create it. Elegance, referring to refinement and simplification, is another attribute. Besemer (2006) explained elegance by adding qualifications such as "little surface decoration, smooth, simple shape" (p. 130). Her definition of elegant was related to a specific historically bounded aesthetic code, according to which elegance equates refinement and simplicity. Such a code is quite popular and mainstream in Western cultures, yet such a definition cannot be said to represent a universal aesthetic code. So, while elegance is an important attribute, as it expresses the aesthetic value of products, its definition should be recast. That said, while style and design appear to be the primary determinants of sales success (Cooper & Kleinschmidt, 1987), elegance shows some power in predicting consumers' willingness to buy products (Besemer, 2000).

Consistent with her objective stance, Besemer developed a measurement scale which could be used by lay people across product domains, the Creative Product Semantic Scale (CPSS; Besemer 1998; Besemer & O'Quin 1999; O'Quin & Besemer, 1989). CPSS is "an objective descriptive assessment measure that provides measurements of the component qualities of creativity in products. Its current version consists of 55 contrasting adjectives, on Likert-type scales from 1 to 7" (Besemer, n.d.). Exploratory and confirmatory factor analyses indicated the construct is consistent with Besemer's understanding of the nature of the creative product. Additionally, statistical evidence asserted that CPSS can reliably detect raters' perceived differences. The measure is gaining in popularity, and a number of authors referred to it in their research (e.g., Andrews & Smith, 1996; Cropley & Cropley, 2000; Cropley, Kaufman, & Cropley, 2011; Im & Workman, 2004; Kristensson, Gustafsson, & Archer, 2004; Puccio, Treffinger, & Talbot, 1995).

Amabile and the Subjective Stance

Creativity researcher Teresa Amabile is at the other end of the theoretical continuum. Amabile (1982) maintained that psychometric creativity tests of the creative person were "built according to the test constructor's or scorer's intuitive assessment of what is creative" (p. 999). By this, she means they are subjective. By extension, she also means that product creativity cannot be defined in an objective manner; it can be present only if appropriate judges agreed that it existed (Amabile, 1982, 1983).

Around the end of the 1970s, Amabile saw in creativity tests a methodological impediment for measuring social and environmental influences on creativity (Amabile, 1982). She went so far as to say that tests "were expressly designed to be sensitive to individual differences…while assessing rather stable individual differences" (p. 999). The essence of her criticism stemmed from her conviction that creativity could not be objectified. Instead, its existence rests in the perception of appropriate observers:

> A product or response is creative to the extent that appropriate observers independently agree it is creative. Appropriate observers are those familiar with the domain in which the product was created or the response articulated. Thus, creativity can be regarded as the quality of products or responses judged to be creative by appropriate observers. (Amabile, 1982, pp. 1000-1001)

Amabile (1982) conceded that some objective characteristics of creative products (i.e., some of those included in her colleagues' creativity scales) might exist, and that such characteristics could also be identified and used by assessors. Nonetheless, her belief that some scales are overtly subjective prompted the creation of the Consensual Assessment Technique (CAT; Amabile, 1982).

The foundation of Amabile's position is that creativity can be recognized when seen. Therefore, experts in particular domains are in the best position to recognize the creativity of domain-specific products. The methodology of the CAT (1982) rests on an assessment protocol; compliance with the protocol assures a valid assessment outcome. The protocol specifies that judges must have some experience in the domain, perform the assessment independently, assess technical features and aesthetic appeal, and rate the products relative to one another.

According to Amabile (1982), the construct validity of the CAT was demonstrated by the consistency of inter-rater reliability. Its discriminant validity—which, she said, should be confirmed with more research—was indicated by the ability of judges to differentiate from technical quality and aesthetics. Subsequent studies using CAT (Baer, 1993; Baer, Kaufman, & Gentile, 2004; Conti, Coon, & Amabile, 1996; Hennessey, 1994; Runco, 1989) confirmed her findings. Factor analysis performed in a number of these studies provided evidence that CAT differentiates creativity from attributes such as technical goodness or style (Baer & McKool, 2009).

Some of Amabile's pivotal assumptions, however, do not seem to have been fully proven. Do judges' ratings prove the appropriateness of the product they assess? While she specified that judges must be selected from a random sample of the population, there is no evidence that the judges in her studies were randomly selected (1982). Instead, they appeared to have different kinds and levels of expertise and experience. Her findings indicated that the level of expertise of the different "judges did not matter as much as expected" (p. 1006), which would seem to mean that the judges did not appear to define creativity in different ways. Further, Amabile (1982) noted that "appropriateness" didn't imply high levels of expertise in the domain, but only "familiarity with the domain" (p. 1006).

Looking Further Afield for Context

Horn and Salvendy (2006, 2009), two scholars in the field of industrial engineering, have published in human factor and ergonomics journals. Their research seeks to understand how product creativity influences consumers' evaluations, and focuses on a pragmatic, business-centered understanding of the creative product.

In a 2006 paper, they offered an integration of the objective and subjective stances. In fact, Horn and Salvendy claimed that product creativity is both objective (as related to the physical attributes of the product) and subjective (as related to the assessor and the context in which the product exists). To support objectivity, they assume a universal set of criteria for the judgment of product creativity, while the judgment of the criterion levels is subjectively dependent on a judge's experience and social agency. Horn and Salvendy's (2006) model is predicated on product, consumer, and context.

When Horn and Salvendy (2009) revisited their model, affect, importance, and novelty were the new dimensions. Affect (i.e., emotional response) is considered the primary influencer of product creativity and consumers' positive perceptions. In particular, affect and novelty contributed in "relatively equal amounts to the overall evaluation of product creativity" (Horn & Salvendy, 2009, p. 235).

Conclusion

No matter whether one agrees that the creative product is the most important of the four Ps, it is concrete evidence that creativity exists.

Theorists, researchers, and experts have shaped definitions, models, and tools showing some validity and reliability. However, much is yet to be done. More comprehensive explorations can come only from cross-pollinating research across domains and cultures. Philosophy, design, marketing, information technology, sociology, and semiotics all yield fundamental bodies of knowledge that can enrich the study of creativity.

"How do I know it is creative?" is just one of the big questions. As research in the field is biased toward the West (Lan & Kaufman, 2012), creative product measurement should also be explored in other cultures. We should also ask if and how social and cultural, linguistic, or genetic aspects impact the way people perceive and appreciate the creative product.

"Product creativity is assumed to have the potential to be an added value" (Horn & Salvendy, 2006, p. 397), so follow-up questions should be investigated. For example, how might business, education, and the arts benefit from the enhancement of the creative product research? Following Getzels' (1982) advice, we should continue to look for the right questions to be able to find the appropriate answer.

References

Amabile, T. M. (1979). Effects of external evaluation on artistic creativity. *Journal of Personality and Social Psychology, 37,* 221-233.

Amabile, T. M. (1982). The social psychology of creativity: A consensual assessment technique. *Journal of Personality and Social Psychology, 43,* 997-1013.

Amabile, T. M. (1983). *Social psychology of creativity.* New York, NY: Springer-Verlag.

Amabile, T. M. (1996). *Creativity in context.* Boulder, CO: Westview Press.

Andrews, J., & Smith, D. C. (1996). In search of the marketing imagination: Factors affecting the creativity of marketing programs for mature products. *Journal of Marketing Research, 33,* 174-187.

Baer, J. (1993). *Creativity and divergent thinking.* Hillsdale, NJ: Lawrence Erlbaum Associates.

Baer, J., Kaufman, J. C., & Gentile, C. A. (2004). Extension of the consensual assessment technique to non-parallel creative products. *Creativity Research Journal, 16*(1), 113-117.

Baer, J., & McKool, S. S. (2009). Assessing creativity using the consensual assessment technique. In C. S. Schreiner (Ed.), *Handbook of research on assessment technologies, methods, and applications in higher education.* Hershey, PA: IGI Global.

Barron, F. (1955). The disposition towards originality. *Journal of Abnormal and Social Psychology, 51,* 478-485.

Besemer, S. P. (1998). Creative Product Analysis Matrix: Testing the model structure and a comparison among products—three novel chairs. *Creativity Research Journal, 11,* 333-346.

Besemer, S. P. (2000). To buy or not to buy: Predicting the willingness to buy from creative product variables. *Korean Journal of Thinking & Problem Solving, 10,* 5-18.

Besemer, S. P. (2006). *Creating products in the age of design.* Stillwater, OK: New Forums Press.

Besemer, S.P. (n.d.). *The CPSS.* Retrieved from http://ideafusion.biz/home/creative-product-semantic-scale

Besemer, S. P., & O'Quin, K. (1986). Analyzing creative products: Refinement and test of a judging instrument. *Journal of Creative Behavior, 20*(2), 115-126.

Besemer, S. P., & O'Quin, K. (1999). Confirming the three-factor creative product analysis matrix model in an American sample. *Creativity Research Journal, 12,* 287-296.

Besemer, S. P., & Thompson, P. (2013). Defining and measuring creativity in product design: Searching for a yardstick. *Innovation: The Journal of the Industrial Designers Society of America, 32,* 53-57.

Besemer, S. P., & Treffinger, D. H. (1981). Analysis of creative products: Review and synthesis. *Journal of Creative Behavior, 15,* 158-178.

Boden, M. (2003). *The creative mind: Myths and mechanisms* (2nd ed.). London, UK: Routledge.

Briskman, L. (1980). Creative product and creative process in science and art. *Inquiry, 23*(1), 83-106.

Christensen, C. M., Cook, S., & Hall, T. (2006). What customers want from your products. *Harvard Business School Working Knowledge: Research Ideas.* Retreived from http://www.mintinnovation.com/links/docs/Research_for_Insights/observing%20what%20customers%20want%20from%20products.pdf

Conti, R., Coon, H., & Amabile, T. M. (1996). Evidence to support the componential model of creativity: Secondary analyses of three studies. *Creativity Research Journal, 4,* 385-389

Cooper, R. G., & Kleinschmidt, E. (1987). New products: What separates winners from losers? *Journal of Product Innovation Management, 4,* 169-184.

Cross, R., & Parker, A. (2004). *The hidden power of social networks*. Boston, MA: Harvard Business Review Press.

Cropley, D. H., & Cropley, A. J. (2000). Fostering creativity in engineering undergraduates. *High Ability Studies, 11,* 207-220.

Cropley, D. H., & Cropley, A. J. (2008). Elements of a universal aesthetic of creativity. *Psychology of Aesthetics, Creativity, and the Arts, 2,* 155-161.

Cropley, D. H., Kaufman, J. C., & Cropley, A. J. (2011). Measuring creativity for innovation management. *Journal of Technology Management & Innovation, 6,* 13-29.

Csikszentmihalyi, M. (1991). *Flow: The psychology of optimal experience*. New York, NY: Harper Perennial.

Getzels, J. W. (1982). The problem of the problem. *New Directions For Methodology of Social and Behavioral Science, 11-14,* 37-49.

Hennessey, B. A. (1994). The Consensual Assessment Technique: An examination of the relationship between ratings of process and product creativity. *Creativity Research Journal, 7,* 193-208.

Horn, D., & Salvendy, G. (2006). Product creativity: Conceptual model, measurement and characteristics. *Theoretical Issues in Ergonomics Science, 7*(4), 395-412.

Horn, D., & Salvendy, G. (2009). Measuring consumer perception of product creativity: Impact on satisfaction and purchasability. *Human Factors and Ergonomics in Manufacturing & Service Industries, 19,* 223-240.

Im, S., & Workman, J. P. (2004). Market orientation, creativity and new product performance in high technology firms. *Journal of Marketing, 68,* 114-132.

Jackson, P. W., & Messick, S. (1965). The person, the product, and the response: Conceptual problems in the assessment of creativity. *Journal of Personality, 33,* 309-329.

Kersting, K. (2003). *What exactly is creativity? Psychologists continue their quest to better understand creativity.* Retrieved from http://www.apa.org/monitor/nov03/creativity.aspx

Kneller, G. F. (1965). *The art and science of creativity.* New York, NY: Holt, Rinehart, and Winston.

Kristensson, P., Gustafsson, A., & Archer, T. (2004). Harnessing the creative potential among users. *Journal of Product Innovation Management, 21,* 4-14.

Lan, L., & Kaufman, J. C. (2012). American and Chinese similarities and differences in defining and valuing creative products. *The Journal of Creative Behavior, 46,* 285-306. doi:10.1002/jocb.19

Loewy, R. (1979). *Industrial design.* Woodstock, NY: The Overlooked Press.

MacKinnon, D. W. (1978). *In search of human effectiveness: Identifying and developing creativity.* New York, NY: Creative Education Foundation Press.

Maher, M. L. (2010). Design creativity research: From the individual to the crowd. In T. Taura & Y. Nagai (Eds.), *Design Creativity 2010* (41-47). London, UK: Springer-Verlag.

Nickerson, R. S., Perkins, D. N., & Smith, E. E. (1985). *The teaching of thinking.* Hillsdale, NJ: Lawrence Erlbaum Associates.

Oman, S., & Tumer, I. Y. (2009, 22-27 August). The potential of creativity metrics for mechanical engineering concept design. In Norell Bergendahl, M., Grimheden, M., Leifer, L., Skogstad, P., & Lindemann, U. (Eds.). *Proceedings of ICED 09, the 17th International Conference on Engineering Design, Vol. 2*. Palo Alto, CA: The Design Society. Retrieved from http://www.designsociety.org/publication/28581/the_potential_of_creativity_metrics_for_mechanical_engineering_concept_design

O'Quin, K., & Besemer, S. P. (1989). The development, reliability, and validity of the revised Creative Product Semantic Scale. *Creativity Research Journal, 2*, 267-278

Parnes, S. J., Noller, R. B., & Biondi, A. M. (1977). *Guide to creative action*. New York, NY: Scribners.

Plucker, J. A., Beghetto, R. A., & Dow, G. T. (2004). Why isn't creativity more important to educational psychologists? Potentials, pitfalls, and future directions in creativity research. *Educational Psychologist, 39*(2), 83-96.

Plucker, J. A., & Mackel, R. A. (2011). Assessment of creativity. In R. J. Sternberg & J. C. Kaufman (Eds.), *The Cambridge handbook of creativity*. New York, NY: Cambridge University Press.

Puccio, G. J., Treffinger, D. J., & Talbot, R. J. (1995). Exploratory examination of relationships between creativity styles and creative products. *Creativity Research Journal, 8*, 157-172.

Runco, M. A. (1989). The creativity of children's art. *Child Study Journal, 19*, 177-189.

Rhodes, M. (1961). An analysis of creativity. *Phi Delta Kappa, 42*, 305-310.

Simonton, D. K. (1999). *Origins of genius*. New York, NY: Oxford University Press.

Simonton, D. K. (2004). *Creativity in science: Chance, logic, genius, and zeitgeist*. Cambridge, UK: Cambridge University Press.

Sternberg, R. J., & Lubart, T. I. (2002). *Defying the crowd*. New York, NY: Free Press.

Taylor, I. A. (1975). An emerging view of creative actions. In I. A. Taylor & J. W. Getzel (Eds.), *Perspectives in creativity* (pp. 297-325). Chicago, IL: Aldine.

Taylor, I. A., & Sandler, B. J. (1972). Use of a creative product inventory for evaluating products of chemists. In *Proceedings of the 80th Annual Convention of the American Psychological Association, 7*, 311-312..

Treffinger, D. J., Isaksen, S. G., & Firestein, R. L. (1983). Theoretical perspectives on creative learning and its facilitation: An overview. *Journal of Creative Behavior, 17*(1), 9-17.

Treffinger, D. J., & Poggio, J. P. (1972). Needed research on the measurement of creativity. *Journal of Creative Behavior, 6,* 253-267.

Ward, W. C., & Cox, P. W. (1974). A field study of nonverbal creativity. *Journal of Personality, 42,* 202-219.

Wiggins, G. (2006). A preliminary framework for description, analysis and comparison of creative systems. *Knowledge-Based Systems, 19,* 449-458.

About the Author

Eva Teruzzi is a change management expert. She has a master's degree in Foreign Languages and Literatures, an International Coach Federation certification, a graduate certificate in Creativity and Change Leadership, and almost 30 years of experience in business. She began teaching new product development at LIUC University in Italy in 2013.

Eva's master's thesis at the ICSC will examine cross-cultural environments in creative product measurement from a consumer perspective. She currently serves as Director, Product Marketing and Business Development, at Fiera Milano. Follow her on Twitter @eva_teruzzi, and on LinkedIn at it.linkedin.com/pub/eva-teruzzi.

What is the Correlation Between Mental Health and Creativity?

Julia Figliotti
International Center for Studies in Creativity
SUNY Buffalo State

Originally published in *Big Questions in Creativity 2014*

Abstract

Since the inception of creativity as a subject for study, there has been the idea that "madness" must be involved in some capacity. Over time, this idea gained momentum and turned into an area of research and inquiry. Over the past five years, many studies, both conclusive and inconclusive, examined the relationship between mental illness and creativity. In an analysis of these studies, this paper reduces the relationship into three major divisions: defining creativity and its characteristics, defining mental illnesses and their symptoms, and exploring relationships between the two. Ultimately, the author concludes, more research must be conducted before arriving at a conclusive verdict.

What is the Correlation Between Mental Health and Creativity?

When considering the query, "What is the actual relationship between mental health and creativity," we must reflect on many different facets. First, how is creativity defined? Which aspects of creativity pertain—divergent thinking, creative self-beliefs, physical invention? Second, how is mental health defined? What particular disorders are we focusing on, and what are their symptoms? This paper attempts to address these supporting questions, one by one, in an effort to understand whether any relationship does exist.

Defining Creativity

In the field itself, creativity is defined in its simplest form as the ability to produce something—tangible or intangible—that is both original and useful (Newell, Shaw, & Simon, 1963). Yet that does not really get to the heart of the matter. Instead of a broad, empirically-accepted definition, a narrower one that focuses on Big-C, Pro-c, little-c, and mini-c creativity (Kaufman & Beghetto, 2009) could cast a brighter light on the subject.

Big-C creativity, also known as eminent creativity, is most commonly referenced in individuals such as Albert Einstein, Sylvia Plath, and Leonardo DaVinci. Lubart (2010) further determined that a society's focus on Big-C creativity often contributes to the culture's perception of creativity as a whole. In that context, contemporary society will not label you as creative if you are not painting the next Mona Lisa, or inventing the next iPad.

Pro-c creativity was defined by Kyaga et al. (2013) as concerning professional creators who are not yet eminent. While not the most commonly-discussed or most obvious form of creativity, Pro-c creativity is particularly prominent in studies regarding mental disorders in creative professions. Little-c creativity was defined by Lubart (2010) as "a form of self-actualization or individual self-development" with no substantial production (p. 270). Essentially, little-c represents creativity on a personal level. Finally, Kaufman and Beghetto (2009) defined mini-c creativity as the "dynamic, interpretive process of constructing personal knowledge and understanding within a particular sociocultural context" (p. 3). In other words, mini-c creativity represents the creativity that is an unavoidable and inherent part of the learning process.

Characteristics of Creative People

Do you know someone who is highly creative? What about that person comes to mind that makes you certain of his or her creative ability? Does she paint? Does he write music? Is she a scientist? Is he an author? Now consider that person's personality. What characteristics stand out?

Lubart (2010) stated several personality traits are associated with creativity across cultures and around the world: cognitive aspects include the "ability to make connections, ask questions, use imagination, think flexibly, [and] experiment with ideas"; personality traits include "independence, self-confidence, [and] assertiveness"; and motivational characteristics included "high energy, ambition, [and] enthusiasm" (p. 270).

Sadre and Brock (2008) included Torrance's (1962) account of the 80-plus characteristics of creative persons in their own list, pointedly noting that not all of these traits must be present for a person to be considered creative. Their list included sensitivity, independence, altruism, energy, industriousness, persistence, self-assertiveness, versatility, a withdrawn nature, attraction to the mysterious, defiance of conventions, independence in judgment and thinking, radicalism, discontentedness, stubbornness, a temperamental streak, possession of odd habits, and an aversion to organization. Chances are, your creative acquaintance possesses several, if not many or all, of these traits.

Defining Mental Disorders

It is challenging to clarify the term "mental disorders" for this analysis. Stein et al. (2010), working from the fourth edition of the Diagnostic and Statistical Manual of Mental Disorders (DSM-IV)*, described the features and considerations of mental disorders as significant patterns associated with distress or disability. They are manifestations of "behavioral, psychological, or biological dysfunction[s]" in affected individuals (p. 1760). The same conundrum exists with creativity; the definition is broad and general. However, unlike creativity, no definition adequately specifies the exact boundaries for the concept of "mental disorder," a concept which understandably fails to take into account all possible situations (Stein et al., 2010).

---

*It should be noted that the fifth edition of the DSM was published in June 2013. However, as all the studies consulted for this paper were based on the DSM-IV, the fourth edition is used herein as the primary reference.

Types and Symptoms

Hundreds of classifications of mental disorders exist in the realms of psychology and psychiatry. However, studies involving a correlation between creativity and mental disorders tend to focus on only a few. In the prominent research from the past five years, the disorders most focused upon by researchers were schizophrenia, bipolar disorder, depression, attention deficit dyperactivity disorder (ADHD), and anxiety (Andreason, 2008; Andreason, 2011; Beaussart, Kaufman, & Kaufman, 2012; Glazer, 2009; Kyaga et al., 2013; Kyaga et al., 2011; Sadre & Brock, 2008; Silvia & Kimbrel, 2010). Of the available studies, only Sadre and Brock's (2008) "Systems in Conflict" delved into the symptoms of the individual disorders.

The DSM-IV described the common symptoms of each of the aforementioned disorders. Characteristic indicators of schizophrenia included "delusions, hallucinations, disorganized speech...[and] grossly disorganized or catatonic behavior" (American Psychiatric Association [APA], 1994, p. 273). Features of bipolar disorder are "abnormally and persistently elevated, expansive, or irritable mood, lasting at least one week" (p. 332), "violent behavior..., school truancy, school failure, occupational failure, divorce, or episodic antisocial behavior" (p. 352). Major depressive disorder (more commonly known as depression) was identified by sensitivity to pain and physical illness, an unsociable nature, physical tiredness, and often suicide (APA, 1994). ADHD was identified by inattention in academic, social, or occupational settings; messy and careless work; difficulty sustaining attention in tasks or activities; daydreaming; shifts in (uncompleted) activities; difficulty with organization; ease of distraction; fidgetiness; excessive and inappropriate running or climbing; excessive talking; impulsivity; impatience; interrupting; and clowning around (APA, 1994). Finally, symptoms of anxiety included difficulty controlling worry, being in a constant state of worry (though the focus may shift), restlessness, being easily fatigued, difficulty concentrating, irritability, muscle tension, and disturbed sleep (p. 433).

The Relationship, Explored

Many symptoms of mental disorders track with the aforementioned characteristics of a creative mind. Bipolar disorder and ADHD in particular have symptoms that parallel characteristics of creative people: temperamental natures, antisocial behavior, aversions to organization, radicalism, high energy, stubbornness, and distraction. Anxiety and depression have a less direct connection, but several components are prominent: disorganization, withdrawn and antisocial behaviors, restlessness, and difficulty concentrating.

The symptoms commonly found in schizophrenic patients have very little in common with the characteristics of creative people. However, one study in this analysis suggested the presence of schizophrenia in an individual has a negligible overall impact on his creativity. According to Kyaga et al. (2013), "individuals with overall creative professions were not more likely to suffer from [schizophrenia] than controls" (p. 83). That said, this study did not account for the field of authors who do empirically show a higher likelihood for creative people to suffer from schizophrenia.

Does this crossover between symptoms and traits mean your creative acquaintance is actually exhibiting symptoms of a mental disorder? Certain studies on the relationship between creativity and mental health might lead to that conclusion. However, there are some researchers who believe that perhaps an individual diagnosed with a mental disorder is actually exhibiting traits of a creative mind.

A 2008 study conducted by Sadre and Brock focused on highly creative children and adolescents who were diagnosed with mental illnesses. They had been placed on anywhere from one to five medications and complained of strong side effects. Many of the children in this study, through counseling and the use of creative outlets, were taken off their medications, and several even had their diagnoses reversed. As the authors implied, when comparing the characteristics of creativity and the symptoms of mental disorders (specifically, ADHD and bipolar disorder), it is easy to see why creativity might be misdiagnosed as a mental disorder (Sadre & Brock, 2008).

Though their study focused solely on children and adolescents, I believe there is a carry-over of misdiagnosed creativity into adulthood as well. This begs the questions: are parents and doctors taking the easy way out by diagnosing a mental disorder and prescribing medications for an "illness"? What might be the benefits of incorporating creativity training into the psychiatric and psychological fields?

Mental Health and Big-C Creativity

Also known as eminent creativity (Kyaga et al., 2013), Big-C creativity studies often portrayed a direct positive correlation between mental disorders and levels of creativity (Andreasen, 2008; Glazer, 2009; Kyaga et al., 2013). These studies were frequently based on biographies and anecdotes, usually because said eminent creators have long since passed away. Andreasen (2008) presented a prime example of this style of research:

> Vincent Van Gogh...suffered from severe bouts of both psychotic mania and psychotic depression, yet he also produced more than 300

of his greatest works [during that time]. Sylvia Plath...suffered from severe mood disorder for much of her life...writing poetry...suggesting intermittent periods of a manic or hypomanic state. Martin Luther suffered from periods of intense despair, but also periods of extremely high energy.... There are many other well-known creative people who suffered from mood disorders, many of them bipolar: Ernest Hemingway, Winston Churchill, and Theodore Roosevelt, to mention a few. (p. 251)

While evidence supports the positive relationship between mental disorders and Big-C creativity, the tie is ultimately anecdotal. Although Glazer (2009) assured us that "it is now generally accepted that the link [between creativity and madness] is empirically grounded" (p. 755), there are those who disagree. Kyaga et al. (2013) retorted that these studies tend to focus on alcoholic authors and painters who were diagnosed long before the publication of the DSM-IV; analyses of long-dead Big-C creators through biographies do not equate to empirical evidence. Without the corroborating evidence of current studies involving living eminent creators, historiometric studies become less credible.

Mental Health and Pro-c Creativity

Pro-c creativity relates to people in creative professions. Of the research collected regarding creativity and mental health, a majority of the non-anecdotal studies focus on Pro-c creativity. Creative professions are usually described in these studies as "scientific and artistic occupations" (Kyaga et al., 2013). Andreasen (2008), for example, wrote a literature review that focused solely on mental disorders in writers. After citing previous empirical studies dating back to 1974 (some of which she had conducted herself), Andreasen (2008) concluded that "the overall literature supporting this association is relatively weak" due to "inadequate definitions of both creativity and mood disorders, reliance on anecdotal and autobiographical or biographic sources..., a lack of control groups," and a narrow range of the types of creativity being studied (p. 254). However, as previously stated, there is evidence in many studies that authors in particular have higher levels of bipolar disorder, anxiety, schizophrenia, and depression (Andreasen, 2008; Andreasen, 2011; Glazer, 2009; Kyaga et al., 2013). For example, Kyaga et al. (2013) noted a higher rate of schizophrenia, bipolar disorder, and anxiety in authors. Overall, though, it seems that very few conclusions on a positive correlation between mental illness and creativity can be drawn from studies focused on Pro-c creativity.

Mental Health and Little-c Creativity

Most people can relate to little-c creativity, which encompasses everything from the songs we sing under our breath when someone is taking too much time at the copy machine to the bedtime stories we make up so the kids will finally go to sleep. Little-c creativity is everyday creativity on a personal, individual level.

In a pragmatic analysis, Silvia and Kimbrel (2010) found that "mixtures of anxiety, depression, and social anxiety predicted little variance in creativity" (p. 2). Their study assessed multiple dimensions of depression and anxiety, and it incorporated a wide range of tasks and measures relating to creativity, including "creative cognition [such as divergent thinking]…everyday creative behaviors… creative accomplishments in different domains…and creative self-beliefs" (p. 3). The data, collected from psychology students at a university, indicated there is neither a positive nor negative correlation between little-c creativity and the presence of select mental disorders.

Few studies exist regarding the relationship between mental disorders and little-c creativity. The area demands further exploration if we hope to get stronger evidence concerning a correlation. If more studies are conducted that focus on everyday creativity, we will close in on more generalizable results.

Mental Health and Mini-c Creativity

Creativity in youth is characterized in the work of Kaufman and Beghetto (2009) as mini-c creativity, or the "dynamic, interpretive process of constructing personal knowledge and understanding within a particular sociocultural context" (p. 3). Its relationship to mental disorders is an area of research that has barely been touched. However, Sadre and Brock (2008) brought it to light in a surprising way: they hypothesized that creative children with mental disorder diagnoses may have been misdiagnosed, and that creativity can treat and sometimes reverse these diagnoses. In a study that compared the characteristics of creative personalities with the symptoms of bipolar disorder and ADHD, they highlighted case examples to support their theory that "a positive meaning for symptoms [creativity] removes the stigma of a mental illness diagnosis, and improves the young persons' self-esteem and behavior" (p. 358).

This study underscored the perils of misdiagnoses, noting that "children as young as 3 years have been diagnosed with bipolar disorder" (p. 366), exposing them to the possible dangers of psychostimulant treatments. Further, it raised the potential for using creativity as a treatment program. This area of research deserves much more attention, both in children and in adults.

Sadre and Brock (2008) offered five case studies of children and adolescents diagnosed with mental disorders who were able to wean themselves off many of their medications through the creative channeling of their energies and passions. Some even emerged from the therapy with fully reversed diagnoses. If these young people can use creativity and creative outlets to overcome their illnesses, shouldn't others be able to do the same? Imagine if our society could acknowledge the possibility that we can help people work past misdiagnoses with something as simple as creativity. This critical area of study is well worth our time and effort.

One Correlation and a Caution

It is imperative to point out a positive correlation between higher levels of mental illness and corresponding levels of creativity in writers. Authors in particular have higher levels of bipolar disorder, anxiety, schizophrenia, and depression, and are more likely to commit suicide than any other creative professionals studied (Andreasen, 2008; Andreasen, 2011; Glazer, 2009; Kyaga et al., 2013). However, these statistics do not act as predictors, and writers need not rush to a psychiatrist based on these findings alone.

Does this correlation hold for all forms of mental illness? Apparently not. In a study that focused on schizophrenia, bipolar disorder, anxiety, ADHD, and depression (and used living people for the study and control groups), Kyaga et al. (2013) found no stronger correlation between most of these disorders and individuals in all other creative professions as compared with a control group.

One's level of creativity is not heightened by mental disorders or illnesses. In fact, several studies suggested that having a mental disorder diminishes creativity levels (Glazer, 2009; Kyaga et al., 2013; Silvia & Kimbrel, 2010). A treatment study cited by Andreasen (2008) showed a full 50 percent of bipolar patients had higher levels of creativity during and after psychiatric treatment, while 25 percent showed lower levels of creativity. This means that, while their symptoms were being controlled, the patients with bipolar disorder were more creative than when their disorder was in full swing.

Conclusion

Although there are many differing views on the correlation between creativity and mental health, most researchers agree that more research needs to be conducted in order for the individual studies and views to attain higher credibility

(Andreason, 2008; Andreason, 2011; Beaussart et al., 2012; Glazer, 2009; Kyaga et al., 2013; Kyaga et al., 2011; Sadre & Brock, 2008; Silvia & Kimbrel, 2010). However, this will be no easy feat. As Silvia and Kimbrel (2010) stated, "There are many disorders and many domains of creativity: crossing the different disorders with the different creative domains yields a massive Disorder by Creativity matrix" (p. 2).

What is the correlation between creativity and mental health? The question is simply too complex to answer just yet. But by focusing more attention on how their many facets intersect, we may one day have a collective answer.

References

American Psychiatric Association (1994). *Diagnostic and Statistical Manual of Mental Disorders, 4th edition*. Washington, DC: Author.

Andreasen, N. C. (2008). The relationship between creativity and mood disorders. *Dialogues in Clinical Neuroscience, 10*(2), 251-255.

Andreasen, N. C. (2011). A journey into chaos: Creativity and the unconscious. *Mens Sana Monogr, 9*(1), 42-53.

Beaussart, M. L., Kaufman, S. B., & Kaufman, J. C. (2012). Creative activity, personality, mental illness, and short-term mating success. *The Journal of Creative Behavior, 46*(3), 151-167.

Glazer, E. (2009). Rephrasing the madness and creativity debate: What is the nature of the creativity construct? *Personality and Individual Differences, 46*, 755-764.

Kaufman, J. C., & Beghetto, R. A. (2009). Beyond big and little: The four c model of creativity. *Review of General Psychology, 13*, 1.

Kyaga, S., Landén, M., Boman, M., Hultman, C. M., Långström, N., & Lichtenstein, P. (2013). Mental illness, suicide, and creativity: 40-year prospective total population study. *Journal of Psychiatric Research, 47*, 83-90.

Kyaga, S., Lichtenstein, P., Boman, M., Hultman, C., Långström, N., & Landén, M. (2011). Creativity and mental disorder: Family study of 300,000 people with severe mental disorder. *The British Journal of Psychiatry, 199*, 373-379.

Lubart, T. (2010). Cross-cultural perspectives on creativity. In J. C. Kaufman & R. J. Sternberg (Eds.), *The Cambridge handbook of creativity* (pp. 265-278). New York, NY: Cambridge University Press.

Newell, A., Shaw, J. G., & Simon, H. A. (1963). The process of creative thinking. In H. E. Gruber, G. Terrell, and M. Wertheimer (Eds.), *Contemporary approaches to creative thinking* (pp. 63-119). New York, NY: Atherton.

Sadre, M., & Brock, L. J. (2008). Systems in conflict: Labeling youth creativity as mental illness. *Journal of Family Psychotherapy, 19*(4), 358-378.

Silvia, P. J., & Kimbrel, N. A. (2010). A dimensional analysis of creativity and mental illness: Do anxiety and depression symptoms predict creative cognition, creative accomplishments, and creative self-concepts? *Psychology of Aesthetics, Creativity, and the Arts, 4*(1), 2-10.

Stein, D. J., Phillips, K. A., Bolton, D., Fulford, K. W. M., Sadler, J. Z., & Kendler, K. S. (2010). What is a mental/psychiatric disorder? From DSM-IV to DSM-5. *Psychological Medicine, 40*(11), 1759-1765.

About the Author

Julia Figliotti is a 2014 graduate of the International Center for Studies in Creativity. She has a B.A. in Writing and an M.S. in Creativity, both from SUNY Buffalo State. Julia is a certified FourSight facilitator and works for Knowinnovation, an international company with a focus on scientific innovation. A professional writer, Julia has been published by National Public Radio, *Gargoyle* magazine, and The Partnership for 21st Century Skills. She is working on the publication of two children's stories, and is creating a website for the remote facilitation of Creative Problem Solving sessions.

What is Creative Economy?

Irina Mishina
International Center for Studies in Creativity
SUNY Buffalo State

Originally published in *Big Questions in Creativity 2013*

Abstract

The current conception of the term *creative economy* is based on the economic activities within creative or cultural industries. This approach misses the essence of the phenomenon the term creative economy is supposed to describe: a paradigm shift, the structural change of the very basis—not only of our economy—but society as a whole. The purpose of this paper is to propose a new, more integrated conception of creative economy as an economic system that is still emerging and is based on the following pillars: (a) ideas as the main factor of economic growth, (b) collaboration, (c) connectivity, (d) entrepreneurship, (e) creative organization, and (f) business model innovation and creative business strategies.

What is Creative Economy?

The concept of *creative economy* gained wide popularity in both academic literature and popular press in the last decade. Although there are some discrepancies as to the origins of the term, it was the work of John Howkins in *The Creative Economy: How People Make Money from Ideas,* first published in 2001 (Howkins, 2007), and of Richard Florida in *The Rise of the Creative Class,* first published in 2002 (Florida, 2004), that brought the topic to broad public attention.

Taking into account that Howkins (2007) defined *creative economy* as the financial volume of transactions with creative products produced within creative industries (he identified fifteen), and Florida (2004) defined his *creative class* based on occupations that he identified as creative, it is not a surprise that the prevailing notion of creative economy is associated with economic activities related to industries and professions that traditionally are deemed creative. Theories of these two authors inspired policy makers around the world to search for new strategies that support the development of creative and cultural industries through investments in cultural facilities, in attempts of forging *creative cities* and attracting members of the *creative class*. The topic gained importance at the highest levels, which resulted in extensive Creative Economy Reports published by the United Nations Conference of Trade and Development in 2008 and 2010 (UNCTAD, 2008; UNCTAD, 2010).

This paper, however, approaches the concept of creative economy from a different point of view. This author considers creative economy as a new socioeconomic system emerging as a result of structural changes we have witnessed and experienced at all levels of our lives in recent decades. This paper attempts to summarize the underlying reasons for the emergence of this new system and to identify its main characteristics.

Current Approach

The tendency to limit the interest in creative economy to creative or cultural industries is understandable if we take into account the high growth rates observed in this sector (Florida, 2004; Howkins, 2007; UNCTAD, 2010). Although the estimation of the scale of the actual economy of creative industries differs depending upon which industries and occupations are actually included, and whether an occupational or industries approach is used, the figures are still worth the attention. The estimations vary from 1% of the U.S. total workforce (Markusen, Wassall, Denatale, & Cohen, 2008) to 30% (Florida, 2004), and from $592 billion of worldwide production in 2008 (UNCTAD, 2010) to $2706 billion in 2005 (Howkins, 2007). It is generally argued that the industries approach tends to overestimate the total value of creative economy, as not all occupations within creative industries require creative labor, and hence not the total volume of transactions generated within those industries represent transactions with creative goods and services (Markusen et al., 2008; UNCTAD, 2010). On the other hand, Florida's (2004) estimations, based on an occupational approach, rendered the highest results (Markusen et al., 2008), which also has caused heated discussions around the validity of his data (Baris, 2005; Donegan, Drucker, Goldstein, Lowe, & Malizia, 2008; Glaeser, 2005; Malanga, 2004; Mishina, 2011). UNCTAD (2010), using the industries approach that divides creative industries into four categories (heritage, arts, media, and functional creations, which includes advertising, design, architecture, research and development, digital services, etc.), admitted that it is very difficult at the current moment to make accurate estimations, as the actual structure of statistical data does not reflect the real creative nature of economic transactions.

Academic literature dedicated to the topic of creative economy tends to revolve around issues related to creative industries and the creative class: the impact of particular industries on economic development (Adler, 2011; Christopherson & Rightor, 2010; Mellander & Florida, 2007), overall impact of cultural production on general societal development (McIntyre, 2008), regional and urban development policies based on support and promotion of creative and cultural industries (Chapain & Comunian, 2010; Cooke & De Propris, 2011; Felton, Gibson, Flew, Graham, & Daniel, 2010; Florida, Mellander, & Stolarick, 2007; Ho, 2009; Hospers & Pen, 2008; Lange, 2011; Ooi, 2010; Vorley, Mould & Smith, 2008), and economic geography of the creative class and creative cities (Boschma & Fritsch, 2009; Waitt & Gibson, 2009).

Attempts at Definition

Without intending to downplay the importance of cultural development, it must be noted that the definition of creative economy based on the economic activities within only certain industries that are classified as creative raises various important issues. The first one is that the most generally-accepted classifications of creative industries support the erroneous opinion of the general public that creativity (a) is domain related, (b) is something related to arts and design, and (c) is a personal talent. Second, the assumption that creative economy is based on what people *do* as opposed to *how* they do it, and that some professions or activities may have more importance for economic and social development than others, creates a basis for social inequality and conflict. Wilson (2010) argued that prioritizing "the rhetoric of the 'creative industries' over and above any further exploration of creativity and its wider role in our economic, social and cultural welfare" threatens the possibility of promoting creativity "as not only an individualistic phenomenon, the preserve of the talented few, but also as a social concept, founded on our relational consciousness, and holding the promise of a genuinely creative economy" (p. 367). "Cultural policy's concern... must surely have a fundamental interest in supporting and enabling the creative potential in all of us" (p. 368).

But what is more important is that such an approach to the concept of creative economy loses from its sight the very deep essence of the phenomenon it is supposed to describe: the structural change of the very basis not only of our economy, but society as a whole. Curiously enough, all major works that constitute the pillars of the current concept of creative economy *do* mention this structural change. Howkins (2005) defined creative economy as an "economy where a person's ideas, not land or capital, are the most important input and output" (para. 2). He added, regarding the nature of creativity, "From [an] economic viewpoint, it is open to all. Not everyone can be a farmer (you need land), or a manufacturer (you need money and factories) or a government official (you need to pass exams). But everyone can be creative" (para. 11).

Florida (2004) claimed, "human creativity is the ultimate economic resource. The ability to come up with new ideas and better ways of doing things is ultimately what raises productivity and thus living standards" (p. xiii). Throughout his work he constantly reminds us that it is important to find ways for anyone, regardless of the type of job one performs, to be creative in what one does. The concept of *creative factory* is one of the interesting examples he provided to illustrate this phenomenon. He also built an argument that creativity has always been, throughout economic history, the primary driver that led the transformation from one economic system to another: the rise of agriculture, the emergence of trade and specialization, the Industrial Revolution, capitalism, the organizational age, and so forth. However, now "we live in a time of great promise. We have evolved economic and social systems that tap human creativity and make use of it as never before" (p. xiii).

UNCTAD (2010) acknowledged: "In the 'creative city' it is not only artists and those involved in the creative economy who are creative. Creativity can come from anyone who addresses issues in an inventive way" (p. 14).

The idea that our socioeconomic system, driven by human creativity, is evolving into a new paradigm, is not new. Peters and Besley (2008) gave an account of the whole line of predecessors to Howkins whose conceptual theories contributed to the notion of the creative economy. The most remarkable were Daniel Bell's (1974) concept of the *post-industrial society*, Peter Drucker's (1969, 1973) idea of the *knowledge worker*, and Paul Romer's (1990) *new growth theory*. The idea of the creative economy is very closely related to, and is sometimes used interchangeably with, the concepts of *knowledge economy* and *new economy*.

New growth theory, forged in the 1990s, considers the underlying causes of growth. In addition to two factors considered by traditional economics theory, *capital* and *labor,* new growth theory adds a third one: *technology,* which is "endogenous." It is a central part of our economic system and increases in proportion to the resources we devote to it, as opposed to the classical view that technological breakthroughs are random (Robinson, 1995). According to this theory, "knowledge and technology are characterized by increasing returns, and these increasing returns drive the process of growth" (Cortright, 2001, p. 2), which makes ideas the ultimate "source of economic progress" (p. 6). Romer, one of the major contributors to the new growth theory, described manufacturing as mere rearranging of physical things. This type of activity is not unique to people; animals can do that, too, and with amazing precision. But producing ideas is inherent to the human being, and this is what distinguishes us from the rest of the animals (Romer, 1993). "New ideas generate growth by reorganizing physical resources (natural, human, capital) in more efficient and productive ways" (Peters & Besley, 2008, p. 94). Florida (2004) identified two main factors that drive creative economy: speed and change (p. 147), and it is undeniable that these two factors are brought to us by the development of technology.

Many authors, while treating the issues related to creative economy, knowledge economy or new growth theory, mentioned Joseph Schumpeter and his concept of *creative destruction* (Cortright, 2001; Florida, 2010; Peters & Besley, 2008; Tong & Liu, 2009). While the combination of production factors (capital, labor, etc.) is optimized in the process of innovation, the old system demonstrated resistance to the new developments. The existing infrastructure is not ready to support this new combination; hence before the progress is noticeable the system seems to retrocede, causing capital mismatch and structural unemployment. The old system must be destroyed so the new, more productive system can take its place. As Florida (2010) described in *The Great Reset*, this is exactly what we are observing with the current state of our global economy. The real creative economy is still emerging, and we do not yet know exactly what form it will take, but by analyzing different pieces of information about the changes we are witnessing and experiencing, we can make an informed prediction of its main features.

This paper suggests that creative economy is an emerging way in which economic and social systems function, based on the following pillars: (a) ideas as the main factor of economic growth, (b) collaboration, (c) connectivity, (d) entrepreneurship, (e) creative organization, and (f) business model innovation and creative business strategies.

Economics of Creativity

"Creativity is not new and neither is economics, but what is new is the nature and extent of the relationship between them, and how they combine to create extraordinary value and wealth" (Howkins, 2007, p. viii). Economics deals with optimizing scarce resources in order to maximize gain. There are several principal differences between the classical view of economics and an economy based on ideas.

First, in a traditional economy the competitive advantage is based on ownership of scarce resources. Human creativity, as the main resource used in creative economy, is limitless. As Romer explained (Robinson, 1995), the potential number of ideas is immense. For example, the possible number of different potential ways of doing something is so large that you never find the best one; hence there will always be a possibility to improve, to innovate.

Second, physical products and services have one peculiar characteristic, that when one person has one thing, another person cannot have exactly the same thing at the same moment. Ideas, on the contrary, are non-rivalrous by nature, that is, if one person has an idea, nothing impedes anyone else from having the same idea at the same time (Howkins, 2007; Romer, 1993).

Third, the cost per unit of producing physical goods and services tends to be constant. With ideas, the situation is very different. It might be difficult and sometimes rather costly to come up with the right idea, but the cost of copying it is close to zero (Coy, 2000; Robinson, 1995). That is why knowledge-intensive companies dedicate the majority of their activities to figuring out the idea. Once the idea is there, reproducing it is the easiest part of the process. This relationship between finding an idea and reproducing it is related, to a great extent, according to Romer (Robinson, 1995), to one technological advancement that stands out among the chain of innovations in human history: computers. Romer claimed that computers are not a simple technological innovation, but that they represent a structural shift in the relationship between research and production. They are the main factor that drives the whole economy to become increasingly like, for example, Microsoft: more and more people dedicate themselves to discovery activities, and fewer to production.

Finally, another crucial difference between traditional and creative economies is the question of property rights. The topic of intellectual rights is rather controversial and raises heated discussions.

Some claim that intellectual rights are the main pillar that sustains an economy based on ideas, and that they must be protected, as they are the only incentive to invest in the research and development of ideas, especially technological ones. In an interview published in *Forbes,* Romer claimed that even monopolies associated with patent rights are good for the economy, a point of view totally opposite that of classical economics (Robinson, 1995). The argument about incentives is refutable, however. Many studies demonstrated that the expectation of a reward has a negative correlation with the creativeness of the result (Hennessey, 2010).

Howkins (2007) also built a substantial case that, at a minimum, demonstrates that the matter is not so straightforward. First, the basis of the current intellectual rights law was created in different times and was built on the principles of *tangible* property, although tangible property has a very different nature from that of *intellectual* property. Second, the current laws give ground to an imbalance in development between prosperous and poor countries. Finally, conceptually it contradicts the notion that society should benefit from new knowledge; hence this knowledge should be public domain. The popularity of concepts like Creative Commons (where creators choose the rights and restrictions they wish to attach to a work, often choosing lesser restrictions than spelled out in statute) and *open source* (where creators make their work freely available, typically so that others might adopt and improve upon it), strongly demonstrates that a different conception of intellectual rights is possible and valid.

Collaborative Society

The development of phenomena like Creative Commons, open source communities, and the more recent emergence of crowdsourcing, is precisely what gives us the key to a new understanding of human collaboration. Moreover, their rapid expansion and apparent perdurance prove the crucial importance collaboration gains in the new socioeconomic order, becoming a systemic feature. Wilson (2010) argued that the danger of the concept of creative economy, limited by the scope of creative industries, is that it promotes an individualistic view of creativity, whereas creativity is actually social by nature. According to Sawyer (2011), "collaboration is the key to creativity." Creative collaboration is an emergent property of the system, and one of its main characteristics is that the final result is greater than a mere sum of its parts (Sawyer, 2010).

Florida has studied extensively the concept of creative clusters (Florida 2002, 2005, 2008; Florida, Knudsen, & Stolarick, 2005). The nature of this phenomenon lies in the fact that creative people, as well as creative entities (e.g., organizations and enterprises), tend to group together spatially, because their proximity to each other generates the environment in which the creativity of each member of the cluster is enhanced and supported. "Co-location and labour mobility provide a further benefit in that knowledge and expertise are constantly circulated and updated across firms and projects" (UNCTAD, 2010, p. 76). Within a creative cluster, information, ideas and other knowledge are freely flowing, interchanging, enriching each other, and serving as inputs for multiple and complex connections that nurture the creative process.

The emergence of the creative economy provides us with a totally new perspective on the dichotomy of "mine" vs. "not mine." Howkins (2007) described it in this way:

> In "collaborative creativity," everyone is given equal, meritocratic access to the same body of knowledge and is able, even encouraged, to contribute to its development in a free, open, and collaborative manner. It is easy, in such a fluid environment, to lose control of one's ideas and products, and to have them replaced by others'. (p.192)

Looking at creativity from the angle of collaboration returns us to the concept of the non-rivalrous nature of ideas and adds a new dimension to the intellectual rights controversy, which is being aggravated by another pillar of the structural change we are undergoing: connectivity.

The Power of Networks

We have seen that the development of technologies, especially the appearance of computers, played the key role in the structural shift between research and production as economic activities, giving fuel to the rise of the new economic system based primarily on ideas. Further advancement of those technologies—which led, for example, to the Internet and its consequent evolution into widespread, interconnected, easily accessible networks—has profoundly changed our lives over the last two decades, and has created conditions for solidification of all other pillars of creative economy. Networks bring structural transformation to how our society and markets function (Peters & Besley, 2008). Through "exponential cost reductions" and collaboration, networks allow us to "produce more, or more quickly, or differently"; they make it "easier to realize an idea and turn it into product"; and they reduce "the cost of failure" (Howkins, 2007, p. 198).

Networks, which everyday become faster and more boundless, foster the free flow of information, a necessary condition for the emergence and flourishing of new ideas. Moreover, fast and widespread networks allow for copying ideas and digital products at no cost, deepening the difference between the traditional economy and the new economic order. Networks and global connectivity are the basis for further thriving of creative collaboration, overturning the bases of the intellectual property laws and leading to the development of new types of organizations and business models. They facilitate access to resources, fostering innovative and entrepreneurial behavior. In short, it is the connectivity factor that binds together all separate pillars of creative economy, turning them from independent concepts into interconnected and interdependent components of a global system.

Entrepreneurial Society

In "Emergence of the Entrepreneurial Society," Audretsch (2009) described how in the 1990s, after the dominance of the organizational age, "entrepreneurship emerged as the engine of growth, innovation, economic development" due to the shift from physical capital to knowledge capital (p. 506). Entrepreneurship is one of the crucial features of the emerging economic order, because it is the link between ideas and their implementation. There is a need in an entrepreneur to bring an idea to the market.

But there is more to it. Leadbeater and Oakley (2001) identified four of "the most powerful forces that drive entrepreneurship" today: (a) technological change, (b) knowledge creation, (c) cultural change that promotes risk-embracing behavior and personal responsibility, and (d) economic change that makes it less appealing to work for a corporation, and more rewarding to work for yourself (p. 81). What do we observe around us? The speed of technological advancement is growing at a rapid pace. Digital technologies and network expansion propels the creation of new knowledge and provides wide access to this knowledge. The labor market is undergoing substantial changes; every day it seems to become more and more difficult to find a job following the old patterns. For example, currently we can observe a clear trend of growth in business outsourcing (Huws & Podro, 2012); and, while unemployment rates remain high, companies' demand for temporary workers grows (Marsh, 2012; Wishnia, 2012). Moreover, it seems that more and more people prefer the flexibility of freelance-type jobs to full-time permanent employment (Erikson, 2012). At the same time, opportunities that digital technologies and the Internet render have lowered the entry levels on many markets, with enormous entrepreneurial possibilities. Entrepreneurship is gaining importance not only as a social phenomena but also as a scholarly discipline (Audretsch, 2012; Sánchez, 2011; Zahra & Wright, 2011).

Entrepreneurship in the creative age is not merely about starting companies. "Entrepreneurship is a matter of everyday activities" (Steyaert & Katz, 2006, p. 180). We all need to start considering ourselves as personal enterprises, as the idea of *personal branding* (Salenbacher, 2010) underscores. Howkins (2007) introduced the concept of the *post-employment job* when referring to this emergence of a new entrepreneurial attitude related to the development of creative economy. To fully embrace the opportunities this paradigm change offers us, we need to switch our mentality from the notion of a job as employment, to a job as "things-to-be-done" (Howkins, p. 141). Salenbacher also suggested that we need a new word for the changing concept of work. Coy (2000) predicted that we would handle "more personal matters at work, and more work matters at home" (para. 16), exactly as Florida (2004) described was occuring with members of the creative class.

There is a great deal we can learn from creative industries in this matter. According to Holt and Lapenta (2010), some studies revealed that in creative industries even employees with "underpaid, generic, repetitive, and often 'uncreative' and alienating" (p. 226) jobs often demonstrated high levels of job satisfaction. It is because they have already embraced the idea of work as vocation, fulfillment and personal growth. The creative economy gives this chance to all of us.

The Rise of the Creative Organization

The expansion of networks, the boost of creative collaboration, and the shift in mentality towards more entrepreneurial behavior, together with other factors of our current economic situation that force market players to search for ways of adapting to the newly emerging system, have led to the evolution of the new type of organization. Florida (2004) provided an account of the variety of arguments about whether the future system will be based on the economic activities of independent entrepreneurs, or if the dominance of big corporations will prevail. While the theorists get lost in the battle, we can observe how the face of the contemporary corporation is changing, integrating the features of both predicted paradigms.

According to various studies (Bughin & Chui, 2010; E-Metrixx, n.d.; Hamel, 2011) the best players are adapting various innovative management practices that are inspired by the principles of the so-called *Web 2.0*. These practices may be grouped into the following categories: (a) horizontal hierarchies, (b) flexible organizational structure based on projects, as opposed to job functions, (c) infrastructures that facilitate free information flow, (d) collaboration, and (e) an organizational climate that gives people a sense of purpose, fosters creative behavior and supports "transparency, openness, and freedom" (Hamel, 2011, p. 3).

It may be that the current development of the creative economy does not provide any indications that the existence of the big enterprises will cease, but these enterprises themselves are changing their organizational form, while they absorb the fundamental characteristics of the creative economy and convert themselves into collaborative entrepreneurial societies. In the new socioeconomic paradigm, a creative organization represents a model of the creative economy itself.

Creative Business Strategies and Business Model Innovation

While global connectivity lowers the cost of entry to the majority of markets, facilitates access to resources, frees the flow of information, and overturns existing markets and creates new ones, it also increases competition to an unprecedented degree. If in the traditional economy the competitive advantage was determined by access to scarce resources, this is no longer the case. The key to victory over the competition lies in the ability to offer a unique value to the customer, brought to life by business strategies that seek not to be *better* than one's rivals, but to be *different* (Kim & Mauborgne, 2005).

While markets are transforming, the old business models stop being functional. This is especially true for the markets plunged into the fundamental restructuring by the digital revolution, such as music, photography, and journalism. The old business models in these industries were based on the traditional notion of tangible property rights. Even intellectual rights were associated with certain tangible products—a CD, a film, a book, and the like. In order to get these products to market the creators had to work through intermediaries who acted as market gatekeepers, restricting access and accumulating the greatest share of the benefits (Foong, 2010). Digital technologies and network expansion, enabling access to the digital copy of the product at literally no cost, have turned this situation on its head and thrown the affected industries into crisis, despite desperate attempts by the major market players to protect the copyright status quo. However, as Howkins (2007) stated, "industries do not collapse because their existing business models are threatened but because they fail to find new ones" (p. 65). As Apple demonstrated by reinventing the digital music market, new business models are possible. Foong (2010) provided examples of brilliant business model innovation based on Creative Commons in different creative industries. The major common feature of these new business models is that, like Apple, they are based on establishing a relationship with a customer, as opposed to simply selling a product or a service.

Digital and networking technologies enable and foster business model innovation outside of the creative industries, too. It has become one of the most important aspects of companies' innovation activities (Osterwalder & Pigneur, 2010). The truth is that business model innovation, combined with creative business strategies, represents an important factor that gives competitive advantage in the creative economy, and the main resource this factor is related to is creative thinking. In addition, not only is this resource available to everyone, but it is an indispensable instrument of success for every agent of a creative economy, whether it is a company, a professional acting within a flexible structure of a creative organization, or an independent entrepreneur. The power of creative thinking is what is driving the evolution of the creative economy.

Conclusions

Creativity has always been an important driving force of economic development. However, technological advancements have finally shifted the balance between research and production to such an extent that ideas have turned into the primary capital responsible for economic growth. This, and not the development of the so-called creative industries, is the main pillar of the emerging creative economy. Our current system is still undergoing the phase of creative destruction, but we already can identify the main features of the new order that is being born. An economy based on ideas is being propelled by digital technologies and networks. They provide a perfect framework for creative collaboration and entrepreneurship. Collaboration and entrepreneurial attitude, together with the network principles of Web 2.0, also constitute the basis of a new type of creative organization. Finally, in a system where growth depends on unlimited resources available to everyone, creative thinking—empowering the development of creative business strategies and new business models—is becoming the ultimate factor of competition.

With the combination of all these conditions, together we can participate in the most exciting process in the whole history of humanity: the unfolding of a new system that appears poised to provide each of us with more opportunities for fulfillment, personal growth and meaning. Welcome to the creative age.

References

Adler, N. J. (2011). Leading beautifully: The creative economy and beyond. *Journal of Management Inquiry, 20*(3), 208-221.

Audretsch, D. B. (2009). Emergence of the entrepreneurial society. *Business Horizons, 52*, 505-511.

Audretsch, D. (2012). Entrepreneurship research. *Management Decision, 50*(5), 755-764.

Baris, M., (2005, November). The flight of the creative class: The new global competition for talent [Review of the book *The Flight of the Creative Class* by R. Florida]. *The Next American City, 9*, 43-45.

Bell, D. (1974). *The Coming of Post-Industrial Society.* New York, NY: Harper Colophon Books.

Boschma, R. A., & Fritsch, M. (2009). Creative class and regional growth: Empirical evidence from seven European countries. *Economic Geography, 85*(4), 391-423.

Bughin J, & Chui, M. (2010, December). The rise of the networked enterprise: Web 2.0 finds its payday. *McKinsey Quarterly.* Retrieved from http://www.mckinseyquarterly.com/The_rise_of_the_networked_enterprise_Web_20_finds_its_payday_2716

Chapain, C., & Comunian, R. (2010). Enabling and inhibiting the creative economy: The role of the local and regional dimensions in England. *Regional Studies, 44*(6), 717–734.

Christopherson, S., & Rightor, N. (2010). The creative economy as "Big Business": Evaluating state strategies to lure filmmakers. *Journal of Planning Education and Research, 29*(3), 336–352.

Cooke, P., & De Propris, L. (2011). A policy agenda for EU smart growth: The role of creative and cultural industries. *Policy Studies, 32*(4), 365-375.

Cortright, J. (2001). *New growth theory, technology and learning: A practitioner guide* (Reviews of Economic Development Literature and Practice: No. 4). Portland, OR: Impresa.

Coy, P. (2000, August 28). The creative economy. In *Businessweek Online*. Retrieved from http://www.businessweek.com/2000/00_35/b3696002.htm

Donegan, M., Drucker, J., Goldstein, H., Lowe, N., & Malizia, E. (2008). Which indicators explain metropolitan economic performance best? *Journal of the American Planning Association, 74*(2), 180-195.

Drucker, P. (1969). *The age of discontinuity.* New York, NY: HarperCollins.

Drucker, P. (1973). *Management: Tasks, responsibilities, practices.* New York, NY: Harper & Row.

E-Metrixx (n.d.). *Organisational creativity* [web page]. Retrieved from http://www.e-metrixx.com/me2-creativity-profit/organisational-creativity

Erikson, T. (2012, September 7). The rise of the new contract worker [web log post]. Retrieved from http://blogs.hbr.org/erickson/2012/09/the_rise_of_the_new_contract_worker.html

Felton, E., Gibson, M. N., Flew, T., Graham, P., & Daniel, A. (2010). Resilient creative economies? Creative industries on the urban fringe. *Continuum: Journal of Media & Cultural Studies, 24*(4), 619-630.

Florida, R. (2002). Bohemia and economic geography. *Journal of Economic Geography, 2,* 55-71.

Florida, R. (2004). *The rise of creative class: And how it's transforming work, leisure, community, and everyday life.* New York, NY: Basic Books.

Florida, R. (2005). *Cities and the creative class.* New York, NY: Routledge.

Florida, R. (2008). *Who's your city: How the creative economy is making where to live the most important decision of your life.* New York, NY: Basic Books.

Florida, R. (2010). *The great reset: How new ways of living and working drive post-crash prosperity.* New York, NY: HarperCollins.

Florida, R., Knudsen, B., & Stolarick, K. (2005). *Beyond spillovers: The effects of creative-density on innovation.* Toronto, Canada: The Martin Prosperity Institute, University of Toronto. Retrieved from http://www.creativeclass.com/richard_florida

Florida, R., Mellander, C., & Stolarick, K. (2007). *Inside the black box of regional development: Human capital, the creative class and tolerance.* Toronto, Canada: The Martin Prosperity Institute, University of Toronto. Retrieved from http://www.martinprosperity.org/projects/project/global-creativity

Foong, S. (2010, December). Sharing with creative commons: A business model for content creators. *PLATFORM: Journal of Media and Communication, A Creative Commons Special Issue,* 64-93. Retrieved from http://journals.culture-communication.unimelb.edu.au/platform

Glaeser, E. L. (2005). Review of Richard Florida's *The Rise of the Creative Class* [Review of the book *The Rise of the Creative Class* by R. Florida]. *Regional Science and Urban Economics, 35,* 593-596.

Hamel, G. (2011, July). *The management 2.0 challenge.* Handouts presented at Harvard Business Review webinar. Boston, MA: Harvard Business School Publishing.

Hennessey, B. A. (2010). The creativity-motivation connection. In Kaufman, J. C., & Sternberg, R. J. (Eds.), *The Cambridge handbook of creativity.* New York, NY: Cambridge University Press.

Ho, K. C. (2009). The neighborhood in the creative economy: Policy, practice and place in Singapore. *Urban Studies, 46*(5&6) 1187-1201.

Holt, F., & Lapenta, F. (2010). Introduction: Autonomy and creative labour. *Journal for Cultural Research, 14*(3), 223-229.

Hospers, G. J., & Pen, C. J. (2008). A view on creative cities beyond the hype. *Creativity and Innovation Management, 17*(4), 259-270.

Howkins, J. (2005, February). The creative economy: Knowledge-driven economic growth. In *Asia-Pacific Creative Communities: A Strategy for the 21st Century.* Senior Expert Symposium, Jodhpur, India. Retrieved from http://www.unescobkk.org/fileadmin/user_upload/culture/Cultural_Industries/presentations/Session_Two_-_John_Howkins.pdf

Howkins, J. (2007). *The creative economy: How people make money from ideas.* (Rev. ed.) London, UK: Penguin books.

Huws, U., & Podro, S. (2012, August). *Outsoursing and the fragmentation of the employment relations: the challenges ahead.* London, UK: ACAS. Retrieved from: http://www.acas.org.uk/media/pdf/p/8/Outsourcing-and-the-fragmentation-of-employment-relations-the-challenges-ahead.pdf

Kim, W. C., & Mauborgne, R. (2005). *Blue ocean strategy.* Boston, MA: Harvard Business Publishing.

Lange, B. (2011). Re-scaling Governance in Berlin's Creative Economy. *Culture Unbound, 3,* 187-208.

Leadbeater, C., & Oakley, K. (2001). *Surfing the long wave: Knowledge entrepreneurship in Britain.* London, UK: Demos. Retrieved from http://www.demos.co.uk/publications/surfing

Malanga, S. (2004). The curse of the creative class. *City Journal.* Retrieved from http://www.city-journal.org/html/14_1_the_curse.html

Markusen, A., Wassall, G. H., Denatale, D., & Cohen, R. (2008). Defining the creative economy: Industry and occupational approaches. *Economic Development Quarterly, 22*(1), 24-45.

Marsh, J. (2012, November 20). Strong demand for temporary staffing [web log post]. Retrieved from http://www.protingent.com/home/news-connections/blog/protingent-blog/2012/11/20/strong-demand-for-temporary-staffing

McIntyre, P. (2008). Creativity and cultural production: A study of contemporary western popular music songwriting. *Creativity Research Journal, 20*(1), 40-52.

Mellander, C., & Florida, R. (2007). *There goes the neighborhood: How and why bohemians, artists and gays affect regional housing values.* Toronto, Canada: The Martin Prosperity Institute, University of Toronto. Retrieved from http://www.creativeclass.com/richard_florida

Mishina, I. (2011). *Debates around the creative class.* Unpublished manuscript, International Center for Studies in Creativity, Buffalo State College, Buffalo, NY.

Ooi, C. S. (2010). Political pragmatism and the creative economy: Singapore as a city for the arts. *International Journal of Cultural Policy, 16*(4) 403-417.

Osterwalder, A., & Pigneur, Y. (2010). *Business model generation.* Hoboken, NJ: John Wiley & Sons.

Peters, M. A., & Besley, T. (2008). Academic entrepreneurship and the creative economy. *Thesis Eleven, 94,* 88-105.

Robinson, P. (1995). Paul Romer. *Forbes, 155*(12), 66-68.

Romer, P. (1990). Endogenous technological change. *Journal of Political Economy, 98*(5), S71-S102.

Romer, P. (1993). Ideas and things. *Economist, 328*(7828), 70-72.

Salenbacher, J. (2010). *Creative personal branding.* Charleston, SC: Jürgen Salenbacher.

Sánchez, J. C. (2011). Emprendimiento: introduccion [Entrepreneurship: Introduction]. *Psicothema, 23*(3), 424-426.

Sawyer, R. K. (2010). Individual and group creativity. In Kaufman, J. C., & Sternberg, R. J. (Eds.), *The Cambridge handbook of creativity.* New York, NY: Cambridge University Press.

Sawyer, R. K. (2011, November). Keynote presented at Creativity World Forum (Unpublished proceedings), Hasselt, Belgium.

Steyaert, C., & Katz, J. (2006). Reclaiming the space of entrepreneurship in society: geographical, discursive and social dimensions. *Entrepreneurship & Regional Development, 16*(3), 179-196.

Tong, G., & Liu, Y. (2009). The affection of independent innovation on employment. *Management Science and Engineering, 3*(1), 36-40.

UNCTAD. (2008). *Creative economy report 2008: The challenge of assessing the creative economy towards informed policy-making.* Geneva, Switzerland: United Nations.

UNCTAD. (2010). *Creative economy report 2010: Creative economy: A feasible development option.* Geneva, Switzerland: United Nations.

Vorley, T., Mould, O., & Smith, H. L. (2008). Introduction to geographical economies of creativity, enterprise and the creative industries. *Geografiska Annaler: Series B, Human Geography, 90*(2), 101–106.

Waitt, G., & Gibson, C. (2009). Creative small cities: Rethinking the creative economy in place. *Urban Studies, 46*(5&6), 1223–1246.

Wilson, N. (2010). Social creativity: Re-qualifying the creative economy. *International Journal of Cultural Policy, 16*(3), 367-381.

Wishnia, S. (2012, August 22). A nation of temps [web log post]. Retrieved from http://www.salon.com/2012/08/22/a_nation_of_temps

Zahra, S. A., & Wright, M. (2011). Entrepreneurship's Next Act. *Academy Of Management Perspectives, 25*(4), 67-83.

About the Author

Irina Mishina is a creative and effective thinking facilitator and coach, specialized in Creative Problem Solving. As a facilitator she works with individuals and groups, helping to apply heuristic thinking methods to situations of complexity, innovation, problem solving, business development and process improvement. As a coach she works with entrepreneurship-minded people, facilitating creative thinking in professional and personal projects, and business idea development.

Irina is a Specialist in Business Management, certified by the American Institute of Business and Economics; a FourSight certified facilitator; and an NLP Master Practitioner. She has a degree in Economics from Moscow State University, and a Graduate Certificate in Creativity and Change Leadership from the International Center for Studies in Creativity at SUNY Buffalo State, where she is currently pursuing a Master of Science in Creativity.

Irina has extensive professional and international experience with various multinational corporations, and is a creative independent professional and entrepreneur, the founder of Ima Blumm Creatiff Consulting, and a managing partner at Seeding Growth. She is also a multidisciplinary artist and writer. Creativity is her life's passion and she is convinced that in our times of constant change that developing creative potential—whether of an individual or of organization—is a requirement for success. Her research interests include creative economy, business strategy and business model innovation, and consciousness development.

Irina is currently based in Barcelona, Spain.

Web: www.imablumm.com, www.seedinggrowth.es
Email: irina@imablumm.com
Twitter: @imablumm

What's Next for Creativity?

Mary Kay Culpepper
International Center for Studies in Creativity
SUNY Buffalo State

Originally published in *Big Questions in Creativity 2013*

Abstract

The study of creativity is actually several kinds of studies, involving psychology, sociology, education, economics, neurology, and more. As a result, the body of both theoretical and empirical research is expanding so vigorously the field risks a potentially damaging fragmentation. Drawing on an existing seven-part concentric schema that moves from the innermost neurological aspect of creativity to the outermost systems approach attempting to explain the place of the field in the universe, the author reviews recently published literature and offers predictions for future directions of study in each aspect. The paper concludes with the assertion that future inter- and intra-disciplinary research should consider the complex interplay of aspects involved in creative thinking and production.

What's Next for Creativity?

Predict, v.t. To relate an event that has not occurred, is not occurring and will not occur.

—Ambrose Bierce

Stepping into the breach to make a forecast is fiendishly foolhardy, just as Bierce—the pioneering American satirist and journalist who died a century ago—implied in that entry in his *Unabridged Devil's Dictionary* (2000). Yet foreseeing the future of a field as wide-ranging as creativity is not just compelling, but possibly essential; as an ever-developing science, creativity is among the most promising constructs of human experience.

Creativity—defined here as the production of products or ideas both novel and appropriate (Hennessey & Amabile, 2010)—is also among the least understood constructs of human experience, though not for lack of research. As practiced in the second decade of the 21st century, creativity study ranged from the intensely personal—such as searching for a genetic basis for creativity (Runco et al., 2011), and exploring the phenomenon of experiencing goosebumps when listening to music or viewing a painting (Silvia & Nussbaum, 2011)—to the broadly civic, including recommending strategies to improve the creativity of entire countries (Villalba, 2010) and cultures (Tsai, 2012). Both popular and scholarly literature reflects this expansiveness; Amazon returned more than 16,000 results for the term "creativity book" ("Books: Creativity," 2013), while Google Scholar listed 1.19 million articles for the term "creativity" ("Creativity," 2013).

Obviously, for anyone looking at the future of creativity research, a great deal of reading is in order. Creativity has been featured in at least a half-dozen academic journals (*Journal of Creative Behavior, Creativity Research Journal, International Journal of Creativity and Problem Solving, Creativity and Innovation Management, Journal of Thinking Skills and Creativity,* and *Psychology of Creativity, Aesthetics, and the Arts*), a constant stream of new compendia, and abundant national and international conferences and symposia (Hennessey & Amabile, 2010).

But psychology and creativity hardly have a monopoly on scholarly research on the subject. In the process of researching this paper, I found relevant, thought-provoking articles in sources as diverse as *Research Policy,* the *Journal of Homosexuality,* and *Brain Research.* The many out-of-field articles point to a growing concern among creativity scholars: Investigators in one arena of creativity often appear oblivious to developments in another. In more than a few cases, the resulting fragmentation has meant that research duplicates, rather than illuminates, the existing body of knowledge.

The focus of this paper, then, is to describe some ongoing currents in a variety of areas in creativity research and suggest developments that might emerge. My hope is that this update, studded with my own opinions about future studies in creativity, will serve as a clarification, and as a milepost past which the next few months and years might be measured.

Bearing in mind Bierce's admonition regarding predictions, I nonetheless bring experience to this exercise. As someone who wrote in the mass media about trends in fashion, architecture, and cuisine, I learned long ago that the secret to forecasting the near future lies in unearthing fresh and reliable resources that possess relevant facts, and piecing the findings together to see what direction they indicate. Therefore, I favored scholarly articles and books published within the last three years. When that was not possible, I relied on established scholars whose work was well known in the field and who had published within the last 10 years.

Four of those scholars guided my methods. I drew initial inspiration from a short piece in the *Los Angeles Psychologist* by Plucker and Kaufman (2008) who described trends in creativity research that are just now coming to fruition. I found a longer, more focused article in the *Annual Review of Psychology* by Hennessy and Amabile (2010) to be especially insightful. Importantly, the authors established a schema of concentric circles to illustrate seven distinct spheres of creativity research: neurological, affect/cognition/training, individual/personality, groups, social environment, culture/society, and systems approach. Their structure framed the discussion with elegance and simplicity, and I use it in the analysis that follows.

What Lies Within: The Neurological Level

Between drugs that appear to enhance behaviors linked to creativity, and technological advances in imaging techniques such as functional magnetic resonance imaging (fMRI), positron emission tomography (PET) scans, and electroencephalography (EEG), the neurology of creativity generates a wide variety of exploration.

For example, Sawyer (2011) summarized and reviewed research in cognitive neuroscience and creativity through 2010. He explained the brain's working mechanisms and cited relevant studies regarding cognitive neuroscience and various creative pursuits. He related that creativity emanates from some 20 regions of the brain, and noted that the complexity studied by cognitive neuroscientists may reveal that the processes involved in creativity are also those involved in everyday, non-creative activity. He concluded, "It may be the case that the construct of creativity simply cannot be defined in terms of cognitive events that occur in one minute or less" (p. 151).

Sawyer's argument found agreement from researchers who warned that the technology of cognitive neuroscience threatens to outpace consensus regarding the meaning of its output. Dietrich and Kanso (2010) organized a meta-analysis of 63 papers on the neural foundations of creative thought, and found the studies investigated three broad categories: divergent thinking, artistic creativity, and insight. "Taken together, creative thinking does not appear to critically depend on any single mental process or brain region, and it is not especially associated with right brains, defocused attention, low arousal, or alpha synchronization, as sometimes hypothesized," they reported (p. 822).

That said, technology continued to tantalize researchers. In asking how the brain "thinks," Andreasen (2011) used fMRI research to bolster her claim that the brain is a continually reorganizing system, guiding an unconscious process, which effectively assists the creative process. Kröger et al. (2012) also employed fMRI to pinpoint brain regions involved during passive conceptualizing, with the goal of assessing the effects of originality and relevance, two elements of creative output. Similarly, other recent fMRI research (Aziz-Zadeh, Liew, & Dandekar, 2012) explored whole-brain activity involved in processing visual creativity.

Another less technical but undeniably intriguing study suggested that alcohol might lubricate the creative process. Jaroz, Colflesh, and Wiley (2012) found that intoxicated subjects performed better on a battery of creativity tests than their sober counterparts. The trio hypothesized that alcohol has a mitigating effect on executive function and inhibition; deficits in both areas are thought to enhance creative problem solving.

Will future studies look even more closely at brainwaves, and will researchers examine the effects of other, more powerful drugs? I predict new machines will capture increasingly detailed information about how the brain works, though it might be years before those machines can measure—and we can fully comprehend—the scope of what happens in our brains when we create.

Future Learning: Affect, Cognition, and Training

What conditions are optimal for the apprehension of creativity? In this sphere of study, researchers examined mood, the processes that underpin creative performance, and the most effective ways of training people to engage their creativity (Russ, 2011). Predictably, with continual research, theories and measures continue to change, and the resulting changes indicate new lines of investigation.

Many researchers have considered positive affect imperative for creativity (Rego, Sousa, Marques, & Pina e Cunha, 2012; Baron & Tang, 2011). But not all of them do; Chermahini and Hommel (2012) posited that divergent thinking promotes positive affect, while convergent thinking promotes a negative one. Both affects are necessary for creative thinking, and this work points to a complicated relationship between them.

Similarly, the picture regarding cognition is open to wide interpretation, and recent work recommended against making sweeping statements about any one model (Simonton, 2012). Accordingly, Ward and Kolomyts (2010) proposed balancing conflicting theories with research that converges both empirical and anecdotal methods.

The same caution exists for those studying creativity training. While training has been shown to yield positive outcomes (Puccio, Cabra, Fox, & Cahen, 2010), the most effective variety appeared to be a detailed and particular kind of training, requiring domain-specific exercises, lectures, practices, and well-researched (if subject to change) cognitive models (Baer, 2012; Caughron, Peterson, & Mumford, 2011).

The appeal of the idea that creativity can be taught and learned will continue to make this sphere an important focus of research, I believe. Because affect, cognition, and training are intimately connected to the neurological study of creativity, further interdisciplinary studies might well identify which specific processes are required for the gamut of creative activities. They could also identify the definitive role of mood, and the true value of creativity training.

Senses of Self: Personality and Individual Differences

What makes creative people tick? According to Feist (2010), having or lacking certain personality dispositions makes a person more or less likely to display creativity. Interestingly, much has been written about the longstanding suspicion of a link between creativity and madness (Beaussart, Andrews, & Kaufman,

2012; Cropley, Cropley, Kaufman, & Runco, 2010). While some research pointing to that link may contain flaws, these studies nevertheless appeared to show a relationship between psychopathology and creative behavior. Such is also the case with a Swedish longitudinal study (Kyaga et al., 2012) which suggested links between some mental illnesses (including depression, schizophrenia, bipolar disorder, and anxiety) and creative writers, though subjects in creative professions in general were not more likely than those in the rest of study to suffer from psychiatric disorders.

Interestingly, new ways of interpreting statistical research point to refinements in regard to personality and cognitive style assessments. Von Wittich and Antonakis (2011) investigated the discriminant and incremental validity of the Kirton Adaption-Innovation Inventory (Kirton, 1999), which purported to measure creativity style preferences, and wondered if the assessment actually measured personality. Martinsen and Diseth (2011) likewise analyzed Assimilator-Explorer cognitive styles (Kaufman & Martinsen, 1991), raising the same issue. Although these studies are open to questions regarding the experience of the subjects as well as the cross-cultural applications of the findings, I believe they will prompt additional experiments examining the role of personality in cognitive style.

Personality also figures into the work of Kink and Woschnjak (2011), who looked at contemporary, jazz, and ballet dancers whose work necessarily varied by creativity demand. Their research associated personality traits with the acquisition and actualization of creative potential; I think this study seemed to promise more research investigating the role of personality in specific creative professions.

Feist (2010) remarked that psychological research in personality was considered a shrinking field in the 1970s and 1980s, when the professional psychological consensus was that personality dispositions either did not exist or were a marginal consideration. His work, however, has been influential in turning the tables. I predict personality research will soon perhaps identify the difficult-to-grasp individual qualities necessary for creative production.

Creating Together: Groups

Two or more individuals make up a group, and just as individuals can be creative, so can groups. Recent research promoted the understanding that the group creative process is more complex than previously thought, and is equally likely to be successful as the individual pursuit (Hennessey & Amabile, 2010).

Indeed, Sawyer (2010) summoned the notion of collaborative emergence, borrowing a concept from sociology to describe the improvisational quality that arises when a group is creating without a structured plan. Because individual-based approaches of explaining creativity stop shy of convincing support for groups, Sawyer believed further investigation should follow. I agree, and find group intuition (Dayan & di Benedetto, 2011) a distinctly exciting focus of that investigation.

Studies involving team openness and creativity (Schilpzand, Herold, & Shalley, 2010), corporate values and group creativity (Valentine, Godkin, Fleishman, & Kidwell, 2010), and the role of leaders in spurring the creativity of their groups (Hemlin & Olsson, 2011), have implications for shaping progress in organizations.

I furthermore think research of how groups create can augur well for diversity and fairness. Cunningham (2011) related sexual diversity within work groups to enhanced creativity, which suggests creativity could help bring about a more equitable future.

Motivation and Reward: Social Psychology

As the science that studied the influences of our situations with respect to how we view and influence one another, social psychology examined the ways people think about and relate to one another (Myers, 2012). Its most important contribution is perhaps to recognize creativity supporters and detractors that exist in society.

Recently published literature in this sphere is concerned with motivation, and the social environment's influence on its intrinsic and extrinsic forms. Intriguing new research indicated that inspiration is the motivational force that rendered the creative process satisfying enough to keep a creator engaged (Conti & Amabile, 2011). Moreover, that same motivation can apparently be bolstered in individuals who regularly journal about their work (Amabile & Kramer, 2011). Indeed, a host of motivations could well be behind the finding that people tend to make more creative decisions for others than they do for themselves (Polman & Emich, 2011).

In my opinion, one of the most promising areas of social psychology research is the networking necessitated by new media. I found this direction appealingly grafts creativity theory to both applied sociology and psychology, revealing in the process how individuals and groups relate and create online. Gauntlett (2011) suggested that online creative networks in particular serve as a kind of "social glue" connecting "people with others in unexpected, unplanned, and perhaps rather anarchic ways" (p. 224). Similarly, Peppler and Solomou (2011) examined creativity networks in a single social media outlet and found distinct patterns emerging.

In a related development, a new American Psychological Association journal, *Psychology of Popular Media Culture*, provides an outlet for research examining the relationship between creativity and media, both old and new.

Where We Live, Work, and Play: Social Environment

This area of study has been the purview of organizational psychologists who have investigated the effect of creative climate on individuals, teams, groups, and even cultures. Moreover, the relatively new field of cultural psychology suggested "that culture shapes how people's minds operate—sometimes in profound ways" (Heine, 2011, p. xix), and it analyzed creativity as well. Furthermore, social scientists such as Mann and Chan (2011) attempted to understand the climate for innovation by drawing together constructs from history, policy, economics, and law, in addition to business and management.

Organizational psychologists continue to turn their attention to social behaviors supporting creativity, including those of leaders (Puccio, Mance, & Murdock, 2011), as well as aspects such as positive affect, autonomy, and time pressure (Hennessey & Amabile, 2010). In the process, this research continually refines management practice both in the U.S. and abroad, as it is more likely than most other creativity literature to be published in the popular press and new media.

Schools are organizations, too, and there is growing public concern about the presence (or absence) of creativity in education. Bronson and Merryman (2010) voiced in a widely read *Newsweek* article that falling creativity scores among American schoolchildren may be the result of a lack of a concerted effort to emphasize creative thinking and processes in schools. As a counter, Smith and Smith (2010) propose that educators be trained in and understand creativity so they can feature it in curricula, establish the usefulness of creativity as the cornerstone of academic growth, and demonstrate the effectiveness of creative approaches across multiple subjects.

To that point, Barbot, Besançon, and Lubart (2011) created the Evaluation for Potential Creativity, an assessment for middle-school students that accounts for domain specificity and measures both verbal and visual modes of expression. Such a measure could monitor students' development and influence curriculum development to feature teaching and training for creativity.

Culture is often viewed by creativity researchers through an organizational lens, and one pressing topic in this arena is the universality of the creative process and the means by which it is expressed in various countries and cultures (Oades-Sese & Esquivel, 2011). I find an interesting direction of this work involves the multicultural experience; people who live in more than one culture could appear more creative because they must consider multiple perspectives (Heine, 2011; Fee & Gray, 2012). With the number of diaspora networks worldwide increasing ("Weaving the world together," 2011), a proven creativity connection between shifting cultures and societal and economic success could change the fortunes of entire countries.

Worlds Within Worlds: Systems Theory

Perhaps no other area of creativity research has changed so radically as the modeling of its theories. During the last three decades, researchers have become increasingly interested in interactive, contextualized depictions of creativity (Moran, 2010). The resulting theories spotlighted the worth of creativity in every aspect of human endeavor, from building knowledge to building organizations (Puccio & Cabra, 2010).

Influenced by general system theories in social sciences, management, and physics, the systems approach placed creativity in a larger ecological (and sometimes cosmological) context that addressed evolution and change (Gabora & DiPaola, 2012; Gabora & Kaufman, 2010), as researchers examined the qualities of human potential and their interaction with society.

One emerging direction lies in examining the interplay between creativity and the construct of worldview, which can be defined as the way we influence the world and the world influences us (Culpepper & Clark, 2012). Mirroring Andreasen's (2011) contention that the brain is a continually reorganizing system, Gabora (2011) maintained that worldview, which is self-mending and self-organizing, is a kind of penultimate creative product, one that occurs in the mind before anything is outwardly visible.

Systems theory, I believe, will evolve to embrace the really big questions facing creativity, including who becomes creative, and whether creativity is a life-long human proposition. That is the point of Miller & Wildman's (2012) proposal to tie creativity to chaos theory, perhaps one day answering questions regarding the creative genesis of the species.

To be sure, new theories will necessarily address each sphere currently studied in creativity, and then some, crossing into disciplines and fields yet unconsidered. Will there ever be one defining theory? I cannot imagine it, given the panoramic scope of the research in the field. But I do think that because creativity is central to our very humanity, we are compelled to keep searching for its DNA.

Binding Things Together: Conclusion

Attempting to cover the gamut of creativity literature from the last couple of years is like going for a very quick dip in a very large pool: bracing, certainly, yet hardly a comprehensive experience. But even this brief splash revealed developing patterns. During the process, I kept seeing a number of words reappearing, like waves in that pool: technology, environment, personality, process, culture, equitability, connectivity. Tantalizingly, they offer clues to what will happen, and maybe what is already taking place.

My readings reminded me that creativity doesn't happen in a vacuum, and neither does its study. Collaboration with other scholars across fields and disciplines is a necessity, one that can be further leveraged when "theorists and researchers work together and understand the discoveries that are being made across domains and analytical levels…. Only by using multiple lenses simultaneously, looking across levels, and thinking about creativity systematically, will we be able to unlock and use its secrets" (Hennessey & Amabile, 2010, p. 590).

Like Montuori (2011), who wrote in the journal *Futures*, I believe "…the imagination of desirable futures can emerge from a creative ethic that stresses the value of generative interactions and contexts that support creativity" (p. 221). As the future shapes our comprehension of the processes that make up creativity, he stated, we will be required to face circumstances with a creative mindset.

So, what's next for creativity? I predict it will be a confluence of work coming from many different disciplines and perspectives, with yet-unimagined connections making a kaleidoscopic future. As prognostications go, that may be vague enough to suit even Bierce. And if I am right, the results—like the future—will take care of themselves.

References

Amabile, T., & Kramer, S. (2011). *The progress principle: Using small wins to ignite joy, engagement, and creativity at work*. Cambridge, MA: Harvard Business Press.

Andreasen, N. C. (2011). A journey into chaos: Creativity and the unconscious. *Mens Sana Monographs, 9*, 42–53.

Aziz-Zaden, L., Liew, S., & Dandekar, F. (2012). Exploring the neural correlates of visual creativity. *Social Cognitive and Affective Neuroscience.* Advance online publication. doi:10.1093/scan/nss021

Barbot, B., Besançon, M., & Lubart, T. (2011). Assessing creativity in the classroom. *The Open Education Journal, 4,* 58-66.

Beaussart, M., Andrews, C., & Kaufman, J. (2012). Creative liars: The relationship between creativity and integrity. *Thinking Skills and Creativity.* Advance online publication. Retrieved from http://dx.doi.org/10.1016/j.tsc.2012.10.003

Baer, J. (2012). Domain specificity and the limits of creativity theory. *Journal of Creative Behavior, 46,* 16-29.

Baron, R., & Tang, J. (2011). The role of entrepreneurs in firm-level innovation: Joint effects of positive affect, creativity, and environmental dynamism. *Journal of Business Venturing, 26,* 49-60.

Bierce, A. (2000). P. In D. Schultz & S. Joshi (Eds.), *Unabridged devil's dictionary* (p. 186). Athens, GA: University of Georgia Press.

Books: Creativity. (2013, January 1). Retrieved from http://www.amazon.com/s/ref=nb_sb_noss?url=search-alias=stripbooks&field-keywords=creativity&x=0&y=0

Bronson, P., & Merryman, A. (2010). The creativity crisis. *Newsweek,* retrieved January 1, 2013, from http://hartfordinnovationcenter.com/~ARTICLES/O-The%20Creativity%20Crisis-07-19-2010.pdf

Caughron, J. J., Peterson, D. R., & Mumford, M. D. (2011). Creativity training. In M. Runco & S. Pritzker (Eds.), *Encyclopedia of creativity, Vol. 1: A-H* (pp.449-455). London, England: Academic Press.

Chermahini, S. A., & Hommel, B. (2012). Creative mood swings: Divergent and convergent thinking affect mood in opposite ways. *Psychological Research, 76,* 634-640.

Conti, R., & Amabile, T. A. (2011). Motivation. In M. Runco & S. Pritzker (Eds.), *Encyclopedia of creativity, Vol. 2: I-Z* (pp. 147-152). London, England: Academic Press.

Creativity. Retrieved January 1, 2013, from http://scholar.google.com/scholar?hl=en&q=creativity&btnG=&as_sdt=1%2C1&as_sdtp

Cropley, D. H., Cropley, A. J, Kaufman, J. C., & Runco, M. A. (Eds.). (2010). *The dark side of creativity.* New York, NY: Cambridge University Press.

Culpepper, M. K., & Clark, C. (2012, September). *The doctor can see you now: Physician worldview, honing theory, and areas for primary care innovation*. Paper presented at the American Creativity Association conference, Philadelphia, PA.

Cunningham, G.B. (2011). The benefits of sexual orientation diversity in sports organizations. *Journal of Homosexuality, 58*, 647-663.

Dayan, M., & di Benedetto, C. A. (2011). Team intuition as a continuum construct and new product creativity: The role of environmental turbulence, team experience, and stress. *Research Policy, 40*, 276-286.

Dietrich, A., & Kanso, R. (2010). A review of EEG, ERP, and neuroimaging studies of creativity and insight. *Psychological Bulletin, 136*, 822-848.

Fee., A., & Gray, S. (2012). The expatriate-creativity hypothesis: A longitudinal field test. *Human Relations, 65*, 1515-1538.

Feist, G. J. (2010). The function of personality in creativity. In J. Kaufman & R. Sternberg (Eds.), *Cambridge handbook of creativity*. New York, NY: Cambridge University Press.

Gabora, L. (2011). Five clarifications about cultural evolution. *Journal of Cognition & Culture, 11*, 61-83.

Gabora, L., & DiPaola, S. (2012, May). How did human beings become so creative? A computational approach. *Proceedings of the International Conference on Computational Creativity 2012*, Dublin, Ireland. Retrieved from http://computationalcreativity.net/iccc2012/wp-content/uploads/2012/05/203-Gabora.pdf

Gabora, L., & Kaufman, S. B. (2010). Evolutionary approaches to creativity. In J.C. Kaufman & R.J. Sternberg (Eds.), *Cambridge handbook of creativity* (pp. 279-300). New York, NY: Cambridge University Press.

Gauntlett, D. (2011). *Making is connecting: The social meaning of creativity, from DIY and knitting to YouTube and Web 2.0*. Malden, MA: Polity Press.

Heine, S. J. (2011). *Cultural psychology* (2nd ed.). New York, NY: W. W. Norton.

Hemlin, S., & Olsson, L. (2011). Creativity-stimulating leadership: A critical incident study of leaders' influence on creativity in research groups. *Creativity and Innovation Management, 20*, 49-58.

Hennessey, B. A., & Amabile, T. M. (2010). Creativity. *Annual Review of Psychology, 61*, 569-598.

Jaroz, A., Colflesh, G., & Wiley, J. (2012). Uncorking the muse: Alcohol facilitates creative problem solving. *Consciousness and Cognition, 21*, 487-493.

Kaufmann, G., & Martinsen, O. (1991). The explorer and the assimilator: A theory and measure of cognitive styles in problem solving. *International Creativity Network Newsletter, 1*, 8-9.

Kaufman, J., & Sternberg, R. (Eds.) (2010). *The Cambridge handbook of creativity*. New York, NY: Cambridge University Press.

Kink, A., & Woschnjak, S. (2011). Creativity and personality in professional dancers. *Personality and Individual Differences, 51*, 754-758.

Kirton, M. (1999). *Kirton Adaption-Innovation inventory manual* (3rd ed.). Berkhamsted, UK: Occupational Research Centre.

Kröger, S., Rutter, B., Stark, R., Windmann, S., Hermann, C., & Abraham, A. (2012). Using a shoe as a plant pot: Neural correlates of passive conceptual expansion. *Brain Research, 1430*, 52-81.

Kyaga S., Landén, M., Boman, M., Hultman, C., Långström, N., & Lichtenstein, P. (2012). Mental illness, suicide and creativity: 40-year prospective total population study. *Journal of Psychiatric Research*. Advance online publication. http://dx.doi.org/10.1016/j.jpsychires.2012.09.010

Mann, L., & Chan, (2011). *Creativity in business and beyond: Social science perspectives and policy implications*. New York, NY: Routledge.

Martinsen, Ø., & Diseth, Å. (2011). The Assimilator–Explorer cognitive styles: Factor structure, personality correlates, and relationship to inventiveness. *Creativity Research Journal, 23*, 273-283.

Miller, I., & Wildman, P. (2012). Demiurgic field: Its patterning role in chaos, creation & creativity. *Scientific GOD Journal, 3*, 474-501.

Montuori, A. (2011). Beyond post-normal times: The creativity of the future and the future of creativity. *Futures, 43*, 221-227.

Moran, S. (2011). The roles of creativity in society. In J. C. Kaufman & R. J. Sternberg (Eds.), *Cambridge handbook of creativity* (pp. 74-90). New York, NY: Cambridge University Press.

Myers, D. (2012). *Social psychology* (11th ed.). New York, N.Y.: McGraw-Hill.

Oades-Sese, G. V., & Esquivel, G. B. (2011). Cultural diversity and creativity. In M. Runco & S. Pritzker (Eds.), *Encyclopedia of creativity, Vol. 1: A-H* (pp. 355-341). London, England: Academic Press.

Peppler, K., & Solomou, M. (2011). Building creativity: Collaborative learning and creativity in social media environments. *On the Horizon, 19*, 13-23.

Plucker, J., & Kaufman, J. (2008). Why is creativity important? Current research and new developments. *The Los Angeles Psychologist, 22*, 6-7.

Polman, E., & Emich, K. (2011). Decisions for others are more creative than decisions for the self. *Personality and Social Psychology Bulletin, 37*, 492-501.

Puccio, G. J., & Cabra, J. F. (2010). Organizational creativity. In J. C. Kaufman & R. J. Sternberg (Eds.), *Cambridge handbook of creativity* (pp. 145-173). New York, NY: Cambridge University Press.

Puccio, G. J., Cabra, J. F., Fox, J. M., & Cahen, H. (2010). Creativity on demand: Historical approaches and future trends. *Artificial Intelligence for Engineering Design, Analysis, and Manufacturing, 24*, 153-159.

Puccio, G. J., Mance, M., & Murdock, M. C. (2011). *Creative leadership: Skills that drive change* (2nd ed.). Thousand Oaks, CA: Sage.

Rego, A., Sousa, F., Marques, C., & Pina e Cunha, M. (2012). Optimism predicting employees' creativity: The mediating role of positive affect and the positivity ratio. *European Journal of Work and Organizational Psychology, 21*, 244-270.

Runco, M., Noble, E., Reiter-Palmon, R., Akar, S., Ritchie, T., & Yurkovitch, J. (2011). The genetic basis of creativity and ideational fluency. *Creativity Research Journal, 23*, 376-380.

Russ, S. W. (2011). Emotion/affect. In M. Runco & S. Pritzker (Eds.), *Encyclopedia of creativity, Vol. 1: A-H* (pp. 449-455). London, England: Academic Press.

Sawyer, R. K. (2010). Individual and group creativity. In J. C. Kaufman & R. J. Sternberg (Eds.), *Cambridge handbook of creativity* (pp. 366-379). New York, NY: Cambridge University Press.

Sawyer, R. K. (2011). The cognitive neuroscience of creativity: A critical review. *Creativity Research Journal, 23*, 137-154.

Schilpzand, M., Herold, D., & Shalley, C. (2010). Members' openness to experience and teams' creative performance. *Small Group Research, 42*, 55-76.

Silvia, P. J., & Nusbaum, E. C. (2011). On personality and piloerection: Individual differences in aesthetic chills and other unusual aesthetic experiences. *Psychology of Aesthetics, Creativity, and the Arts, 5*, 208-214.

Simonton, D. K. (2012). Quantifying creativity: Can measures span the spectrum? *Dialogues in Clinical Neuroscience, 14*, 100-104.

Smith, J. K., & Smith, L. F. (2010). Educational creativity. In J. C. Kaufman & R. J. Sternberg (eds.) *Cambridge handbook of creativity* (pp. 250-264). New York, NY: Cambridge University Press.

Tsai, K. C. (2012). The interplay between culture and creativity. *Cross-Cultural Creativity, 8,* 2, 15-20.

Valentine, S., Godkin, L., Fleishman, G., & Kidwell, R. (2010). Corporate ethical values, group creativity, job satisfaction, and turnover intention: The impact of work context on work response. *Journal of Business Ethics, 98,* 353-372.

Villalba, E. (2010). Monitoring creativity at an aggregate level: A proposal for Europe. *European Journal of Education, 45*(2), 314-330.

Von Wittich, D., & Antonakis, J. (2011). The KAI cognitive style inventory: Was it personality all along? *Personality and Individual Differences, 50,* 1044-1049.

Ward, T. B., & Kolomyts, Y. (2010). Cognition and creativity. In J.C. Kaufman & R.J. Sternberg (Eds.), *Cambridge handbook of creativity* (pp. 93-108). New York, NY: Cambridge University Press.

Weaving the world together (2011, November 19). *The Economist, 401*(8760), 72-74.

About the Author

Mary Kay Culpepper is a 2013 graduate of the International Center for Studies in Creativity at SUNY Buffalo State, where she was named a Mary C. Murdock scholar in 2011.

Acknowledgments

There have been many invaluable contributors to these editions. We give special thanks to our colleagues at the International Center for Studies in Creativity at SUNY Buffalo State: Gerard Puccio, Creative Studies department chair, Selcuk Acar, John Cabra, Roger Firestien, Jon Michael Fox, Marie Mance, Sue Keller-Mathers, and Jo Yudess. We were assisted over the years by Julia Figliotti, copy editor extraordinaire, and Kevin Opp, our book designer. We must also thank the spouses who support our annual labors, Andy Burnett, Cullen Clark, and Eleanor Reali.

Finally, our deepest appreciation goes to the 40 contributors to the *Big Questions in Creativity* series. They and the many scholars who pass through the ICSC are standard-bearers for creativity, carrying out our mission to ignite creativity around the world, every day, in ways both exquisite and breathtaking.

About the Editors

Dr. Cyndi Burnett is an Associate Professor at the International Center for Studies in Creativity at Buffalo State. She has a Bachelor of Fine Arts in Theater, a Master of Science in Creativity, and a Doctorate of Education in Curriculum, Teaching and Learning, all of which she uses to help "ignite creativity around the world." Her research interests include: the use of creative models and techniques with children, creative thinking in higher education, and current trends in creativity. Her work includes projects such as: working with educators to bring creative thinking into the classroom, connecting communities of creative thinkers via social media, and designing and running a Massive Open Online Course (MOOC) on Everyday Creativity.

Dr. Burnett is devoted to creating engaging lessons in education. In addition to teaching creativity professionally, she serves on the Board of Trustees for Elmwood Franklin School in Buffalo, is a Learning Advisor for DIY.org, and is a consulting editor for the Journal of Creative Behavior. She was featured in an article in the New York Times titled, "Creativity Becomes an Academic Discipline." She is the co-editor of the *Big Questions in Creativity* book series and co-author of the books *Weaving Creativity into Every Strand of Your Curriculum* and *My Sandwich is a Spaceship: Creative Thinking for Parents and Young Children*.

Twitter: @CyndiBurnett
Facebook: https://www.facebook.com/cyndiaburnett
Email: argonac@buffalostate.edu
Web: cyndiburnett.com

Mary Kay Culpepper is a visiting lecturer and doctoral researcher at the Communications and Media Research Institute of The University of Westminster in London. She holds a bachelor's degree in journalism from the University of Mississippi and her career as a writer and editor developed her drive to know more about the contexts in which people create. After receiving a master's degree from the ICSC at SUNY-Buffalo State, she began to teach creativity studies to undergraduate and graduate students. Her Ph.D. project examines the supports and barriers a person encounters on the way to developing a creative identity. In addition to editing three editions of the *Big Questions in Creativity* series, she has contributed a chapter on creativity and affordance theory to the upcoming *Palgrave Handbook of Creativity at Work*.

Twitter: @MaryKCulpepper
Email: marykayculpepper@gmail.com
Web: MaryKayCulpepper.com

Paul Reali is the founder of OmniSkills, LLC, a training and facilitation firm, and co-founder of Charlotte Center for Literary Arts, Inc., a nonprofit arts center in Charlotte, North Carolina. He is also the Managing Editor of ICSC Press. Paul has an M.S. in Creativity from the International Center for Studies in Creativity at SUNY Buffalo State, and an M.B.A. from Syracuse University, with a major in innovation management. He is the co-author of *Creativity Rising: Creative Thinking and Creative Problem Solving in the 21st Century,* and the co-editor of *Big Questions in Creativity 2013* and *2016,* published by ICSC Press. He is the principal contributor to creativeproblemsolving.com, a resource for CPS practitioners, and has published articles on business and creativity topics in more than a dozen regional, national, and international publications. He is a regular presenter at the annual Creative Problem Solving Institute.

Email: paul@omniskills.com
Twitter: @paulreali
LinkedIn: linkedin.com/in/paulreali
Web: omniskills.com, creativeproblemsolving.com, paulreali.com

About the International Center for Studies in Creativity

The International Center for Studies in Creativity (ICSC) is known around the world for its personally transformative undergraduate, graduate and distance programs that cultivate skills in creative thinking, innovative leadership practices and problem solving skills.

ICSC is the first program in the world to teach the science of creativity at a graduate level: Our Graduate Certificate program includes six courses that focus on creative process, facilitation, assessment, training, theory and leadership. With an additional four courses, including a master's project or thesis, students can complete a Master of Science degree in creativity and change leadership. Graduate students can pursue their degree on campus or via the distance program, which offers a blend of on-campus and virtual classrooms.

For 50 years, ICSC is proud to have contributed to seminal research to the field of creativity. ICSC is part of Buffalo State, The State University of New York.

To learn more, please visit creativity.buffalostate.edu.

About ICSC Press

Created in 2012, ICSC Press is the imprint of the International Center for Studies in Creativity. The mission of the press supports the vision of the Center to ignite creativity around the world, facilitating the recognition of creative thinking as an essential life skill. ICSC Press's goal is to put the work of our best teachers, thinkers, and practitioners into the hands of a wide audience, making titles available quickly and in multiple formats, both paper and electronic. Our titles include:

Books

Big Questions in Creativity 2016, Paul D. Reali & Cynthia Burnett, Eds.

Why Study Creativity? Reflections & Lessons from the International Center for Studies in Creativity, Jon Michael Fox & Ronni Lea Fox, Eds.

My Sandwich is a Spaceship, by Cyndi Burnett & Michaelene Dawson-Globus

Big Questions in Creativity 2015, Mary Kay Culpepper & Cynthia Burnett, Eds.

Big Questions in Creativity 2014, Mary Kay Culpepper & Cynthia Burnett, Eds.

Big Questions in Creativity 2013, Cynthia Burnett & Paul D. Reali, Eds.

Creativity Rising: Creative Thinking and Creative Problem Solving in the 21st Century, by Gerard J. Puccio, Marie Mance, Laura Barbero Switalski, & Paul D. Reali

Journals

Business Creativity and the Creative Economy, Mark A. Runco, Ed.

Journal of Genius and Eminence, Mark A. Runco, Ed.

To learn more, to purchase titles, or to submit a proposal, visit icscpress.com.

www.ingramcontent.com/pod-product-compliance
Lightning Source LLC
Chambersburg PA
CBHW020648300426
44112CB00007B/285